THE SAN JUAN ISLANDS

Afoot & Afloat

NOTICE: A winter storm that raked the San Juan Islands in December of 1990 caused severe devastation to old-growth trees in numerous parks. The state marine parks at Jones, Hope, and Doe islands will be closed to the public until May 1992 in order to clean up downed timber, which poses a fire hazard as well as a physical danger. DO NOT GO ASHORE ON THESE ISLANDS IF THEY ARE POSTED.

SECOND EDITION

THE SAN JUAN ISLANDS

Afoot & Afloat

SECOND EDITION

MARGE & TED MUELLER

THE MOUNTAINEERS • SEATTLE

THE MOUNTAINEERS: Organized 1906
" . . . to explore, study, preserve and enjoy
the natural beauty of the Northwest."

5 4 3 2 1
7 6 5 4

Published by The Mountaineers
1011 S.W. Klickitat Way, Suite 107
Seattle, WA 98134

Published simultaneously in Canada by Douglas & McIntyre, Ltd.
1615 Venables Street, Vancouver, British Columbia V5L 2H1

Edited by Miriam Bulmer
Designed by Judy Petry; layout by Ted Mueller
Maps by Marge Mueller
Cover photos: Anchorage at Patos Island Marine State Park; inset: trail to Bell
Point, British Camp, San Juan Island National Historical Park

Title page photos: (Left) Lime Kiln Point State Park; (right) killer whales (orcas) in
the San Juan Islands

Photos by the authors
Printed in the United States of America

Library of Congress Cataloging in Publication Data

Mueller, Marge.
    The San Juan Islands, afoot & afloat / Marge & Ted Mueller. — 2nd ed.
    p.   cm.
    Bibliography: p.
    Includes index.
    ISBN 0-89886-157-8 :
    1. San Juan Islands (Wash.) — Description and travel — Guide-books.
I. Mueller, Ted.   II. Title.   III. Title: San Juan Islands, afoot and afloat.
F897.S2M79 1988
917.97'74 — dc19   88-12261
                                                                        CIP

Afoot & Afloat

Contents

9. THE NORTHERN BOUNDARY 207

APPENDICES 229

INDEX 236

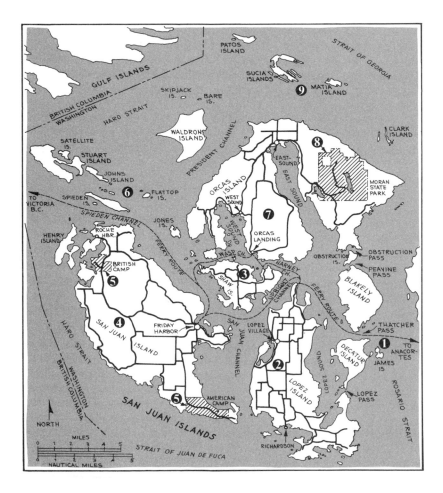

Preface

As its title indicates, this book deals with a broad spectrum of good, clean, healthy, active, and largely nonpolluting recreation available in the San Juan Islands, either on land or on water. Yet the reader thumbing through these pages for his or her favorite sport will soon note that island recreation does not divide itself into two neat categories, for some hikes and campgrounds are accessible only by boat, fishing can be from either boat or land, scuba diving can be boat or shore-based, and many beaches can be reached either by land or sea. And to achieve a catchy title, bicycling was not implied at all, although it certainly is one of the most delightful pastimes in the San Juans, and one that is frequently mentioned in these pages.

While this is a guide to recreation rather than facilities, at the same time it is recognized that any visitor to the San Juans needs to have at least a general idea of what to expect in the way of amenities. Commercial facilities listed in this book are mentioned primarily on a "need to know" basis, such as where to find food, lodging, fuel, moorage, and other necessities. For visitors interested in specifics regarding island facilities, a number of tourist and commercial publications are available that list names, addresses, and phone numbers of businesses in the islands.

The recreations discussed are active, "doing" sorts of things, but they are also take-it-easy, stop-and-smell-the-flowers diversions. The islands aren't very big—one could rush through the three larger ones in a day and claim to have "seen" the San Juans. We urge the reader to stop and think about the history of the Indians who first arrived here in long cedar canoes, and the Spanish and English explorers who came later in sailing ships. Take time to notice the unique birds, flowers, and animals, and the special quality of the clouds piled high above the long, horizontal reaches of the islands. The more you look, the more there is to see.

The places in the book were surveyed over a period of several years, and rechecked just prior to publication. Changes to facilities do occur, however. The authors and The Mountaineers Books would appreciate knowing of any changes to facilities so future editions can be updated. Please address comments to: The Mountaineers Books, 306 Second Avenue West, Seattle, Washington 98119.

We have attempted to make this book accurately reflect the concerns of residents and agencies in the San Juan Islands. We are grateful to the following people who supplied information and checked sections of the manuscript: Darryl Radclift, Chief Ranger of Moran State Park; Dr. Richard Strathmann of the University of Washington Friday Harbor Laboratories; Steve Gobat, Head Ranger, San Juan National Historical Park; and Kevin Barry, San Juan County Parks Department.

Marge and Ted Mueller

Introduction

Tucked away in the northwest corner of the state of Washington, a cluster of emerald gems, set in shimmering azure, lie like a sequestered treasure, awaiting a very special, quiet time to be taken out, examined, and enjoyed.

Tops of an ancient mountain range that over eons settled and became inundated by the sea, the islands were sculpted by massive glacial ice sheets that completely covered them, grinding off the tall peaks, gouging out watery channels and estuaries, and depositing great piles of gravelly debris.

Only the granite hearts of the mountains remain, still bearing the marks of the glaciers' southward journey. Soft glacial till in lowlands has fostered the growth of forests, thickets, and meadows. The buffeting of wind and water on mile upon mile of coastline has carved myriad shapes, ranging from wide, bay-bottom tide flats and long, curving, golden sandspits to narrow, wave-cut bedrock benches.

By definition the San Juans are generally accepted as being those islands lying north of the Strait of Juan de Fuca, south and east of the Canadian boundary and west of—aye, there's the rub! Where do we draw the eastern boundary? San Juan County uses Rosario Strait as its line of demarcation, but islands eastward ache to be called San Juans, too, and with some reason. But holding to bureaucratic boundaries, this book covers those islands lying within San Juan County. Outlying islands are left to be described in another book.

The Skagit County islands of Fidalgo, Guemes, and Cypress serve as an entrance to the San Juans, since a majority of the traffic passes among them, either on the ferry from Anacortes, or through Deception Pass or Swinomish Channel. And it is here that the visitor first sees the forested hills reaching down to placid bays, and the rock buttresses enclosing narrow silvery channels that characterize this ultimate melding of land and water.

And how many San Juan islands are there? As difficult as the territory may be to define, it's even harder to catalog. Figures range from 172 to more than 700! If that seems a startling discrepancy, consider: When is an island merely a rock? How many rocks make a reef? Is a reef an island? What about tidal changes that cause rocks and reefs to appear and disappear and split apart or join together? The problems are legion.

The figure of 172 theoretically includes all of those named islands or groups of named islands within San Juan County, but don't try to count them—you'll never come out with that number. For now let's say "around 200," and go on to other things.

GETTING AROUND IS HALF THE FUN

A watery highway system of broad straits and fjordlike channels links the San Juan Islands. Green-and-white ferries cruise the waters, busily "busing" people, cars, bicycles, trailered or car-top boats, and a startling range of other conveyances from island to island. All ferry routes begin at the city of Anacortes on Fidalgo Island and usually stop at four of the larger islands—Lopez, Shaw, Orcas, and San Juan—and occasionally continue on across Haro Strait to Sidney, B.C., on Vancouver Island.

Passengers view what is advertised as "the most scenic ferry ride in the world" from picture windows in the comfort of the ferry's interior, or from breezy open decks, resembling balconies above the water. At times the vista is a broad panorama of sparkling sea and receding layers of gray-green islands backed by snowcapped distant mountains. Other times rugged rockbound shores seem within touching distance as the ferry threads through narrow passes.

Depending on the season and the luck and sharp eye of the observer, jumping salmon, curious seals, soaring eagles, flocks of migrating waterfowl or even a pod of killer whales may be seen. At each time of day, each change of weather, each advance of season, the islands are painted in infinite variety: the vivid hues of a perfect summer day, the drifting mists of a springtime fog, the blaze of an evening sunset.

Of course private boats, too, travel these waterways—do they ever! Seeking nirvana in salt-scrubbed air and crystal water and tranquil anchorages, they arrive, drove upon drove. Unfettered by such things as stodgy ferry schedules, they wander freely among all the islands, visiting big and little, and particularly frequenting the numerous boat-in marine state parks.

But the non-ferry-served islands are not reserved for affluent yacht owners alone. Even a kayak, canoe, or rowboat will do to reach some, for several of the state parks lie in protected bays within paddling distance. Islands across broader channels can be reached by boats brought via the ferry to launching spots on the larger islands; marinas within the San Juans offer a wide variety of boats to be rented for the hour or day, or chartered for extended cruises. Charters are also available at the nearby cities of Anacortes, Bellingham, and Victoria.

San Juan, Orcas, and Lopez islands have small airports; San Juan Airlines maintains a regular schedule year-round to and from San Juan and Orcas airports, with added flights in the summer. Air services based at San Juan Island and in Anacortes and Seattle charter either small land or seaplanes for flights throughout the islands. Seaplane floats are maintained at Friday Harbor and Roche Harbor. Many of the other islands have single-landing-strip airfields used by private planes or charters.

Many tourists leave their automobiles at the parking lot at Anacortes and walk on the ferry with bicycle or backpack and hiking boots, prepared to enjoy the islands to the fullest at a slower pace. Roads on the ferry-served islands are gently rolling, traffic is light, and the slow and quiet traveler will see far more wildlife and far more beauty than those who rush from here to there in automobiles. Some campgrounds have special areas set aside for hikers and bikers.

THE FLY IN THE OINTMENT

Most paradises have their flaws, and unfortunately the San Juans have theirs, for they are loved almost too much and they can be crowded—exasperatingly crowded! Long ferry lines can mean up to a three-hour wait (and in extreme cases a four- to five-hour delay) for car passengers (foot passengers never have to wait), overnight accommodations can be filled; marinas can be congested and parks can be overflowing with people . . . from June to September.

After Labor Day the tourist crowds almost magically disappear and, except for an occasional sunny winter holiday, the islands are returned to their grateful residents. So be forewarned—expect to wait in a ferry line, make reservations ahead for overnight accommodations, and realize that campgrounds may be filled, forcing you to go elsewhere (signs attempt to notify prospective campers of this before they board the ferry in Anacortes).

Is it worth it? You bet it is! But you must be prepared to be patient and relax (that's one of the great secrets of the island magic). If the ferry leaves you at the dock, there's always another one soon, and no matter how many people there are, the scenery is big enough for everyone to share.

Does that mean that the islands aren't any good off-season? Shhh—that's the best kept secret of all. They're often better. The mobs are gone (but won't be if the secret gets out), and although the weather's cooler and a bit more unpredictable, on a crisp fall day when Indian summer paints the forests, or on a blustery winter day when waves lash furiously at beaches, or on a damp spring day when wildflowers fill hedgerows and lambs cavort in fields, the islands truly show the many subtle nuances of their beauty.

So You've Decided to Take the Ferry . . .

For the novice ferry user, the system may at times seem bewildering; even for the experienced ferry commuter accustomed to cross-sound runs, the procedure in the San Juans is different. In addition, the system can change from year to year, depending on the demand, operating funds available, and new ideas to streamline the operation.

WHICH FERRY TO TAKE

Two types of ferry runs operate through the islands—the domestic and the international. Some years there is also an inter-island run. In the summer departures are about hourly; however, not all ferries stop at all islands. Confusing? It certainly can be. Just remember: it is up to you to be sure you are on the right ferry for your destination. Read the ferry schedule carefully, and when in doubt ask the ticket agent.

For the domestic runs only round-trip tickets are sold at Anacortes, eliminating the need for collecting fares for the return trip. If you buy a ticket for an early stop, such as Lopez Island, and then choose to continue west to a different island, an additional fare will be collected.

The international run takes reservations for vehicles destined for Sidney, so space for additional vehicles on that ferry may be very limited.

If you travel from Anacortes to the San Juans you do not go through customs, even if you are on the international run; however, if you should happen to catch the international run on its return from Sidney on Vancouver Island you will be slightly delayed by the customs inspection in Anacortes.

Ferry schedules (which, by the way, change quarterly) are available at the various ferry terminals and at many businesses in ferry-served cities. Schedules and other information can also be obtained by writing to Washington State Ferries, Pier 52, Seattle, Washington 98104, or by telephoning the number listed in the back of this book.

WALK-ON PASSENGERS

Riding the ferry is a simple matter if traveling by foot: simply buy a ticket and walk on board when the boat arrives, relax by a window, and enjoy the beautiful ride—no hassle, never any wait, and very inexpensive. You may spend the day cruising through the islands, enjoying the changing scene from the breezy decks or enclosed cabins of the ferry. Maps posted on one of the main decks show the route through the islands. A coffee shop on board sells snacks and sandwiches and beverages.

As destinations are neared they are announced on the loudspeaker. Although foot passengers embark and debark via an overhead ramp at Anacortes, at island destinations the car deck is used; watch where other passengers are headed. If you arrive on the auto deck once unloading has begun, use extreme care to avoid moving vehicles.

BICYCLES

This increasingly popular mode of transportation also causes few problems on the ferries, although some people wonder if the day won't come that a ferry will be so filled with bicycles that there won't be any room for cars. There is a small charge for bicycles in addition to the regular foot passenger fare. Passengers are responsible for loading, and unloading, and for the safety and security of their own equipment.

Ferry arriving at Shaw Landing

Bicycles are usually loaded and unloaded as a group, ahead of other vehicles—follow the directions of the ferry crew. After leaving the boat, be aware that a long line of cars with some possibly frazzled drivers are coming right behind you. Stay well to the side so you don't hold them up.

HAND-CARRIED BOATS

Recently paddlers have added a leaf to the Indians' book on portaging by carrying canoes and kayaks onto the ferries, then launching them from nearby public access for tours of the islands. These boats are loaded and unloaded along with bicycles, and also pay a slight charge, in addition to the foot passenger fare.

VEHICLES

Oh, you want to take your *car*? Well, that's another matter. The first question is—won't you reconsider? Will you really need it on the island? Call ahead and see what transportation arrangements can be worked out, for there are many alternatives: if you are visiting friends, perhaps they will pick you up at the terminal; many resorts will meet their customers and drive them to their destination; if you are chartering a boat the same arrangements may be possible. Car rentals and taxi service are available on San Juan Island; bicycles and/or mopeds can be rented on San Juan, Orcas, and Lopez. Or consider car-pooling with a friend.

However, if you're convinced your car or camper is necessary, remember that ferry travel by vehicle can be a delight or an aggravation—it depends largely on the frame of mind of the traveler. Arrive fifteen to twenty minutes ahead of the time of departure to allow time for purchasing tickets and obtaining information.

Peak hours are in the early morning and early evening. Busiest days are Friday through Sunday and, of course, holidays. If possible, avoid these times.

Purchasing Tickets. At Anacortes and Sidney tickets are purchased at a toll plaza, prior to parking. At other locations drivers who are westbound to other island destinations must park first and walk to the ferry landing to purchase tickets. Eastbound travelers do not need to obtain tickets. On the islands the ticket office will not be open until about twenty minutes before the arrival of a ferry.

Lane Assignment. To achieve smooth and quick unloading, cars are assigned lanes at the landing, when purchasing tickets. The lanes are usually signed by destination; however, if you are uncertain check with the agent to see that you are correctly parked.

Do not be upset if later-arriving cars are assigned to shorter lanes. Space on the ferries is apportioned, depending on typical traffic, with more spaces allowed for Orcas and San Juan islands, and fewer for Lopez and Shaw. The system is as fair as possible. At times the ferry will leave the dock with cars still waiting, but open space still obvious. This is done only when it is necessary to save room for cars already waiting on another island.

Most important of all—don't try to crash the line. In addition to being in very bad taste, it can be injurious to your health. After waiting in line for an hour or more, motorists have been known to become pretty irate at people who do not play by the rules, and fistfights have occurred. While this type of retaliation is not recommended, be forewarned—it can happen.

The word is *relax*, be patient and courteous, stay alert, and follow directions. Ferry employees have a monumental task in properly loading cars for the various destinations and assuring that space is fairly allocated to all. Don't hassle them—they know what they're doing. Aside from medical emergencies, they cannot grant special favors to passengers.

Stopovers. The ferry agent will ask your destination; tell the agent your *first* planned stop. If you plan to stop at one island before continuing on to another, be sure that you are parked in the lane for your *first* destination, not your final one.

Overloads. There will be times when there are too many vehicles for a particular ferry to hold. Those waiting will be given priority on the next available boat. Sometimes additional boats will be put on, if they are available. The ferries will keep running until all waiting traffic is handled.

If you anticipate waiting in line, take along a book to read (this one is highly recommended), a pillow to take a nap, or a deck of cards to play games with the kids. (Drain the dog in the bushes, please.)

Get out of your car and walk around, browse through nearby shops, but don't stray too far, for at times during peak traffic hours an extra ferry may be put into service, and can appear without warning. Ferry schedules are often loose during times of heavy traffic, as the boats hurry to provide maximum service. Be alert for ferry arrivals and departures.

Friday Harbor and Orcas have restaurants or cafes overlooking the terminal where passengers can eat while waiting; Anacortes and Lopez have snack bars. If you plan to dine in a restaurant, find out from a ferry attendant when your boat is due, and when you order inform your waitress or waiter what your time schedule is. They may be able to hurry your service along if necessary.

A reservation system would be the ideal solution; unfortunately, no workable system has yet been devised that would be fair to both residents and visitors, taking into account the complexity of loading for multiple destinations.

OVERSIZED VEHICLES

On the ferries there is an extra charge for large RVs, vacation trailers, and trailered boats. In addition, only limited space is allotted for large vehicles, so it is possible that during peak hours you may have a longer wait if you drive this type of camper. Ferry attendants try to load as many customers as possible. As the ferry approaches capacity it is easier for them to shoehorn in six Volkswagens and Toyotas than one pickup camper pulling a boat.

Also be aware that you may be asked to *back* your vehicle on or off the ferry, depending on how it is loaded for inter-island stops. To some drivers, negotiating an unwieldy combination up a ramp in close confines may present a problem.

Now that you've made it on board you may leave your car and go topside to enjoy the most scenic boat ride in the world. The loudspeaker will announce when your destination is near, giving you ample time to return to your vehicle.

Recreation in the San Juans

BOATING

Boating in the San Juans is such a broad category, indulged in by so many people in so many different ways, that it becomes difficult to discuss. Cruisers have one point of view, sailors another, fishermen another, and kayakers yet another. The authors of this book are sailors, and thus are especially concerned about such unpleasant things as scraping keels across rocks and running aground (this perhaps also accounts for the take-it-easy point of view).

Comments regarding boating are as general as possible, touching on as many situations as possible; however, in no way can this book supplant a *good nautical chart* and boating know-how. Charts covering the San Juans are listed in the back of this book.

There are many hazards, both in the islands and inherent to boating. Before attempting any cruising, boaters are urged to take a boating safety course. The U.S. Power Squadron's classes in small boat handling are excellent; information regarding the course can be obtained through the U.S. Coast Guard.

In many places throughout the text cautionary comments refer to "small boats," a vague category including dinghies, rubber rafts, canoes and kayaks, or, in general, any watercraft that is paddled or has minimal power. These cautions can also apply to boaters in larger boats who have had little experience in handling adverse conditions, whatever the size of the craft, for they too should use extra care in navigating San Juan waters.

Many canoe and kayak trips are possible in the San Juans, ranging from quiet paddles around protected bays to extended open water excursions. Canoeists and kayakers should have training in ocean traveling before attempting any open water trips, and *any* boater, before beginning any trip, should check on local weather conditions.

Tidal currents in the San Juans vary from one to six knots, with the strongest currents usually occurring in Spieden Channel. The more severe currents can cause small boaters serious problems, and a strong beam tide can even create difficulties for larger boats navigating in a dense fog.

Tidal current *is not the same as the tide*, although one does give rise to the other. Tides measure the vertical distance water rises and falls above the sea floor due to the gravitational attraction of the sun and moon as well as more obscure forces. Tidal currents represent the horizontal flow of water resulting from this rise and fall of the tide.

Tidal current tables (*not* tide tables), which are printed annually, are keyed to station points on the small craft portfolio charts. The approximate time of maximum velocity of the current can be computed by referencing the tidal current tables to the station point. Although many other factors enter into the actual surface velocity and even the direction of the current, general knowledge of the predicted current is invaluable to safe navigation.

FISHING

The state of Washington requires licenses for both saltwater salmon fishing and freshwater fishing. Licenses are not needed for other types of saltwater angling. The water around the San Juan Islands is open to fishing year-round; be sure to check state regulations for possession limits and other restrictions.

A few of the lakes in San Juan County are open year-round; others have seasons. A brochure published by the state Department of Wildlife lists all regulations and seasons. Lakes within the state parks are subject to these same restrictions.

SCUBA DIVING, SEAFOOD HARVESTING, AND BEACH FORAGING

Numerous publications are available that give suggestions on digging clams and catching crabs and shrimp. Several are listed in the back of this book. To many capturing fresh food for the dinner table is one of the greatest delights of a visit to the beach. Unfortunately this resource is not limitless, and heavy use can seriously deplete areas.

Empty seashells, small rocks, and driftwood may be taken by beachcombers, although many of them may harbor tiny marine life. Check to see if it's inhabited before taking it home. Overzealous beachcombers are often seen hauling off buckets of beach treasures. Most of it is eventually discarded in someone's backyard. While there is certainly pleasure in having a small souvenir of a San Juan trip on a coffee table or mantel, please use restraint in the quantities you take.

Licenses and Limits. Scuba divers, beach users, and boaters trapping crab and shrimp must observe all state regulations on the taking of fish, shellfish, and any other food animal. The saltwater sport fishing pamphlet, published by the state Department of Fisheries, is available in most sporting goods stores, and lists bag limits and other restrictions.

Family bicycling on Lopez Island

If you dig clams, you should know that state law requires that all holes be refilled. It may take several turns of the tide for displaced sand to be leveled, and in the meantime small marine animals trapped in the pile may smother, while others may die from exposure to the sun.

Marine Sanctuaries. All of the seashores and seabed of San Juan County and around Cypress Island in Skagit County are a marine biological preserve. The taking or destruction of any living specimen, except for food use, is prohibited by state law. Special permission may be granted in the case of scientific research; such permission may be obtained by writing the Director of the Friday Harbor Laboratories, P.O. Box 459, Friday Harbor, Washington 98250.

Paralytic Shellfish Poisoning (red tide). When the state Department of Health periodically issues a "red tide warning" and closes particular beaches, the public usually reacts with confusion or skepticism. A clearer understanding of the phenomenon of red tide will lead to a greater respect for its dangers.

The name "red tide" itself contributes to some of the public's confusion, for it is not always visibly red, it has nothing at all to do with the tide, and not all red algae are harmful. Paralytic shellfish poisoning (PSP) is a serious illness caused by *Gonyaulax catanella*, a toxic, single-celled, amber-colored alga that is always present in the water in small numbers. During spring, summer, and fall, certain environmental conditions may combine to permit a rapid multiplication or accumulation of these microscopic organisms. Most shellfish toxicity occurs when the concentrations of *G. catanella* are too sparse to discolor the water; however the free-floating plants sometimes become so numerous that the water appears to have a reddish cast—thus the name "red tide."

Bivalve shellfish such as clams, oysters, mussels, and scallops, which feed by filtering sea water, may ingest millions of the organisms and concentrate the toxin in their bodies. The poison is retained by most of these shellfish for several weeks after the occurrence of the red tide; butter clams can be poisonous for much longer. When the concentration of the toxin in mollusks reaches a certain level, it becomes hazardous to humans who eat them. The toxins cannot be destroyed by cooking and cannot be reliably detected by any means other than laboratory analysis. Symptoms of PSP, beginning with the tingling of the lips and tongue, may occur within a half-hour of ingestion. The illness attacks the nervous system, causing loss of control of arms and legs, difficulty in breathing, paralysis, and, in extreme cases, death.

Shellfish in all counties on Puget Sound are under regular surveillance by the state Department of Health. PSP (or red tide) warnings are issued and some beaches are posted when high levels of toxin are detected in tested mollusks. Warnings are usually publicized in the media; the state toll-free hotline listed in the back of this book has current information as to which beaches are closed to shellfish harvesting. Crabs, abalone, shrimp,

Cascade Lake trail, Moran State Park

and fin fish are not included in closures since there have been no recorded cases of PSP in the Northwest caused by eating any of these animals.

WALKING, HIKING, AND BICYCLING

Roads in the San Juans are narrow, often without shoulders. Although traffic usually is light, care must be taken not to endanger yourself and drivers. Walk on the left, facing oncoming traffic, but bike single file on the right, moving with traffic. Stop to rest only where there are turnouts, *not* on the narrow shoulder, on hills, curves, or in ditches. Wear light-colored and bright clothing so that you are easily seen. Flags are an excellent addition to bicycles.

Restrooms are often few and far between in the rural areas—plan ahead. "Taking to the woods" is often trespassing.

CAMPING

In addition to city, county, and state parks that have camping areas, a number of resorts also have campgrounds. Moran State Park and several commercial campgrounds take reservations in summer. *In summer, do not go to the San Juans unless you are sure of overnight lodging.* At other times of the year, if you have not made prior reservations, check for space as soon as you arrive at your destination, and go elsewhere if accommodations are not available. Campground managers will usually be helpful in suggesting alternatives, and sometimes will call around to help you find a place for the night.

Welcome to the San Juan Islands

No rose is without its thorns, and unfortunately the San Juans, for all their beauty, have theirs. Prices can be high, recreational lands can be crowded, and the residents can be less than welcoming. The county has a population of less than 10,000, and the arrival of several times that number of tourists, almost all during the three months of summer, places severe strains on facilities and on the humor of those who live here year-round.

SOME HARD ECONOMIC FACTS

Some visitors to the San Juans have squalled loudly when they discovered that prices are higher than for comparable goods on the mainland, a few miles away. In a few cases prices can run 30 percent higher. Residents are *not* out to gouge the summer visitor—residents have to pay those high prices too.

The problem is that the islands produce relatively few hard goods, and it is tough to earn a living here. Many of the people who live here are retired; a few others make a living by commuting to mainland jobs; some are writers, artists, and craftsmen whose jobs are not dependent on local suppliers. In the 1980s only two people in the entire county were engaged in full-time farming; the fishing industry is but a shadow of what it once was; aquaculture holds some promise for the future, but it is severely restricted by environmental constraints. Tourism is the number one industry here, and as such it must pay for itself. The people who live here and provide services to tourists still have to pay taxes and feed their families all year, even after the tourists have gone home.

The available public lands (especially parks and campgrounds) are heavily used by tourists, and there is a constant cry for more. Unfortunately every bit of land that is put in the public trust for recreational use narrows the tax base, placing a greater financial burden on those remaining landowners. Additionally, the more tourists that arrive, the greater the burden on public utilities such as power, water, and sewer, and public services such as road maintenance, fire protection, and law enforcement—all of which are paid for by local taxes.

Consider also that nearly all goods that are consumed here must be brought in by ferry. Gasoline, for example, is brought by tanker trucks on special night runs, after the regular passenger runs, due to its hazardous nature. After carrying fuel the ferries must be completely hosed down to eliminate any possible danger from spilled fuel. The cost of this special service must be passed on to the consumer. Although this is one of the more extreme examples, it illustrates the reasons goods and therefore services frequently cost more in the San Juan Islands.

The people who live year-round in the islands do so because they love it here—but they aren't making a killing on the tourists. With this in mind, don't resent it if residents expect a fair price for their goods and services, or expect to be paid for the use of their property.

OF "NO TRESPASSING" SIGNS AND OTHER AGGRAVATIONS

One of the most negative aspects of the San Juans, and most noticeable to those of us devoted to good, clean public recreation, and lots of it, is the proliferation of "No Trespassing" signs from every fence post and every beach, screaming, "Stay away, we don't want you here!" Under such duress the meek become paranoid and the feisty grow defiant.

San Juan residents aren't unfriendly—in fact they're some of the nicest folks around, and most of them feel that tourism is a vital function of their islands. These people are simply tired of boorish boaters who come ashore to relieve themselves and their dogs on private beaches, leaving feces and toilet paper strewn about; they're tired of fences ripped down and campfires built in dry timber and grasslands by campers; they're tired of farm animals shot and children endangered by overzealous hunters; they're tired of ignorant disregard of privacy and outright vandalism and thievery.

The horror stories are plentiful—enough to make fellow tourists ashamed of their breed. But we know we're not all like that, in fact few of us are, so don't take "No Trespassing" signs as a personal affront. Instead, heed them and respect the rights of the people who own the property, who keep the islands functioning with their tax money, and who are doing their best to keep it unspoiled for the future.

Even if lands are unposted, do not assume they are public, or that no one cares if you trespass. Unless clearly designated as public land, *stay off*, somebody owns it. The growth of public recreation in the San Juans lies largely in the hands of the residents. More lands are available for development now, and more could become available in the future, but it will take a favorable position by these residents, convinced that tourism is really good for the economy, before there is any marked increase in public recreation facilities.

PROBLEMS IN PARADISE

San Juan County has trouble coping with pressures created by its own residents and newcomers, let alone hordes of visitors. Many ask, how far can the islands stretch? With an educated, cooperative attitude tourists can minimize the impact on these islands, and somewhat ease the pressures.

Water. "Water, water, everywhere, but not a drop to drink," may soon become the theme of the San Juans, for at present there's barely enough to go around. Some of the small marine park islands have none at all, and wells at several of the other parks frequently run dry by midsummer. Even in the towns water is at a premium, with new construction of homes and businesses limited in some areas by unavailability of water hook-ups. Heavy demands on wells and catch basins are causing these water resources to be depleted.

Sign on faucet at Spencer Spit State Park

As ridiculous as it may sound, when visiting the San Juans, *bring water!* Fill up camper and boat water tanks at home or at the last mainland stop, and once you're there, take it easy. There's enough water at present to assure reasonable cleanliness for everyone, but don't let faucets run unnecessarily at campgrounds, don't rinse down boats with fresh water at marinas, and don't use a gallon of water when a quart will do.

Fire. Going hand-in-hand with the water problem in the islands is the problem of serious fires. There are no convenient fire hydrants on every street corner (and very few street corners). In remote areas reaching a fire is very difficult, and putting it out more so. By late summer roadside grasses and thickets can be tinder dry, so please be extremely careful with matches, cigarettes, and campfires.

Pets. It may come as a surprise, but good old Fido is not exactly welcome in the San Juans. In this largely rural country, city dogs and farm animals often do not mix well, and every year there are many tragic instances of domestic animals being slaughtered by dogs roaming free. The perpetrators were not vicious watchdogs, trained to attack, but friendly, sit-by-the-fire family pets. The San Juan County dog ordinance states that any unlicensed dog found at large in rural areas may be shot. This applies to dogs of residents and visitors alike. Leave your pet at home or keep it on a leash at all times.

Public Lands

Public-owned lands in the San Juans are a calico quilt of city, county, state, and national parks, lands owned by the state Department of Natural Resources (DNR), Coast Guard-maintained lighthouses owned by the U.S. Bureau of Land Management, fishing lakes owned by the state Department of Wildlife, and wildlife refuges operated by the U.S. Fish and Wildlife Service.

Not including the wildlife refuges, this public property presently totals in excess of 12,000 acres, scattered about more than fifty separate locations (the wildlife refuges are an additional 650 acres on eighty-four individual sites). All of these lands except the wildlife refuges (which have two exceptions that will be noted later), and the lighthouse reserves are open to public recreation. Facilities vary from excellent parks with complete camping facilities to primitive patches of land with no improvements whatsoever.

The public sites together offer a rich variety of recreation—boating, fishing, scuba diving, beachcombing, shellfish gathering, hiking, birdwatching, camping, sightseeing, and many other activities.

In addition, The Nature Conservancy, a private conservation organization supported by memberships and donations, has purchased some environmentally important property in the islands, and holds it as nature preserves.

Turnstones on offshore rocks (photo by Bob and Ira Spring)

Rules and regulations in the various areas are set up to preserve the natural environment and to maintain the safety and pleasure of all visitors. The observance of these regulations is especially important in San Juan County, where many local residents view public use lands with an uneasy eye, fearing that public abuse of such lands will flow over to neighboring private property. Additionally, many long-time islanders have a strong paternal feeling toward these areas, for they loved and cared for them long before any mainland tourist ever set foot on them.

WHAT'S A WILDLIFE REFUGE DOING IN THE MIDDLE OF A TOURIST PARADISE?

Before the coming of man, birds nested throughout the San Juans and raised their young here, while migratory birds used the islands as resting stops. Seals and sea lions hauled out on rocks and foraged the waters. Then civilization began encroaching on the most desirable of the islands, leaving only remote offshore rocks for these timorous creatures.

Anticipating man's insatiable demands for home and recreational sites, eighty-four of these islands have been set aside as the San Juan Islands National Wildlife Refuge, providing sanctuaries for pelagic birds and animals. The U.S. Fish and Wildlife Service, which administers these sanctuaries, recognizes that safeguarding of such lands enhances the human benefits associated with wildlife and its environment.

The history of the wilderness area goes back to 1914, when Smith and Minor islands, located in the Strait of Juan de Fuca, were first designated as wildlife refuges. Jones and Matia islands became refuges in 1937, and in 1960 Turn Island, Bird Rocks (in Rosario Strait), Williamson Rocks (west of Fidalgo Island), Colville Island (south of Lopez Island) and Bare Island (north of Waldron Island) were established as a collective San Juan Islands National Wildlife Refuge, with a total of fifty-two acres of land.

Since that time other islands have been added as refuges, and in the 1970s seventy-nine of them (excluding Turn, Jones, Smith and Minor islands, and five acres of Matia Island), achieved wilderness status. Turn and the Matia area remain as National Wildlife Refuges, permitting some recreational use. These protected islands today total 646 acres and range in character from barren reefs, which at high tide are little more than inhospitable offshore rocks, to wooded islets that support deer, raccoons, foxes, rabbits, river otters, weasels, and other small mammals, as well as birds and seals.

As stated in the public use policy statement for the San Juan Islands Wildlife Refuge, which was adopted in 1979, going ashore on any of the islands of the wilderness area at any time is prohibited in order to protect the wildlife there. Special permission may be granted in the case of scientific research. Such permission must be obtained from the Refuge Manager of the Nisqually National Wildlife Refuge, 2625 Parkmont Lane, Building A-2, Olympia, Washington 98502.

DEPARTMENT OF NATURAL RESOURCES BEACHES

Some 78 percent of the tidelands in the San Juan Islands are state owned and open for public use. For the most part these are only the lands lying below the mean high water level, even though upland property is privately owned. In some cases these shores may be so steep and rocky that they are unapproachable. Some beaches, however, are suitable for recreation, but they should not be confused with privately owned property.

In the past the state Department of Natural Resources attempted to locate and identify all public beaches throughout the state utilizing an on-site marking system. Unfortunately, in the initial program such a large number of beach markers were destroyed by vandalism or natural causes that the marking project was abandoned. A booklet published by the DNR, *Your Public Beaches, San Juan Region*, has photos and maps of every one of these DNR beaches in the islands, so most are not described in here.

At Obstruction Pass, Point Doughty, and Griffin Bay the DNR has upland areas that have been developed as parks and are described in this book. These parks are maintained by state parks personnel, by agreement between the two agencies. This arrangement provides more efficient servicing of the camp areas.

THE PARKS—RULES, REGULATIONS, AND COURTESY

The following comments apply specifically to the parks in the San Juans operated by the Washington State Parks and Recreation Commission. In general, these same rules, where relevant, also apply to city, county, and DNR parks. Many of the parks have specific rules and regulations prominently posted on a bulletin board, or have pamphlets available at park headquarters. Check local regulations when using any area.

Some activities listed here may not be specifically covered by park rules, but many do affect the aesthetics of the area and the enjoyment of others. While visiting, be courteous and considerate of other park users and treat the park itself with care. It is not the wish to set down a long, pedantic list of "don'ts" here, in order to restrict the freedom and pleasure of recreationists, but it must be recognized that in any public-use facility one must bend a little to the needs of others, perhaps sacrificing some individual freedom for the benefit of all.

Camping. Camp only in designated areas; camping is limited to seven consecutive days. Do not ditch tents, cut green boughs for beds, hammer nails into trees, or in any other way mutilate nature in the quest for a perfect campsite.

Garbage. Trash cans are provided in all but the undeveloped state parks; please use them, rather than depositing litter on the beaches or in the campgrounds. However, with the increasing waste disposal problem in the San Juans, a sensitive visitor will take garbage back home whenever possible. In areas where garbage cans are not provided, all trash *must* be removed.

When on boats, do not "deep six" debris, whether it is beverage containers, orange peels, or chicken bones. It does not usually come to rest six fathoms down, but will eventually wash up on some beach as ugly litter.

Fires. Build fires only in designated fireplaces and fire rings. This park regulation is vitally important due to the extreme fire hazard during the summer months, and the difficulty of handling fires on the remote islands. Before leaving, be sure your campfire is out. Beach fires are prohibited in order to maintain the beaches in a nearly natural state. Report any out-of-control fire immediately—see Appendix A in the back of this book.

Some boaters cook on portable charcoal-burning barbecues or hibachis that they place on the float alongside their boat. Such cookers have badly charred some of the docks; when using any such stove on the dock be sure the wood is properly shielded from the heat of the cooker. Some places forbid the use of such stoves on the docks.

Driftwood. Small pieces of driftwood may be taken from the beaches for use in fireplaces; however, the use of a chainsaw for the cutting of wood is discouraged, and in some parks is prohibited. State law forbids the removal from beaches of any logs that are considered "marketable," except by licensed patrols.

Living Plants. Green wood may not be gathered from the forests for fires or any other purpose (it doesn't burn well, anyway). Plants may not be dug up nor flowers picked.

Vehicles. Motorized vehicles or bicycles are prohibited on service roads and trails. Observe posted speed limits on public roads within parks.

Boats. In the moorage area of marine state parks the boat speed limit is three mph (no-wake speed). In addition to being extremely annoying to other boaters, hot-rodding or racing, even in small outboard-powered dinghies, can create a wake that may swamp other small craft, send hot food flying from a cruiser's galley range, or cause other damage. Boaters are legally responsible for any damage caused by their wakes.

Moorage. Buoys and floats are on a first-come, first-served basis. The practice of individuals attempting to "reserve" space by tying a dinghy to a float or buoy is not legal in the state parks. Moorage on floats or buoys is limited to thirty-six consecutive hours (or two nights).

It is courteous to use the minimum moorage space possible on a float. Beach small boats whenever you can, instead of tying up to a float. Berth small cruisers or runabouts as far forward as possible, leaving the end of the float for larger boats that require deeper water and more maneuvering space.

During the busy summer season, it is considerate (and often more fun) to raft together with a friend on a buoy, thus freeing a moorage for another boater. Observe restrictions posted on the buoys limiting the number and size of boats. Too many boats rafted together can displace a buoy.

When anchoring, be sure your hook is properly set and you are not drifting, and that the swing of your anchorage will not permit you to collide with others. While artists may paint pretty pictures with boats all neatly swinging in unison, in real life it doesn't always work that way, as the shape of the hull greatly affects the way wind and tide push a boat, and the maximum northerly swing of one boat may coincide with the maximum southerly swing of another. Be sure your anchorage is secure before leaving your boat or retiring for the evening, or the "things that go bump in the night" may be you.

Pets. Pets must be on a leash no longer than eight feet and be under control at all times. Some boat-bound yachtsmen regard the land facilities of state parks merely as handy places to allow their dogs to relieve themselves. Even the most devout animal lovers find it hard to think kindly of these pets while trying to scrape doggy droppings from the grooves of their Topsiders. State park regulations dictate that pet owners must clean up after their pets. Violators are subject to fines.

Fees. There is a fee for use of campsites at Deception Pass, Moran, and Spencer Spit State Parks. Fees are charged for moorage on the state park floats, whether you are tied directly to the float or rafted alongside. The fee schedule is published in newspapers and boating periodicals in the spring. Since some of the marine parks have a self-register system with fees deposited in a locked box, boaters should have the proper change on hand.

Noise. Since sounds carry greater distances over water, use care that radios or boisterous noises do not penetrate to nearby boats or campsites.

Vandalism. It probably does little good to talk about intentional vandalism here. The damaging or removal of park property is, of course, illegal and when observed should be reported to the proper authorities.

Some acts of vandalism, however, are committed out of thoughtlessness or ignorance. Spray painting or scratching graffiti on rocks or other natural features may not be recognized by park visitors as vandalism until they are confronted with a lovely sandstone wall turned ugly with mindless scrawling. Such defacement is prohibited in all parks.

Digging into banks with shovels, picks, or any similar tool is also prohibited. Holes dug in beaches for clams or for any other purpose must be refilled.

Marine Life. Observe state Department of Fisheries regulations on the taking of fish and shellfish in saltwater areas; in freshwater lakes the regulations of the state Department of Wildlife apply. All of the seabed of the San Juan Islands is a marine preserve. It is unlawful to remove from beaches any living animals such as starfish, sand dollars, or sea anemones, except those edible varieties defined and regulated by the state Department of Fisheries.

Wildlife. Hunting or harassing of wildlife and discharge of firearms is prohibited within the state parks.

Emergencies or Complaints. In parks where rangers are not on duty, the proper authority can be reached by marine or Citizens' Band radio if immediate action is necessary. A list of park addresses is included in Appendix A at the back of this book. In matters of less urgency, the rangers should be contacted by telephone or in writing. Some state parks have telephones on the grounds.

Emergency Assistance

Overall legal authority in the San Juan Islands rests with the county sheriff. The emergency number is 911. Complaints or other business should be referred to the sheriff's office number listed in the back of this book.

The U.S. Coast Guard has primary responsibility for safety and law enforcement on the water. Marine VHF channel 16 is continuously moni-

Helicopter evacuation of injured hiker at Jones Island

tored by the Coast Guard and should be the most reliable means of contact in case of emergencies on the water. The Coast Guard monitors Citizens' Band channel 9 at some locations and times, but it has no commitment to full-time radio watch on this channel. Several volunteer groups do an excellent job of monitoring the CB emergency frequency and will assist as best they can with relaying emergency requests to the proper authorities.

Boating and beach travel entail unavoidable risks that every traveler assumes and must be aware of and respect. The fact that an area is described in this book is not a representation that it will be safe for you. The areas described herein vary greatly in the amount and kind of preparation needed to enjoy them safely. Some may have changed since this book was written, or conditions may have deteriorated. Weather conditions can change daily or even hourly, and tide levels will also vary considerably. An area that is safe in good weather at low or slack tide may be completely unsafe during inclement weather or at times of high tide or maximum tidal current. You can meet these and other risks safely by exercising your own independent judgment and common sense. Be aware of your own limitations, those of your vessel, and of conditions when or where you are traveling. If conditions are dangerous or if you are not prepared to deal with them safely, change your plans. Each year many people enjoy safe trips in the waters and on the beaches of the San Juan Islands. With proper preparation and good judgment, you can too.

Ferry entering Harney Channel; Obstruction Pass and Mt Baker beyond

1. Thatcher Pass

The "front door" to the San Juan Islands, Thatcher Pass is the main thoroughfare for much of the islands' pleasure boating and all of its ferry traffic. Although the ½-mile-wide channel has ample room for all the vessels that pass through it, it may seem snug quarters for sailboats trying to make way in light wind when a monstrous green-and-white ferry is hard astern. The only navigational hazard in the pass is Lawson Rock, at the northeast side of the channel, which is marked with a daybeacon.

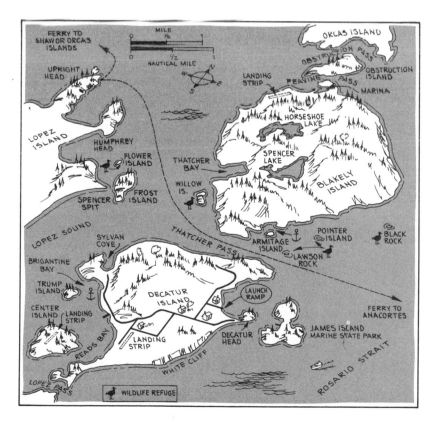

31

Willow Island from the ferry

Thatcher Pass provides westbound ferry passengers with their first close-up views as the boat threads its way between Decatur and Blakely islands. Tourists "ooh" and "aah" at little Armitage Island and the twin bays behind it, and perhaps with a start they notice that there is a stately bald eagle perched atop a fir snag returning their stares.

At times, depending on tide and traffic conditions, the ferry comes seemingly within arm's reach of little Willow Island, on the southwest side of Blakely Island. This 9½-acre rock is one of the islands of the San Juan Islands National Wildlife Refuge. The broad streak of white guano visible on the south side of the island marks the nesting area for a small colony of pigeon guillemots. With its black body and white wing patches, this member of the auk family resembles a pigeon in coloring and size, and early settlers called it a sea pigeon. Although its beak is as sooty black as its body, the inside of its mouth (which it opens wide during mating rituals) and its legs are bright red, making it a very distinctive bird when sighted.

Blakely Island

Facilities (marina at Peavine Pass): Guest moorage, diesel, gas, groceries, marine supplies and repairs, laundry, showers, picnic shelter, fireplace

Poised at either side of Thatcher Pass, Blakely and Decatur islands stand as protectors of the inner channels of the San Juans, their eastern shores bearing the brunt of storms whipping up Rosario Strait. Blakely Island, the larger, higher, and more imposing of the pair, lies to the north of the passage. Although the island covers only seven square miles, within that space its forested slopes rush steeply upward to a height of over 1,000 feet. Underwater the shores drop off just as sharply, providing only a few skimpy beaches.

On the far northern end of Blakely Island, facing on Peavine Pass, is a marina—the island's only commercial facility. Fuel and temporary moorage are available at the long float in the outer harbor, while a few additional overnight moorage slips are in the inner harbor behind a rock breakwater. The entrance to the inner harbor is shallow but well marked; favor the breakwater side of the channel for the deepest water. The island airport is immediately to the southwest.

The marina store is well stocked—since it is the only store on the island it provides groceries for residents. A nearby picnic shelter with a nice view of Peavine Pass has tables, sinks, and a fireplace for the use of visitors. Don't plan on extended shore leave here, for all island roads are private and are gated just beyond the marina.

Visiting boaters can find nice anchorages behind pretty little Armitage Island on the southeast end of Blakely Island, just east of Thatcher Pass. All buoys and floats in the bay are private, as is the shoreline. Tidelands of Armitage Island itself are public below mean high water level; however, the shoreline drops off so steeply that the tidal shelf is very narrow. The bay, as well as the channel around the island, has more than ample depth for boats of almost any draft.

Thatcher Bay, on the west side of Blakely, north of Willow Island, looks like an appealing spot for a stopover, but it is quite shallow, especially on its south side. Safe anchorage can only be had well out from shore. At times the bay is used for storing rafted logs.

Most of Blakely Island is owned by a small corporation that purchased the land from a logging company. It sells only a few home sites each year in order to ensure the island's orderly development. Such exclusiveness stems not from snobbery or for a desire for inflated real estate prices, but from a great love for this delicate island and concern for the welfare of the people who build their homes there. Boaters should respect their intent and admire the island from the water, but stay off private property.

Seattle Pacific University has been deeded several sections of the island, including beach lands and property bordering on two lakes, totaling about one-fourth of the island's acreage. The property was donated to the university to be used in its natural state for biological and environmental research and educational programs. The university has constructed a small library, laboratory, dining hall, and dormitory. In order to keep the island natural, only small groups of students use the facility.

Black Rock, Pointer Island, and Lawson Rock, lying east of Blakely, along Rosario Strait, along with Willow Island on the west side, are all part of the San Juan Islands National Wildlife Refuge, offering protection to nesting seabirds.

Decatur Island

Just half the size of its neighbor to the north, and with less dramatic contours, Decatur Island may not seem as exclusive as Blakely, but all property here also is privately owned, and there are no stores. The only public boating facility is a boat launch ramp on the north end of the island at the end of the county road that crosses the island. A short dock located on the southwest end of the island on Reads Bay at the community of Decatur is for use by residents only. Nearby is the island airplane landing strip.

Several good spots to drop a hook can be found around the island. Brigantine Bay, a bit to the north behind Trump Island, has good anchorages quite close to shore; however, when southerlies blow, the flat southern tip of Decatur offers no protection. Shrimp pots set here usually bring in enough of the tasty crustaceans to enhance a galley dinner.

Around a rocky headland is another fine anchorage at Sylvan Cove, known locally sometimes as Kan Kut Bay. The neat buildings and velvet grasslands at the head of the bay are an idyllic scene from the water. The largest of the buildings was a boat-in restaurant many years ago, but today all property surrounding the cove, including the dock and buoys, are part of a private real estate development.

On the east shore of Decatur Island is a large, unnamed, curving bight with a gentle, sandy beach punctuated by the dramatic round knob of Decatur Head. The south end of the bight offers some anchorages to over-flow crowds from James Island Marine State Park, but there is precious little wind protection from any quarter. Care must be used anchoring here, as it is quite shallow, especially on the west side. The county boat launch ramp faces on this bay.

Decatur Head, which is known geologically as a tombolo, was once a separate little island, but the action of wind and waves over centuries of time built up the sand neck that now joins it to the larger island. Spencer Spit, on Lopez Island just to the west, is an example of such a neck in the process of being formed as it stretches out toward Frost Island.

James Island Marine State Park

Park area: 113 acres; 12,340 feet of shoreline
Access: Boat
Facilities: Campsites, picnic tables, picnic shelter, fireplaces, latrines, dock with float, mooring buoys, portable toilet dump, *no water*

Lacking the broad beaches and sheltered harbors of other San Juan marine parks, James Island is often ignored by visitors in favor of more spacious and glamorous spots. Its coves are frequently used only as an overnight stop for southbound boaters awaiting the turn of the tide at

Boat moored on the east side of James Island

Deception Pass. Nevertheless, the park offers pleasant camping and scenic hikes to those who linger awhile.

The park lies 4 nautical miles west of Sunset Beach or Flounder Bay on Fidalgo Island, the nearest point where trailered boats can be launched. Hand-carried boats can be launched at Spencer Spit on Lopez Island, which is 4 nautical miles to the west. Passage from Lopez Island to James in a very small or paddle-powered boat must consider tidal currents that can reach 2 knots in Thatcher Pass. Heavy boat traffic in the channel may add to the hazard.

James Island is one of the most rugged of the San Juan Island Marine State Parks, with high, steep bluffs broken by coves on opposing sides of the island. The eastern side of the island has two small adjacent coves holding two mooring buoys each. These anchorages are open to weather and waves from Rosario Strait. A cove on the west side, sheltered by Decatur Island, contains a dock with float large enough for three or four boats. Decatur Head lies immediately west across the ¼-mile-wide channel, tethered to its parent island by a narrow spit of land.

Since moorage is so limited at James Island, be considerate by tying up boats to occupy the least amount of dock space, and do not take up dock space with dinghies. Dock space or buoys cannot be reserved by tying a dinghy to them.

The deep water of the island's coves and the strong current, especially on the west side, make anchoring difficult if the buoys and float are occupied, but small boats can be easily beached at either place. The western cove is a favorite scuba diving area; while fish are few, the invertebrate life is varied and colorful.

Scattered in the trees on the narrow neck of land between the coves, a picnic shelter and a dozen campsites provide picnic tables, fireplaces, and pit toilets. Campers must furnish their own fresh water.

From the camp area a broad, signed trail meanders into deep forest, arriving in ½ mile at a tiny beach on the far edge of the western cove. Two campsites lie in the forest above the beach. A secluded driftwood-strewn beach on the south flank of the island can be reached by boat or overland exploration.

Many ill-defined paths lace the island, some of them marked with colored plastic streamers. Use care in following these paths along the high grassy bluffs as many of them dwindle away. Overzealous explorations can leave a hiker hung up on the cliffs; an unwary step can result in a bad fall into the rocks or water.

Persons planning to camp should be forewarned of a greedy horde of masked bandits that lie in wait onshore—raccoons. Although they may seem cute early in the evening as their bright eyes glimmer at the edge of your campfire, their charm palls when you awake at 2 a.m. to find them rattling cook pots and rifling groceries. To discourage these persistent pests, secure everything back on your boat or inside your tent.

Mackaye Harbor

2. Lopez Island

Cow country—and sheep, and goats and horses, too. A green patchwork quilt of fields and pastures, interrupted by sections of velvety forest rolling down to the edge of the sea; farmyards with chickens busily scratching around great piles of fishing nets; arrow-straight roads, edged by fences and hedgerows, disappearing into soupy San Juan mists. At the island's southern tip the level land tilts upward to form steep, craggy cliffs and deeply notched, rocky bays; as if to compensate for its meek, pastoral nature, here Lopez Island presents some of the most rugged shoreline to be found in any of the San Juans.

Lopez, the most level of the three largest San Juan islands, was once a major agricultural supplier for western Washington. Its dry climate favored crops of grain and orchards of fruit. Dams built on the Columbia River

during the 1930s later brought irrigation to the arid lands of eastern Washington, converting them to bountiful farmland with which the San Juans could not compete. Agriculture, and with it the islands' economy, declined. The few farms still in operation today primarily provide food for residents.

Lopez Island does not display as much distinct marine flavor as Orcas and San Juan islands. Its shoreline does not attract the usual San Juan hordes of yachtsmen, since it lacks the good harbors necessary for such activity. Bays on the north are quite shallow, while southern ones are farther from the boating mainstream, and those facing on the Strait of Juan de Fuca are subject to bad weather and uncomfortable swells. Nevertheless,

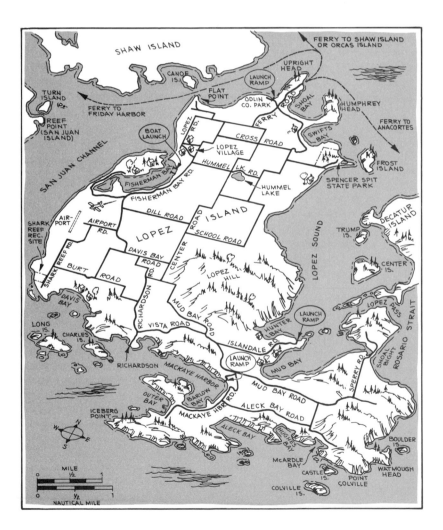

several choice spots along its shores do make fine stopovers for boating tourists, and the gently rolling heartland is a joy to hikers and bicyclists.

The island is reached by ferry from Anacortes (about a forty-five-minute trip), or from Sidney, B.C., on Vancouver Island (slightly less than two hours away). The ferry landing is in a cove at the tip of Upright Head, where the only tourist facility is a small coffee shop. A brief, steep grade up from the ferry landing challenges trailer-pulling vehicles and bicyclists before the flat of the island is reached. City folk visiting the San Juans for the first time have been known to unload their cars at Lopez, drive down the timber-bordered road of Upright Head, make a quick loop around the island, and scurry back to the next departing ferry, shocked at the lack of such amenities of "civilization" as shopping malls, fast-food chains, or movie theaters.

Lopez Island can also be reached by San Juan Airlines, which stops at the local airfield, by prior reservation. Charter airlines also provide service to the island.

The only island "business center" is at Lopez Village and on the nearby road that runs along the east shore of Fisherman Bay. Businesses here include a grocery store, several small shops, and two marinas, one with a restaurant and overnight lodging. Meals are offered at inns located at Fisherman Bay and on the south end of the island at Mackaye Harbor. The historic general store at Richardson was destroyed by a fire in the fall of 1990. Boat fuel is still available at the Richardson dock; auto fuel is also available there, as well as at service stations at the intersection of Mud Bay and Mackaye Harbor roads and at Lopez Village.

An increase in campsites over the last few years at Odlin County Park and Spencer Spit State Park, the only two car campgrounds on the island, has raised the total number of available sites to 75. If these areas are all filled, it may be necessary to go elsewhere—check in early in the day to be sure you have a site. Camping along island roads is prohibited.

Among an entire bevy of islands described as friendly and relaxed, Lopez is considered to be the friendliest and most laid-back of all. The common phrase here is: "Wave, you're on Lopez." First-timers are surprised to find that drivers passing each other on the road offer a salutory wave, and wonder if they have been mistaken for someone else. Usually it dawns on the tourist that this is simply a charming practice unique to an island where the population is so small that everyone is known, and even "outlanders" are welcome.

Although accommodations in campgrounds, inns, and bed-and-breakfast establishments may be filled in the summer, don't overlook off-season. The San Juans receive only half the amount of rain that falls on Seattle and other Puget Sound areas, so the dry climate can make spring and fall touring the most delightful of all. The crowds are gone, but the beauty remains—and is even enhanced. In spring, shores and pastures are filled with awakening life; by fall the scent and colors of autumn permeate the waysides, and bays host flotillas of migrating waterfowl.

All facilities are open year-round, and visitors are especially welcomed off-season. Reservations are usually not needed, but check ahead to be sure.

The North End

ODLIN COUNTY PARK

Park area: 80 acres; 4,000 feet of shoreline
Access: Ferry to Lopez Island, boat
Facilities: 30 campsites, picnic tables, fireplaces, picnic shelters, group camp, drinking water, pit toilets, boat launch (ramp), dock with float, children's play equipment, ball field, hiking trails
Attractions: Beachcombing, fishing, boating, paddling, swimming, clam digging, hiking, scuba diving

Truly a family park, with a beached rowboat where youngsters can play at "going to sea" with driftwood oars, an old artillery gun to climb on, a softball diamond for family ballgames, a volleyball net, and an open field for Frisbee matches. All this and an outstanding beach, too!

Odlin County Park is located within minutes of the ferry terminal at Upright Head. To reach it, follow Ferry Road south from the ferry landing for 1¼ miles; at the first two-way intersection turn right (west), and follow the road downhill for 300 yards to the campground.

Odlin County Park

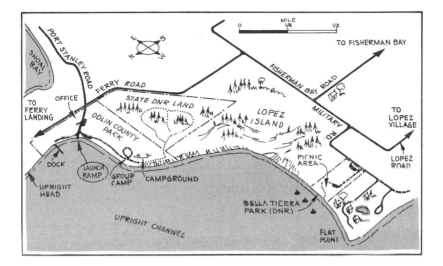

The park, on a curving, sandy bay, makes a nice quick stop for lazing in the sun while waiting for the next ferry—you may even decide to linger awhile and catch a later one. Just offshore the ferry sails by in Upright Channel on the run to Friday Harbor that bypasses Wasp Passage.

A boat launch for trailered boats is straight ahead at the end of the park's main road; a narrow road branching to the south leads past the ball field (complete with bleachers) to the camping area. The first of the park's 30 campsites are just above the beach, with elbow-to-elbow picnic tables and fireplaces.

The park road continues south into the trees to more private, sheltered sites and a small grassy clearing for group get-togethers. Bicycle and walk-in campsites are found beyond the road end, along the bank overlooking the bay. In summer the beachfront campsites are frequently more heavily used than those at Spencer Spit State Park, where sites are farther away from the water, in timber some distance above the shore.

By boat, Odlin County Park lies 3½ nautical miles southeast of Orcas, and 5½ nautical miles northeast of Friday Harbor. A dock with a float at the north end of the park is available for loading and unloading—no overnight moorage. The soft bottom of the shallow bay provides good anchoring. At the north side of the park, near the dock, the bottom begins to drop off quite steeply.

Scuba diving is excellent near the pier and along the sheer rock walls and submerged boulders on the west side of Upright Head. A rainbow assortment of sea stars cling to the rock, and schools of curious fish swim by. Tidal currents outside of the bay are quite strong. The sandy bottom of the bay is habitat for sea pens, sea cucumbers, and striped nudibranchs.

The fine sandy beach invites swimming, sand-castle building, and barefoot walks. At low tide dig clams—if those ahead of you haven't found them already. Uprising cliffs halt beach walks on the north side of the park. South, the gradual shoreline can be followed all the way to Flat Point, 1½ miles away.

Trails out of the campground circle around in a flatland of second-growth timber and brush. Although they make nice walking, none have particular destinations; some dead-end, others loop back on themselves. Good mushroom picking in season. A primitive shore-side trail goes past the last two walk-in campsites and along the gradually steepening embankment, 100 feet above the water. Use care here, as the edge is undercut and can be dangerous—not recommended for children.

BELLA TIERRA PARK (DNR)

Access: Ferry to Lopez Island, boat
Facilities: Picnic tables, fireplaces, latrines, water, mooring buoys
Attractions: Picnicking, boating, beachcombing, clam digging

Newly developed by the Department of Natural Resources, Bella Tierra Park is a welcome addition to the day-use recreational facilities on Lopez Island. The park has two picnic sites nestled in dense brush upland from the beach, two other picnic sites with fire braziers, and water in a grassy clearing on the bluff above the beach. Three offshore mooring buoys are provided for visiting boaters.

To reach the park by land, drive south on Ferry Road, and at a T intersection turn west on Fisherman Bay Road. When this road heads south, continue straight ahead on Military Road. In ¼ mile Military Road heads north, then shortly turns west again. West of this last corner is a parking lot, gated except during daylight hours. A second gate requires visitors to walk the short distance down the service road to the picnic areas and the steps of the path to the beach.

A gently sloping gravel beach with tide-line driftwood and beach grass looks out on Upright Channel. Over 1½ miles of shoreline can be enjoyed by walking east to Odlin Park or west around Flat Point to the end of the public beach 300 yards south from there. At the Flat Point residential area, only the beach below mean high tide level is public.

LOPEZ VILLAGE

Access: Ferry to Lopez Island, boat (walk from Fisherman Bay)
Facilities: Groceries, restaurants, stores, historical museum

The tiny hamlet of Lopez Village, at the entrance to Fisherman Bay, has a number of stores, but no adjacent dock. The motel, restaurant, and marinas are ¾ mile down the road to the south.

On weekends during the summer a "farmer's market" in the village offers fresh produce from local gardens. A pharmacy and a few additional businesses are located along the road south of the marinas.

A block north of the village stores, the Lopez Historical Museum, which is open on weekend afternoons, houses a collection of island photographs and memorabilia. Old farm equipment recalls the days when fruit, grain, and vegetables grown on the island flowed to dining tables in cities throughout Puget Sound.

The only public beach in the vicinity is the road end just west of the post office, although a 20-foot-high bank and precarious access discourage use of the limited beach.

To reach Lopez Village and Fisherman Bay by land from the ferry terminal, follow Ferry Road south for 2¼ miles. At a T intersection turn right (west), and in ½ mile head south on Fisherman Bay Road. In 2 miles the road to Lopez Village is on the right; turn here or continue on to Fisherman Bay, 5½ miles total distance from Upright Head.

FISHERMAN BAY

Access: Ferry to Lopez Island, boat
Facilities: Guest moorage with power and water, boat launch (sling, ramp), boat rental, marine supplies and repair, diesel, gas, restrooms, showers, laundromat, picnic area, restaurant, snack bar, stores, motel, swimming pool, bicycle rentals
Attractions: Boating, paddling, bicycling, fishing, crabbing, clam digging

Fisherman Bay could more aptly be named Fisherman Lagoon, for with its shallow bottom, stagnant water, and mud-flat barrier built up by wave action, it is more closely related to the small lagoons found throughout the San Juans than the clear, deep-water bays. But such a lagoon!

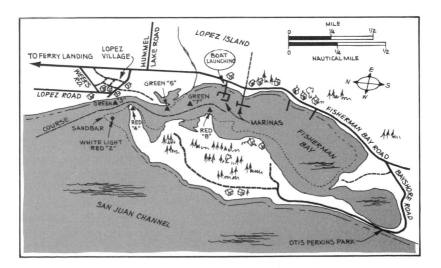

Checking out a crab pot at Fisherman Bay

Nearly ½ mile across and more than a mile in length, with shimmering, tranquil waters and evening sunsets that bring tears to the eyes.

Many boatmen bypass Fisherman Bay, feigning disinterest: actually they are apprehensive about the shallow entrance channel. Once this barrier is conquered, however, any yachtsman can lean back with the air of an experienced salt and play one-upsmanship with less accomplished skippers. It is claimed by businesses inside the bay that any boat that does not draw more than 4½ feet can enter the bay safely if the tide is not below zero. If that statement does not totally reassure a pilot, enter on a rising tide to avoid the embarrassment of being stuck on a sand bar through a change of tide.

The accompanying map should be helpful when navigating the channel. Once into the channel keep red, even-numbered markers to starboard, green, odd-numbered to port when entering, the opposite when leaving.

If the anxious moments of the channel can be forgotten, the ½-mile journey is delightful, especially to large boats unaccustomed to such close quarters—cruising through the front yards of quaint little waterfront homes, with the banks almost within arm's reach. Moorage, fuel, boat servicing, supplies, and launch and haul-out facilities are available at one of two marinas on the east shore. Picnic tables and bicycle service and rentals are also in the vicinity. Perhaps treat yourself to dinner at the restaurant or an inn farther down the bay. Good anchorages can be had anywhere once you're within the harbor.

The bay is superb for small boat paddling. Put in hand-carried boats at the marina and explore the channel and around the bay. Drop off a crab pot near the western shore and return in the morning to find it filled with Dungeness—perhaps.

OTIS PERKINS PARK

Park area: 1 acre; 60 feet of shoreline on San Juan Channel, 600 feet on Fisherman Bay
Access: Ferry to Lopez Island
Facilities: Picnic tables, *no water*

A startling sight from the road at Fisherman Bay, especially at high tide, are cars virtually driving on water across the low sandspit at the head of the bay to reach a forested peninsula. This narrow neck of land is interesting to drive or bike, but spectacular to walk. To reach it, turn west at the south end of the bay on Bayshore Road and follow the road as it curves around the mudflat.

At the south end of the Fisherman Bay spit, facing on San Juan Channel, is tiny Otis Perkins Park. The park is named for a long-time Lopez Island resident who generously donated the land.

A pair of picnic tables and trash cans are the extent of the park's facilities, unless one counts the sweeping views up and down the length of San Juan Channel, across to San Juan Island, and back to the lagoonlike stretch of Fisherman Bay. Prevailing westerlies whipping off the Strait of Juan de Fuca over the "toe" of San Juan Island can make the site quite breezy.

Park cars here and walk along the narrow spit, either on the beach or at road's edge. Within a few feet of one another are two entirely different saltwater environments. Inside the bay is grassy, saltwater marsh, where crabs, clams, tiny fish, and myriad other small critters live, and where seabirds gather to feed and rest. Outside is smooth, clean beach with wave-swept sand and silvered driftood, but relatively little shore life. The constant movement of waves from San Juan Channel prevents the growth of marine life here.

The road continuing on to the forested peninsula dead-ends at private property, and offers no further public access or even views of either the bay or San Juan Channel.

HUMMEL LAKE

Access: Ferry to Lopez Island
Facilities: Boat launch (ramp)
Attractions: Fishing (freshwater), birdwatching, paddling

Here's a modest little pond that packs a lot of interest into its 36-plus acres of surface. It is a favorite for fishermen, a pleasant spot for wildlife

Hummel Lake

watchers, and is large enough for boaters to take a brief paddle; boats with gasoline motors are not permitted. The lake is stocked with trout, bass, and bluegill.

Hummel Lake is located on the Hummel Lake Road, ¾ mile east of the village of Lopez. To reach it from the ferry landing, follow Ferry Road south for 2¼ miles to a T intersection. Turn left (east), then in ¼ mile turn right onto Center Road, which can be followed to the lake, about 4½ miles total distance from the start. The public boat launch ramp and parking area, which is maintained by the state Department of Wildlife, is on Center Road, just south of the Hummel Lake Road intersection. Ample parking; a latrine is also available adjacent the parking area.

Cattails and blackberry brambles edging the lake rustle with bird life, including marsh wrens and colorful red-winged blackbirds. Virginia rails nest among the reeds—their narrow bodies and strong toes are adaptations for living in the muck and tightly packed reeds of marshes. The bird's assortment of odd calls, ranging to a piglike grunt, is often mistaken for frogs in the still of a spring night. The rail's close relative, the American coot, or "mud hen," also nests here.

Since the lake is only 12 feet deep at its maximum, the water warms early in the spring, and it soon blossoms with algae. Although the green growth may seem unappealing, it is harmless to swimmers.

SPENCER SPIT STATE PARK

Park area: 129 acres; 7,840 feet of shoreline
Access: Ferry to Lopez Island, boat
Facilities: 45 campsites, picnic tables, fireplaces, picnic shelters, beach fire rings, drinking water, restrooms, pit toilets, telephone, trailer dump, mooring buoys
Attractions: Boating, paddling, fishing, beachcombing, clam digging, crabbing, shrimping, birdwatching, hiking

The popularity of Spencer Spit State Park on Lopez Island grows with each new "discovery" by campers, bicyclists, and boaters. Visitors delight in the marine view and the many activities the beaches and waters offer. To the north, tiny Flower Island nestles against the imposing backdrop

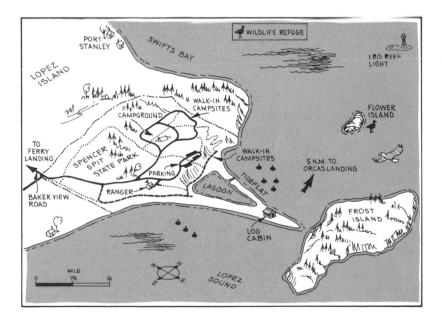

Clam digging at Spencer Spit

of Orcas Island. At sunset the channel is bathed in afterglow and the lights of ferries glimmer against Orcas's dark silhouette.

To reach the park from the ferry landing at Upright Head, drive 1¼ miles to the first road junction, and turn left on Port Stanley Road. At 3¾ miles turn left onto Baker View Road, continuing straight ahead to the park at 5 miles. The route is well signed. The park is 8 nautical miles by boat west of Anacortes, the closest point on the mainland where boats can be launched.

Inside the park entrance a spur road leads to two loops of timbered campsites on the hillside above the beach. Almost half of the sites have space for trailers, although none have hook-ups. In the center of the northernmost loop are walk-in camps and two large shelters equipped with bunks for the use of families or groups. Fifteen more walk-in campsites for cyclists and boaters are strung along the beach.

Vehicles are permitted to drive on the service road from the park office to the beach only for loading and unloading. A group picnic area is located at the top of the bluff next to a parking lot; trails from there lead to the beach. Restrooms (no showers) are located at the camping and parking areas, while lower sites along the beach make do with pit toilets. Fire rings, stoves, and picnic tables located on the beach invite daytime picnicking and evening bonfires. Build fires only in designated areas.

Scattered on either side of the spit, 16 mooring buoys accommodate boaters, with plenty of space for additional boats to drop anchor. There is no trailered boat launching at the park; however small boats can easily be hand carried the short distance to the beach from the loading area.

Winter storms toss up driftwood and shells for beachcombers on the mile-long sandy beach. Butter, horse, and littleneck clams can be dug during summer low tides, and the waters yield crab, shrimp, and bottomfish. During warm summer days the broad beaches heat the usually frigid water to bearable swimming temperatures.

Spencer Spit is an excellent example of a sandspit enclosing a saltchuck lagoon, commonly found in the San Juans. These lagoons are formed over a long period of time by the action of wind and tide on sandy beaches. In many cases lagoons of this type eventually fill with sediment and no longer contain water. The perimeter of the lagoon displays a rainbow of colors from various algae and saltwater plants.

A wide variety of birds pause at the lagoon during migration, including several kinds of gulls, a dozen types of ducks, great blue herons, kingfishers, black brant, and Canada geese. A billboard display near the parking lot explains the geology and ecology of this unique lagoon.

Rabbits tunnel in the sandy hillside behind the beach and at dusk the long-eared residents appear. Raccoons, too, roam the beaches at night, scavenging for tasty sea creatures. These animals, as well as the local black-tailed deer, can usually be seen during a quiet evening stroll along the beach or park roads.

A log cabin on the end of the spit has been reconstructed in the original style and on the site of a beach cabin that was built here more than fifty years ago. Some of the logs are from the original cabin, others were scavenged from the beach. The historic old structure now serves as a picnic shelter. A second picnic shelter, built in the remnants of the old Spencer family home, is located at the base of the hill above the spit.

Frost Island lies just a stone's throw off the east end of the spit. Although all of its shores below the mean high water level are a public DNR beach, the rocky shoreline drops off so steeply that it is not walkable except at very low water. Do not trespass on property above the tideland, as it is all privately owned. When boating around the island in small craft navigate with care, as the tidal current can be strong in the channel.

Trails beginning at the lower campground road climb up the hill to the other camp areas and beyond into the thick timber of the hillside. No views due to the heavy growth, but still a lovely, cool hike on a warm summer day. These trails are primarily firebreaks terminating at the park boundary.

Boats framed by the cabin at the end of Spencer Spit

FLOWER ISLAND AND LEO REEF

Less than ½ mile offshore north of Spencer Spit State Park, Flower Island is part of the San Juan Islands National Wildlife Refuge. While the shores are interesting to explore by kayak or dinghy, do not go ashore, for such intrusion by man disturbs nesting birds. Harbor seals and sea lions are often seen sunning on rocks or peering curiously from the nearby water.

Leo Reef, ½ nautical mile farther north, is also a favorite haul-out spot for these animals. Passengers on the state ferry are almost assured of seeing them on the rocks or in the water as the boat passes by. The highest of the rocks has a lighted navigation sign. Boats should give the reef a wide berth, as there are a number of submerged rocks in the vicinity.

Lopez Sound

One of the prettiest little cruising corners of the San Juans, with rock-bound islets trimmed with ragged fringes of "bonsai" evergreens, secluded bays, and a narrow pass with a bit of a navigational challenge—just to keep things interesting. Squeezed between long Lopez Island and the "comma" of Decatur, Lopez Sound is just enough off the beaten path that it does not suit the boater hurriedly headed for somewhere else. Instead it attracts cruisers willing to leisurely putt by, inspecting the shoreline, or sailboats looking for some wind.

Fortress, Crab, and Skull islands, between Hunter and Mud bays, are bird sanctuaries of the San Juan Islands National Wildlife Refuge; seals can sometimes be seen basking on their sunny rocks.

The Sperry Peninsula, the rounded tombolo south of Lopez Pass joined to the island by a slim neck of land, is the site of a summer youth camp. An authentic Indian dugout canoe belonging to the camp can often be seen drawn up on the shore by the camp, or being paddled in the water of Lopez Sound. A host of white tepees dot the woods above the shore.

At the head of the sound, the Lopez Pass exit is guarded by the pro truding reef of Rim, Rum, and Ram islands. Here skippers heading out through the pass must continue south 200 feet beyond Ram Island to avoid kelp-flagged rocks tagged by a red daymark, then make a hairpin turn to the left to run the tight little pass into Rosario Strait.

Some recent charts show Rum Island renamed as Cayou Island—evidently the State Board of Geographic Names gave it that title, not realizing it already had a dandy one; however Rum it will always remain to anyone who has a shred of whimsy in their heart.

Rum (or Cayou, if you will), the middle island, is part of the San Juan Islands National Wildlife Refuge. Ram, the larger wooded island on the south, is privately owned, but has been designated as open space, and the public is permitted to go ashore. Approach only with small boats, and even then use care, as the surrounding water is fouled with submerged rocks.

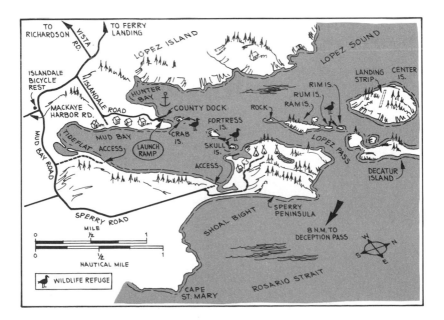

HUNTER AND MUD BAYS

For boaters waiting to cross Rosario Strait and catch a favorable tidal current at Deception Pass, Hunter Bay offers peaceful anchorages in 20 feet of water. A short county dock with a float and a launch ramp on the southeast side of the bay provide land-to-water access. The tidelands on the tip of the peninsula separating Hunter and Mud bays is a public DNR beach, although the shores drop off so steeply that there is little space for walking. Uplands are private.

To reach the county dock by land, follow Mud Bay Road south from the Center Road intersection for about 2 miles, and turn left (east) on Islandale Road, then left again in another ¾ mile. Continue downhill on the narrow road, avoiding private drives, to the boat ramp and dock. There is parking for cars and boat trailers alongside the short spur road to the dock and ramp.

Mud Bay, at the extreme south end of Lopez Sound, is quite shallow for dropping an overnight hook, but it has more extensive stretches of public tidelands—the obvious solution is to anchor in Hunter Bay and dinghy around to Mud Bay for beach walking, clam digging, and exploration.

Two upland accesses on Mud Bay provide a place for land-bound visitors to reach the beaches. A public access near the head of the bay is reached by taking the first road east of the end of Mud Bay heading north

Mud Bay at Sperry Road access

along the shore; it is marked "dead end." Beach homes are passed on a single-track dirt road, ending in ½ mile at a fence and parking space for a couple of cars. An easy scramble leads down to a beautiful flat beach. Most of the beach to mean high tide on Mud Bay is undeveloped state parks land. Avoid any posted beaches and all upland property.

A final access is on the northeast edge of Mud Bay; to find it continue on Mud Bay Road past the head of the bay and turn left on Sperry Road, heading north. When the main road curves right, a single-lane dirt road continues straight ahead for 300 feet to a turnaround at the road end. Here boats can be hand carried the short distance to the water. The nearby lagoon and pebbled beach make interesting exploration by boat or foot.

ISLANDALE BICYCLE REST

A bit of land adjacent to the Lopez Island fire station has been provided as a welcome stop for bicyclers journeying down the island. Trees give shade to one of the two picnic tables at the site. Latrines also offer welcome relief. The rest stop has no drinking water; however, a service station across the road does have water, as well as bicycle repairs and air for tires.

The rest area is at the intersection of Mud Bay and Mackaye Harbor roads, about 11½ miles south of the ferry landing, depending on the route taken.

The Southwest Shore

SHARK REEF RECREATION SITE

Park area: 39 acres
Access: Ferry to Lopez Island
Facilities: Latrines, *no water*

State land at Shark Reef, the legacy of a former military reservation intended to guard the entrance to San Juan Channel, now guards precious marine mammal and bird life, and climax forest. The land, held by the Department of Natural Resources, was scheduled to be logged to provide money for funding state schools. At the behest of local groups it was wisely decided that educational interests would be better served by preserving this unique forest as a wildlife sanctuary. In 1982 it was set aside by the state as a park.

To reach the recreation site turn west on Davis Bay Road 1 mile north of Richardson, and follow the signed route to a parking area at the trailhead to the beach; pit toilets are near the beginning of the trail. No garbage cans are provided—please pack out all your trash.

A level ten-minute hike through the forest leads to the rock and grass bluffs above the turbulent tidal currents of San Juan Channel. Shark Reef itself actually lies nearly a mile north of the park, and view of it is blocked by Kings Point. The jumble of islets lying only 400 feet offshore from the park is a reef that is unnamed except for Deadman Island, the largest and highest of the rocks. With binoculars, harbor seals and sea lions can be seen ponderously heaving themselves along the rocks to favored sunny sites, or slipping into the water with the grace of a dancer. Harbor seals breed here, and glaucous-winged gulls and oystercatchers nest in rocky crevices.

The forest is one of the few remaining old-growth and late-succession second-growth forests on Lopez Island. Cavities in the trees provide nesting sites for screech owls and saw-whet owls; insects in rotting wood sustain a variety of woodpeckers. Four bald eagle nests are known to be in old trees in the vicinity.

Vague trails wind along the cliffs above the water south for another ¼ mile, with views of nearby rocks and across the channel to the end of San Juan Island. The gull cacophony from across the channel at Goose Island serves as atonal background music for the rugged scenery. Above, Cattle Point Lighthouse serves its lonely mission. A place to rest, observe, and meditate.

The Shark Reef property was formerly a military reservation. During the late 1800s the U.S. military strategy was to develop "harbors of refuge" that were safely out of range of the capabilities of naval bombardment at the time, and that could be protected by land-based weaponry. Griffin Bay was designated as such a harbor of refuge, and land was set aside for military reservations on Lopez, Shaw, and San Juan islands.

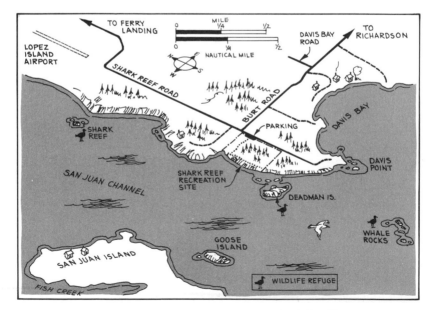

Shark Reef Recreation Site

It was intended that the bay would serve as a safe haven for both commercial and military vessels when adjoining waterways were blockaded by superior naval forces of the enemy. Ships coming in or going out of the Strait of Juan de Fuca could hide here until it was possible for them to make a run for their destination.

About this time the strategy of military combat changed, with the U.S. Navy no longer taking a passive defensive role by protecting home shores, but assuming an aggressive stance and taking the battle to the enemy. The military reservation land in the San Juans was no longer needed; over the years some of it was transferred to the DNR or other government agencies, and some was sold off to private interests. The parks at Shark Reef on Lopez Island and the DNR campground facing on Griffin Bay on San Juan Island are a result of these land holdings.

Boaters should stay well away from Shark Reef, Deadman Island, and all the adjacent rocks. Numerous rocks lie under the kelp-filled water, and currents are strong and tricky. Only experienced kayakers should attempt negotiating the narrow slot between the rocks and the island.

RICHARDSON

Access: Ferry to Lopez Island, boat
Facilities: Diesel, gas, dock (no float)

Looking directly into the Strait of Juan de Fuca from behind the limited protection of Iceberg Point and offshore islands, Richardson is the southern outpost of the San Juans. At the turn of the century it was one of the major ports of the islands, shipping produce from the farms and orchards of Lopez Island via steamship to Puget Sound markets. A large fishing fleet, comprised of nearly fifty outfits, was based here, unloading their catches at the wharf, or taking them directly to mainland canneries.

During this time, it is told, San Juan Channel ran thick with salmon, and at times nets were so full they could not be lifted into the boats. Today the great runs of fish are depleted and fishermen are fewer and must go farther afield for their catches. Purchasing offices for a cannery are still located on Barlow Bay, at the head of Mackaye Harbor, and gillnetters and purse-seiners still raft together in the harbor during fishing season, but the activity does not nearly approximate the days when the harbor bustled with commerce.

Paradoxically, Lopez Island may see the revitalization of the fishing industry, although in a far different way then the hardy fishermen of the early 1900s would have envisioned. At Shoal Bay, east of Upright Head on the north end of the island, efforts are being made to raise salmon in pens for sale to commercial markets. Starting with a strain of wild coho, the biologists here are attempting to develop domesticated stock that will flourish despite the stress of captivity. If this pilot venture is successful, and at present it seems to be doing well, it could mean an entirely new method of providing food fish, as well as a boost to the island's economy.

The historic general store at Richardson, built on pilings over the water, was tragically consumed by fire in the fall of 1990. The fuel tanks and dock were saved, so the only facilities remaining are the fuel dock for boats, and two gas pumps for autos. There are no current plans to rebuild the store.

When approaching Richardson by boat be wary of numerous rocks around Charles Island, and be forewarned there is no float, only a stationary pier—crew members may be needed on hand to fend off shiny fiberglass from creosoted pilings. If the strait is kicking up a bit, strong surges can make docking difficult. Richardson lies 12 nautical miles across Rosario Strait, west of Deception Pass, and 9 nautical miles southwest of Friday Harbor, via San Juan Channel.

To reach Richardson by land, follow Ferry Road, then Center Road south from the ferry landing. In about 8½ miles, where Center Road ends at a T intersection, turn right, then in ¼ mile, left on Richardson Road; total distance is about 10½ miles.

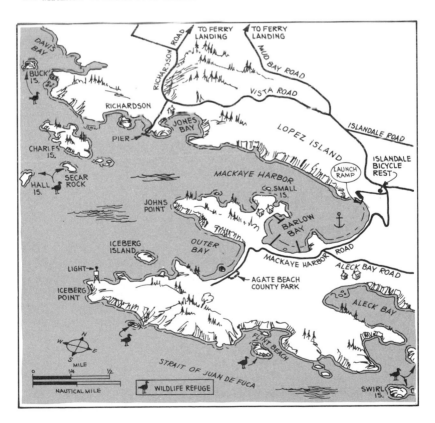

The tour down-island is a pleasure for bicyclists, with gently rolling black-topped roads passing neat farms and cattle-filled pastures. Birds call from hedgerow and marsh, and the San Juan rabbits dash across the road — perhaps just a breath ahead of a hawk. Watch for eagles soaring above the range of low hills to the south.

MACKAYE HARBOR

Mackaye Harbor, lying east of Richardson, offers some good anchorages at the east end of the harbor and in its southern extension, Barlow

Launching kayaks on Mackaye Harbor

Bay. An inn at the head of Mackaye Harbor, within dinghy distance of the anchorages, provides fine meals for boaters tired of galley food. Two commercial fishing docks occupy the south shore of Barlow Bay; the dock on the point to the northwest is privately owned.

At Islandale turn south from Mud Bay Road onto Mackaye Harbor Road, and in a few hundred feet turn right on a single-lane dirt road, signed "Boat Ramp." The narrow road swings downhill to meet the northeast corner of Mackaye Harbor at a single-lane concrete launch ramp. An adjacent parking lot can accommodate a dozen cars and trailers. A rib of submerging rocks on the north side of the ramp is marked with a pole at its outer end.

Boats launched here can explore the multitude of bays and niches along the south shore of Lopez Island. Remember to stay well away from the offshore islets and rocks of the San Juan Islands National Wildlife Refuge.

AGATE BEACH PICNIC AREA

Park area: 2 acres; 600 feet of shoreline
Access: Ferry to Lopez Island, boat
Facilities: Picnic tables, pit toilets, *no water*
Attractions: Beachcombing, scuba diving

Nothing pretentious, but a welcome resting spot and a lovely beach to walk. To reach the park, turn east onto Vista Road ¼ mile north of Richardson and follow it for 1¼ miles to its intersection with Mud Bay Road. Turn right (south) onto Mud Bay Road, then leave it in 1 mile, turning right again onto Mackaye Harbor Road, which circles the shore of the harbor, crosses a neck of land, then contours Outer Bay. The small, grassy picnic area is located near the middle of the beach, on the east side of the road.

Across from the picnic area a stairway descends to the pebbled beach on Outer Bay, facing out to the "toe" of distant San Juan Island. Lying just offshore a distinctive smooth rock shaped like a shark's fin beckons to kayak explorers. Perhaps it can be reached on foot at low tide. What else does low tide bring? Agates? Crabs? Stop and find out. Farther offshore is tiny Iceberg Island, an undeveloped state park property.

Outer Bay is a favorite with scuba divers, who explore the sand and cobblestone beach and offshore rocks. Sea urchins grow in particular abundance here. Strong current can present a problem in the outer portions of the bay, and in summer kelp growth is heavy in some areas.

HUGHES BAY COUNTY PARK

A small, enchanting sand and gravel pocket beach on the east shore of Hughes Bay was acquired by the county in 1989. The beach is rimmed by a high, steep bank. In 1990 storms destroyed the newly constructed wooden staircase down to the beach; although the county plans to replace the stairs, the beach will be inaccessible by land until this occurs. To reach the park, turn south from Mud Bay Road onto Watmough Head Road, and in ½ mile continue straight ahead on Huggins Road. Take the next dirt lane heading right, which leads to the parking area above the beach.

ICEBERG POINT AND POINT COLVILLE

Two stretches of land on the far recesses of Lopez Island are held by the Bureau of Land Management as lighthouse reservations. Iceberg Point houses a navigational beacon, Point Colville does not. At present these two areas can be reached only by boat, as land access is closed.

The shorelines beneath the points are extremely rugged. The difficulty of landing boats varies with the tide level and the turbulence of the water. Between these rocky "toes" of the island are lodged a succession of intimate bays. The looming rock shorelines make these the most spectacular to be found in the San Juans.

The most easterly is Watmough Bay, facing east on Rosario Strait. It is sometimes used as an overnight stop for boaters headed for Deception Pass. Although the narrow slot is well protected from weather, its rocky bottom may present some difficulty in getting anchors to hold.

Farther west, around Watmough Head and Point Colville, are McArdle and Hughes bays. These two south-facing harbors are quite open to weather off the straits and are only marginal holding ground, especially in winds and waves one may encounter.

Aleck Bay, which trends northwesterly for nearly ¾ of a mile, is the jewel among these bays, with good protection and a muddy bottom for holding hooks. Clear days reveal a glorious sight—views all the way down Puget Sound to the crystal mass of Mt. Rainier.

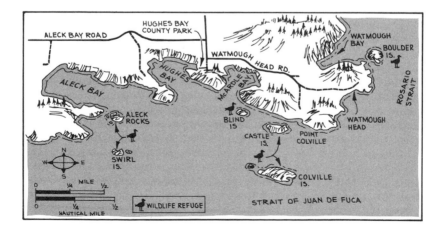

Wildlife Refuge Islands

More than two dozen barren rocks and islets lifting out of the sea off the tip of Lopez Island have been set aside for wildlife management. These bits of rock, along with numerous others located throughout the San Juans, with a total of 352 acres at eighty-four distinct locations, comprise the San Juan Islands National Wildlife Refuge, administered by the U.S. Fish and Wildlife Service.

Islands holding this status in the vicinity of Lopez Island are Shark Reef, located on the west of Lopez near San Juan Island's Cattle Point; Buck Island and Mummy Rocks near Davis Bay; Secar Rock and Hall Island south of Richardson; Aleck Rocks and Swirl Island south of Aleck Bay; 9-acre Castle Island and 11-acre Colville Island (largest of the bird refuges in the vicinity), off Point Colville; Boulder Island east of Watmough Head; Crab, Fortress and Skull islands in Lopez Sound; and numerous other small, unnamed rocks.

The sanctuaries were established primarily to protect nesting birds. They are also important as resting areas for seals and sea lions, and these pelagic mammals, as well as dolphins and whales, forage in surrounding waters.

Glaucous-winged gulls, cormorants, murres, pigeon guillemots, and

Deadman Island near the south entrance to San Juan Channel

Cormorants drying on offshore rocks

black oystercatchers nest in large numbers on the islands, while nearly 50 other species of seabirds are known to stop here during their migration on the Pacific Flyway.

It is well established that the numbers of these birds have dramatically diminished in the last century; civilization is almost totally responsible. In early days Indians looted the rookeries for eggs and killed the birds for food and for their decorative value. The parrotlike beaks of tufted puffins were valued for ceremonial rattles and as adornment, and large numbers were killed just for that purpose. Despite this predation, the great flocks survived.

Today man threatens the existence of these birds with subtler methods: he preempts their habitat, depletes their food sources, and poisons their environment. Aside from the moral and aesthetic issues raised by the loss of huge numbers of birds, this tinkering with one of the important links of the food chain must ultimately affect man, too.

These scattered, inhospitable rocks, swept by heavy seas from the Strait of Juan de Fuca, rarely attract recreational boaters; however, the area is growing in popularity with scuba divers. At this time their numbers are small enough so they do not constitute a serious problem; increased activity could seriously disrupt the rookeries. The presence of humans also prevents seals and sea lions from hauling out on the rocks to rest and warm themselves, a necessary function for these animals.

Boaters and fishermen in the area are urged to stay at least 300 feet away from the wilderness area islands to avoid disturbing the seals and nesting birds. Discharge of firearms is, of course, prohibited.

Spring Passage from Yellow Island; Waldron Island in the distance

3. The Central Channel

Splitting the San Juans from east to west, a central waterway comprised of Harney Channel and Wasp Passage forms a saltwater freeway used by most boats traveling in the islands. Broad and deep throughout most of its length, the channel is constricted only at its western end, where the capricious architect of the sea dumped a load of rocks known as the Wasp Islands.

On this sheltered waterway the Washington state ferry makes three of its four island stops to discharge passengers. When the route that continues

west through Wasp Passage is used, tourists look down from the heights of the ferry onto everyone's dream of a vacation retreat—private little islands and points and bays, each decorated with a summer cabin or retirement home, a bit of a dock, and a bobbing sailboat.

Shaw Island

With a total of only 4,937 acres, Shaw Island is the smallest of the islands served by the ferries. The paucity of water on these rocky acres has limited the real estate development, and most Shaw Islanders prefer it that

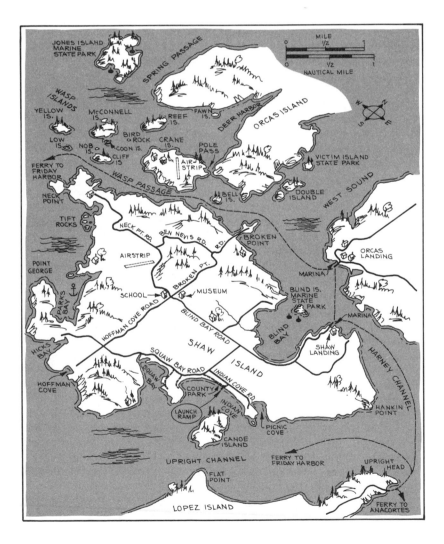

Shaw Island Marina

way. Its population of around a hundred permanent residents swells to about three times that in the summer, and that is about all these shores can support.

Most Shaw Island roads are inland, with few views of San Juan waters, and no access to bays. Instead, the roads roll gently through heavy timber and past small fields edged by bird-filled hedgerows. Here are not the wide agricultural expanses of Lopez Island, but instead small acreages with a few cattle and crops. Hike or bike the byways and enjoy the catharsis of rural island life. The most scenic road on the island is the one following the west shore of Blind Bay, with views across the bay to Orcas Island; it dead-ends at private property.

Arrive on the morning ferry and spend the day on the island, but plan to leave on the evening boat unless you are fortunate enough to claim one of the twelve campsites in the county park or have a good friend on the island. There is no other place to park a camper or pitch a tent, and there are no motels or cabins.

SHAW LANDING

Access: Ferry to Shaw Island, boat
Facilities: Guest moorage, diesel, gas, outboard mix, restrooms, laundromat, service station, groceries, bait, fishing tackle, hardware, gift items

The island's sole "commercial" development is the combination general store/post office/ferry terminal/gas station/marina at the ferry landing. Since 1976 the store has been operated by a small group of Franciscan nuns. The Little Portion store was named by the nuns after an Italian church named Portuncula, meaning "little portion of earth"; the small stone church was the favorite spot of Saint Francis of Assisi. The store is closed Sundays.

The U-shaped docks of the small marina lie east of the ferry landing, in a basin protected by the pilings of the ferry landing and a jutting rocky headland. It has dockside fuel and a few overnight moorages for visiting boaters.

BLIND ISLAND MARINE STATE PARK

Park area: 2 acres; 1,396 feet of shoreline
Access: Boat
Facilities: Campsites, picnic tables, pit toilet, mooring buoys, *no water*, no garbage collection
Attractions: Beachcombing, fishing, shrimping

This 2-acre rock stuck in the entrance to Blind Bay boasts only limited public facilities, a couple of tenacious trees, two sparse campsites—and an unparalleled nighttime spectacle! After sunset, ferries ablaze with lights ply Harney Channel, stopping at times at Shaw and Orcas. Small craft cruise by, resembling nautical fireflies, their reflections glimmering in the darkened sea.

On the southwest side of the rocky island, four buoys give moorage to boaters, although in rough weather better anchorages can be found farther

Boat moored at Blind Island Marine State Park

into the bay. Rocks around the island are a navigational hazard; a large one that has claimed a number of boat hulls lies southeast of the island, midway in the channel. It is marked with a locally maintained caution sign on a pole. Boaters approaching the mooring buoys should enter the bay on the east side of Blind Island, but favor the Blind Island side of the channel. Reefs west of Blind Island make entry via that route even more hazardous.

Low tide exposes rocky beaches all around the island; at that time the best landing site for small boats is on the northeast side. Hand-carried boats may be put in at the marina next to the ferry landing at Shaw Island, ¼ nautical mile away, or at Orcas Landing ¾ nautical mile across Harney Channel. Boating traffic is usually heavy in the channel and can present a danger to small boats. Bring a sleeping bag and stay overnight to watch the evening show.

"LITTLE RED SCHOOLHOUSE"

The main "point of interest" on Shaw Island is near the center of the island at the intersection of Blind Bay Road and Hoffman Cove Road, where a classic one-room schoolhouse stands. Known as "The Little Red Schoolhouse," the building is on the National Register of Historic Places. Instead of sending their children by boat to larger schools on Orcas or San Juan islands, as residents on most of the other small islands do, Shaw Islanders prefer to operate this school for their small population of elementary-aged students.

Across the road is the island's library and historical society. A reef netting boat is displayed on the lawn. The library and an adjacent one-room log cabin that houses a historical collection are open to the public in the afternoon on Tuesdays and Saturdays, and in the morning on Thursdays.

SHAW ISLAND COUNTY PARK

Park area: 65 acres; 3,249 feet of shoreline
Access: Ferry to Shaw Island, boat
Facilities: Campsites, pit toilets, picnic tables, fireplaces, picnic shelter, drinking water, boat launch (ramp)
Attractions: Beachcombing, hiking, clam digging, crabbing, swimming, fishing, birdwatching

Facing on Indian Cove, Shaw Island County Park encompasses 65 acres of prime Shaw Island real estate and one of the best sandy beaches on any of the San Juans. The land, once a military reservation, was purchased by Shaw Islanders for public use. Express your gratitude to these farsighted residents by observing posted regulations and respecting private property bounding the park.

To reach the park from the ferry landing, follow Blind Bay Road, which heads south and then curves westward, to an intersection with Squaw Bay Road in 1¼ miles, signed to South Beach Park. Turn left

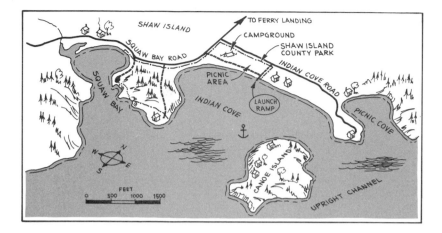

(south); in ½ mile more, an inconspicuous sign points left to the South
Beach Park camping area. There is another entrance from Indian Cove
Road ¼ mile east of its intersection with Squaw Bay Road.

The day-use picnic area is located on a slight embankment above the
shore of Indian Cove. A planked ramp at the end of the entrance road on
the east side of the park provides launching for trailered boats; however,
due to the shallow beach it is usable only at high tide.

Up the road, away from the beach, the campground contains twelve
sites for the fortunate few. Some overflow camping is permitted in the
grassy playground area, but don't expect more—the fragile ecology of the
area cannot tolerate the intrusion of hordes of tourists.

Indian Cove lies just 3½ nautical miles east of Friday Harbor, where
boats may be rented. Small boats are easily beached on the shore; deep keel
vessels will have to anchor well out in the bay as it is extremely shallow.

Canoe Island, a lovely, 45-acre forested enclave on the southeast side
of the bay, is the site of a unique summer camp for teenagers. Although the
camp has the usual summer activities of swimming, sailing, tennis, and ar-
chery, the focus is on lessons in the French language, along with related
subjects such as French cooking and French folk dancing.

The protected, sandy beach of the county park slopes gradually outward for several hundred feet. Sand dollars and heart cockles lie near the
surface; dig deeper to find more tender clams, and perhaps even the mighty
geoduck. On hot summer days the water of the bay warms enough for
wading and swimming.

A forested thumb of land on the west that separates Indian Cove from
Squaw Bay is also part of the park. Tides permitting, circumnavigate the
peninsula on sandy beaches that turn to rock as they round the point. On
the east side of the peninsula, a dirt road goes through forest to reach the
privately owned tip of the island, where a summer home is located. No

Beach at Shaw Island County Park

parking and only minimal turn around space; do not trespass. The road is pleasant enough as it leads through second-growth cedar and Douglas fir, but has few water views and no beach access.

A single-track road on the west side of the peninsula is more attractive. Although it is driveable and has parking at its end for half a dozen cars, it is more interesting to park at the road junction and walk, enjoying the gentle murmur of the forest and views of Squaw Bay. At road end a trail continues less than 50 feet beyond to two tiny coves, embraced by overhanging madronas. They are accessible by an easy rock scramble down to the beach.

No overnight camping here, and no fires; just peaceful forest, beach, and water to enjoy by day.

Squaw Bay, which nearly drains at low tide, is a favorite feeding and resting area for numerous species of birds; others nest in nearby rushes. The lagoon and sandspit at the head of the bay are privately owned, but birds can easily be seen from the road. A roadside sign at the head of the bay tells that herons, kingfishers, cormorants, mergansers, scaups, and eagles are but a few of the many species of birds frequently spotted here.

REEF NETTERS

Commercial reef netting fishing boats working in Upright Channel between Shaw and Lopez islands can often be seen from Shaw Island County Park. Boats are sometimes anchored at the entrance to Squaw Bay.

This unique fishing method was originated long ago by Indians in the San Juans who used dugout canoes and nets fashioned from thin strips of willow or cedar bark. Pioneers adopted the method, and its use has continued to the present time, only being updated by the use of skiffs or barges with large outboard motors, modern nets of synthetic materials, and powered winches to haul in the catch.

Reef netting, which is most commonly utilized for sockeye and humpback salmon, employs the use of two boats with high, ladderlike lookout towers in the bow. These boats are anchored 50 feet apart in shallow water or around reefs, with a 50-foot square net stretched between them and weighted down at the bottom. When the lookouts spot a school of fish swimming into the net, it is quickly pulled up and the catch dumped into holding nets. Very clear water, such as is found in the San Juans, is necessary for this fishing method.

Ferry and reef netters in Upright Channel, from Shaw Island County Park

PARKS BAY

On the southern end of the island, land surrounding Parks Bay and all of Point George is held by the University of Washington's Friday Harbor Laboratories as a biological preserve. Property here has been donated, purchased, or leased in order to maintain the shores and uplands in a nearly natural condition for research and educational purposes. Parks Bay is an excellent boat anchorage in 15 to 30 feet of water; however, going ashore is not permitted, due to its status as a nature preserve.

TIFT ROCKS

On the northeast side of Shaw Island, just north of Parks Bay, lie Tift Rocks. These grass-covered rocks snuggled close to the shore of the island usually go unnoticed by passing boaters. The northernmost and largest of the islands holds the deteriorating stone walls of a cabin that was built by a recluse who once lived here.

The rocks are part of the San Juan Islands National Wildlife Refuge and now host nesting seabirds and a number of seals who haul out to warm themselves in the sun. Going ashore is forbidden, but the animals and the rock walls of the cabin can be seen easily from the water.

The Wasp Islands

Ferry passengers may be treated to a close-up view of the Wasp Islands if the inter-island ferry squeezes through narrow Wasp Passage. Choice of the route through Wasp Passage, or the less scenic route south of Shaw Island through Upright Channel, depends on the weather, tide, and the inclination of the captain of the ferry making inter-island stops. Hope for the intimate and beautiful Wasp Passage route.

The group of assorted islets and rocks at the west end of Wasp Passage, known locally as "the Rock Pile," received its name not from the pernicious insect, but from the American warship *Wasp*, which distinguished itself during the War of 1812. Jones Island to the north was named for the *Wasp*'s commander, Jacob Jones.

Early pioneers frequently rowed sheep to these small islands for summer grazing, and since most are dry, it was also necessary to haul over regularly barrels of drinking water for the flocks.

Much of the colorful history of the San Juans, when pirates and smugglers frequented these waters, centers around the Wasp Islands. McConnell Island was the family home of Victor McConnell, one of these early-day racketeers—until his relatives discovered his activities and requested his absence.

In the late 1880s, the U.S. closed its doors to Chinese immigrants eager for jobs in this bountiful nation, and smuggling these aliens, who had made their way from their homeland to Canada, became a lucrative profession. Along with them came cargoes of heavily taxed opium (which was legal at the time), silk, and other commodities. A few years later when imported wool was slapped with a stiff duty, enterprising boats slipped north to Canada to purchase fleece that could be mixed with the San Juan product and innocently resold, causing revenuers to wonder at the productivity of island sheep.

When Washington went "dry" in 1916, four years before the Volstead Act decreed nationwide Prohibition the smuggling flotilla heeded the cry of the thirsty and dutifully swung into action, importing everything from fine bonded Canadian whiskey to watered-down rotgut from the stills of willing northern neighbors.

The San Juan archipelago is ideally suited to such clandestine activities, with its maze of channels spotted with rocky hiding places and soupy fogs clinging about the shoulders of the islands. Local sailors in small, fast-moving craft knew every inch of the waterways and every trick of the trade. One favorite ploy was to slip on the lee side of a ferry and sneak by under the very noses of watchful revenue boats.

Romantic as it may sound, smuggling was not an innocent pastime, for those were the days of undercover agents, hijackings, bloody shootouts, mysterious disappearances of crews and boats, and blatant murders. Frequently cargoes were hurriedly "deep-sixed" by smugglers fearing apprehension. At least one instance is reported of Chinese aliens being forced overboard; their bodies, with hands and feet bound, later washed up on nearby shores.

Charged with the enforcement of Prohibition, the Coast Guard, with its larger, slow-moving boats, was hard-pressed to apprehend the elusive rumrunners. However, the government boats knew a few tricks too, and one skipper in particular, Lorenz A. Lonsdale, captain of the tug *Arcata*, gave such good account of himself that he was in constant danger of being relieved of command and "kicked upstairs" by pressure exerted by corrupt politicians, dismayed by his successes.

Life today is much more sedate along this central channel. Instead of woolly flocks, the islands are dotted with summer homes—although it is still necessary to import water to many of their occupants. On foggy mornings it is easy to imagine ghosts of early smugglers slipping furtively past the mist-cloaked shores.

Crane Island, with many private residences on its 222 wooded acres, is the largest and most developed of the Wasp group. Planes that land on the airstrip in the center of the island provide transportation and bring supplies to residents. The only public lands on the island are two sections of narrow, unappealing rock beach on the north and west sides.

Smaller Bell Island to the east and Cliff, Coon, McConnell, and Reef islands scattered to the west are singly owned, with one or two summer hideaways on each. All of Coon Island's tidelands, which include a few small pocket beaches, are public. McConnell Island has 2,000 feet of public tidelands along its southern half. The public lands are only those areas below the mean high water level. Do not trespass onto private property.

A tiny rock on the northeast side of McConnell Island, which at low tide is joined to the larger island by a sandy spit, is owned by the state, although it is undeveloped. It is an excellent spot to beach small boats or kayaks for a brief rest.

Down the scale of "ownership," the barren, inhospitable rocks that cannot even support a shack are given over to seabirds and seals. Bird Rock east of McConnell Island, the Nob Island group, Low Island west of Cliff Island, and an unmarked low-tide rock west of Yellow Island are all part of the San Juan Islands National Wildlife Refuge.

Boaters enjoy exploring the watery nooks and crannies of the Wasp Islands, but extreme care must be used for there are many submerged rocks and reefs. Kelp marks many of these danger spots, but a slow speed and vigilant eye on the navigational chart are the pilot's best allies. Smaller, unpowered boats should also be wary of wakes from other boating traffic.

YELLOW ISLAND

Area: 11 acres
Access: Boat
Facilities: Hiking trails, drinking water

Yellow Island, the most westerly of the Wasp group, was purchased in 1980 by The Nature Conservancy as a nature preserve. The island's

Harvest brodiaea blooming on Yellow Island

woodlands, open meadows, and rocky shoreline support more than 180 varieties of wildflowers (nearly every species to be found in the San Juan Islands), ranging from cactuses to the endangered calypso orchid. At the peak of the blooming season, from late April through early June, the island becomes a riot of color. Meadows brim with the yellow, white, and pink blossoms of spring gold, Queen Anne's lace, and sea blush. Even later in the season the dainty lilac-pink blossoms of nodding onion and white swaths of yarrow grace the island slopes.

Going ashore is permitted, subject to restrictions necessary to maintain this as a nature preserve: remain on designated trails; no pets, picnicking, camping, or fires; no collection of plants or animals; prior permission must be obtained for groups of more than six.

Small boats can be landed on gravel beaches at the eastern and western tips of the island, however, offshore rocks and reefs preclude approach by larger boats at these points. A tenuous anchorage can be had in a small rocky cove on the south side of the island near the caretaker's cabin; the buoys here are for the use of the residents.

Two cabins on the island, one on the south shore and another above the western point, were built by Lew and Elizabeth Dodd from driftwood gathered from the beaches and rocks and other native materials from the island. The Dodds bought the island in 1946 and lived here in contented solitude for fourteen years. The Nature Conservancy purchased Yellow Island from the Dodds' children, and the cabins are now used by the resident caretakers.

The Dodds' sensitive care of Yellow Island is evident in the bounty of native plants that grow here, in spite of the heavy impact of civilization on neighboring islands. A bronze plaque beside the trail in the eastern

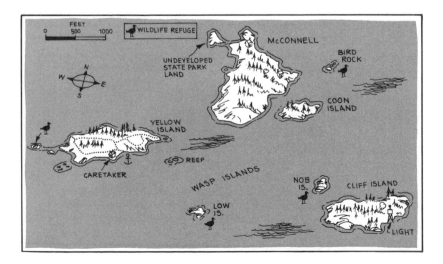

Kayakers at east end of Yellow Island

meadow memorializes Lew Dodd with a poem that he wrote expressing his unending joy of life in this, his personal paradise.

Two trail loops have been carefully laid out to provide maximum appreciation of the island vistas and flora. Due to the fragile nature of the land, hikers *must* stay on the trails.

One loop leaves the south shore cabin for the west point and the western meadow, with views across Spieden Channel and north to Spieden, James, Flattop, and Waldron islands and Spring Passage. As this loop meanders back to its starting point through old-growth pine and madrona, a second trail heads east to reach the east point and circle the eastern meadow. Occasional faint side trails signed "Otters Only" are for the use of the only ones exempt from staying on the main trails.

JONES ISLAND MARINE STATE PARK

Area: 188 acres; 16,368 feet of public tidelands
Access: Boat
Facilities: Float, mooring buoys, campsites, picnic tables, fireplaces, portable-toilet dump, drinking water (well frequently goes dry by midsummer)
Attractions: Beachcombing, clamming, crabbing, abalone, fishing, hiking, scuba diving

A choice little island with welcoming bays and bountiful shores, located so near the main highways of Wasp Passage and San Juan Channel that most passing tourists drop in for a brief visit—and many fall in love and linger awhile.

Jones Island is located less than ½ mile off the southwest tip of Orcas Island, and 2 nautical miles from Deer Harbor Marina. Boaters approaching Jones Island through Spring Passage should be cautious of several rocky shoals just off the east shore.

A cove deeply notching the north side of the island holds a dock with float and a few mooring buoys. On nice summer weekends this bay is always filled with small boats drawn up on the beach and larger ones tied to the float, rafted together on buoys, or bobbing on a hook.

Anchoring in this bay can be tricky, especially with a bit of wind or a strong tidal current to complicate matters. The bottom is rocky and steeply sloping, making it difficult to set a hook solidly. Savvy seamen will often drop a second anchor or will row a stern line ashore and tie up to a tree to keep their craft in position. If unsure about the security of your anchor or that of nearby boats, do not leave your boat unattended. A favorite pastime among those familiar with the bay is sitting on deck with the air of an "old salt" (once one's own boat is solidly nailed down), and watching the embarrassment of the uninitiated as they drift on their anchors.

On the south side of the island is a wider, shallower bay, split by a rocky headland. The three additional buoys placed here are more open to tossing by wind and waves.

The park attracts many visitors in small boats who overnight ashore in the campgrounds overlooking the two bays. At the north cove fourteen campsites with picnic tables and fireplaces are clustered in cool timber; on the south bay a large grassy meadow, fringed with the remains of an apple orchard, offers four sunnier sites with views of the Wasp Islands and pass-

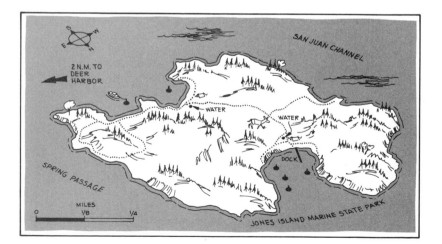

Moorage in the north cove at Jones Island Marine State Park

Deer at Jones Island Marine State Park

ing ferry traffic. Two additional campsites are found on the headlands defining the bay.

Crossing the narrow waist of the island, a ½-mile trail connects the two anchorages. At the approach of a low tide, boaters traipse southward along the path, armed with shovels and buckets, headed for the clam beds on the far shore. Even without the incentive of clams, visitors will enjoy the forest walk through the deep green of the island's interior. Cedar, hemlock, sword fern, and salal suddenly give way to the warm golden meadow on the south bay. Halfway along the trail, just north of the two water tanks, is a magnificent example of a cedar nurse log. The downed giant, several hundred feet long, has two 200- to 300-foot offspring growing from its root base.

An unmarked spur leaves the cross-island trail just above the north campground and heads west to a small cove and west-side beaches.

A small herd of black-tailed deer that inhabits the island often grazes in the meadow. Many are now so accustomed to the crowds of visitors that they will venture to be hand-fed. Although they are appealing, they should not be fed "people food"—to do so may actually harm them. Raccoons, weasels, and martens, which are occasionally spotted at dusk, swim across Spring Passage to raid the nests of seabirds; some of the bolder raccoons also check out the garbage cans by the campgrounds.

Several sketchy trails circle eastward on low bluffs looking down into little one-boat bays facing on Spring Passage. Use care scrambling about the rocky embankment, as footing can be insecure; hikers have been injured here.

The west shore, at the edge of San Juan Channel, is a favorite spot for salmon fishermen. Prized abalone that cling to the rocky western skirts of the island are harvested by skin divers or can be pried off the rocks by beachcombers at low, low tide. Dungeness crab, which migrate around the island at some primitive whim, can sometimes be trapped in the south bay.

Until 1982, Jones Island was owned by the federal government as a part of the San Juan Islands National Wildlife Refuge, and leased by the state for use as a marine park. Since the throngs of people using the island were not particularly compatible with its wildlife status, the U.S. Fish and Wildlife Service relinquished its claim and turned it over to the state in return for several smaller, more remote, state-owned islands.

Jones Island, in a microcosm, reflects many of the problems besetting the San Juans as a whole. With its many attractions and convenient location, it may ultimately be "loved to death" by the squadrons of boaters who arrive on its shores in greater numbers each year.

Today ignorant visitors scar campgrounds by "ditching" their tents, injure trees with nails driven to support tent ropes, strip branches from anything green to fuel their campfires, pockmark the beach and shore with randomly built bonfires (and also risk setting the entire island ablaze), trample undergrowth by careless hiking, frighten the wildlife, and kill or cart away even the inedible living beach creatures. Even the well-intentioned camper who treats the land with care, simply by his presence has a negative impact on the environment. The space requirements and waste disposal logistics of tens of thousands of visitors create problems that must be dealt with.

As with all of the San Juans, Jones Island simply cannot tolerate the pressures of unlimited use and abuse by demanding recreationists. Without careful development and management, and sensitive, responsible use, the future may well see its beaches stripped naked, its meadows ground to dust, its forest destroyed, and its wildlife departed.

Heavy-weather sailing in San Juan Channel; Cattle Point beyond

4. San Juan Island

Verdant, pastoral country, punctuated by forested mountains—most populated of the islands—home of the county seat and its largest (and only incorporated) town—center of commerce and industry—home port for the local fishing fleet—crossroads of these boundary waters, with a steady flow of international traffic through its two customs offices. The archipelago's busiest island.

Yet "busy" is a relative term in this slow-paced paradise. Even in summer, when tourists stream from crammed-full ferries, and harbors and bays swarm with boats, the customary tempo only slightly quickens. Many visitors, understanding the ambiance of the island, arrive on bicycle or on foot with backpack, prepared to enjoy the country at a leisurely rate.

The early Spanish explorer Lopez Gonzales de Haro, who sailed through here in 1791, noted the important strategic location of the island facing on two major waterways and its outstanding physical features, and named it San Juan, principal landfall of this archipelago. Arriving later, British settlers claimed it for the queen and changed its name to Bellevue Island, but eventually the original Spanish designation was restored.

Pioneers recognized San Juan as prime real estate, with its gently rolling farmland ideal for cattle and crops, its thick forests ripe to be turned into cabins, fences, and firewood, and its fine harbors providing sheltered access to the shores. Generation after generation they sank their family roots into the island soil.

Today's San Juan settlers are retirees, artists, authors, and dropouts from the rat race who prefer their air without smog, their beaches without pollution slicks and beer cans, their highways without traffic jams, and their starry nights without obliterating city lights.

San Juan Island can be reached by Washington state ferry from Anacortes or Sidney, B.C., to Friday Harbor, about a one-and-a-half-hour trip either way. For quicker access, San Juan Airlines has regularly scheduled flights from Seattle and Bellingham to the airports at Friday Harbor and Roche Harbor. Other air services offer charter flights.

Private boats visiting the island will find transient moorage and supplies at Friday Harbor and at resorts on Roche Harbor and Mitchell Bay. Numerous fine anchorages are found around the island, as described in the following text; however, public access to the shore is limited.

Hikers and cyclists will enjoy the gently rolling roads edged by pastures and forests, sometimes dropping down to round a salty bay, other times skirting the edge of a bluff, offering marine panoramas. Nearly all roads are two-lane blacktop with very little shoulder, but traffic moves at a relaxed pace, and traveling the roads is quite safe if simple precautions are observed. There are, unfortunately, a few sections of county road on the south and west of the island that are teeth-jarring gravel washboards.

Virtually all facilities and services that are found on San Juan Island

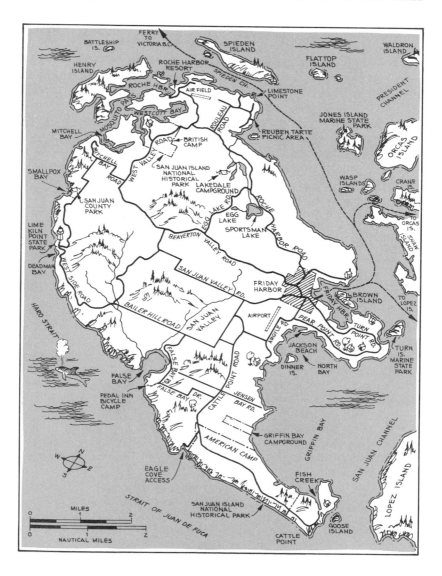

are located at Friday Harbor. Small stores at Roche Harbor and Mitchell Bay pump fuel and carry supplies for campers, boaters, and fishermen, but the selection is limited.

A handful of resorts, hotels, and motels at Friday Harbor and a few other locations on the island provide overnight accommodations by day or week, ranging from modern motels to rustic beach cabins. A few homes that have been converted to bed-and-breakfast establishments offer overnight lodging in a gracious, homey atmosphere. Advanced reservations are essential in summer for all lodging.

In addition to the county campground at Smallpox Bay, commercial camping facilities are available at a trailer park in Friday Harbor, at Islandale near Sportsman Lake, and at the marina at Mitchell Bay. There is also a bicycle campground about a mile west of False Bay. Some campgrounds will make reservations; call for current information. Parking or tenting overnight along the road is not permitted.

Friday Harbor

Access: Ferry to San Juan Island, boat
Facilities: Groceries, stores, gas, diesel, marine repair, boat launch
(sling), boat rental and charters, guest moorage, dock with water and electrical hookups, showers, laundry, fishing tackle and bait, hotels, restaurants, movie theater, bicycle and moped rentals, car rentals, tour buses, U.S. Customs
Attractions: Boating, paddling, fishing, shopping, sightseeing, marine laboratories, museums

An enchanting mix of old and new establishments, some "shopping-center modern," some elderly but beautifully renovated, still others nostalgically decrepit—all with a dash of salt thrown in. Shopping facilities are within walking distance of the ferry landing and public boat moorages. Grocery stores provide delivery service to boats on the docks, fine restaurants cater to tourists, galleries offer quality work by local artists and craftsmen, while other shops have selections of souvenirs, books, and gifts for the folks back home.

Ferries from Anacortes and Sidney arrive regularly during the day to disgorge their passengers, their window-rattling whistle blasts barely noted by local residents. Sometimes two of the green-and-white behemoths are in the harbor, one patiently treading water in the outer bay, awaiting its turn at the slip.

Friday Harbor is virtually a nautical "Times Square" of the Northwest—stand there long enough and eventually every cruising boat that you know will pass by. The public dock plays host to around 20,000 overnight transient boats annually, and an equal number stop briefly to refuel, shop, or clear customs.

A major expansion, completed in 1984, more than doubled the capac-

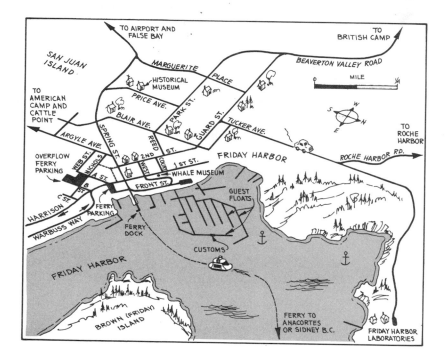

ity of the marina, bringing the total moorages to 463, 94 of which are guest slips. Guest slips are on both sides of G and the inside of H docks, the first two encountered upon entering the moorage area. In addition, both sides of the A breakwater, the inside of B breakwater, and both sides of C breakwater provide another 1500' of guest moorage. If unable to find overnight moorage space in the visitors' floats, check with the dock office for available space in the permanent moorages. Do not tie up to a permanent moorage without permission from the dock office.

If unable to secure a space, the bay northwest of the docks or near the University of Washington Laboratories provides some anchorages within dinghy range of the floats. Use care to anchor well out of the path of the ferries. A large rock showing on charts near the end of the docks has been removed.

The building at the head of the Port of Friday Harbor dock complex houses the harbormaster's office and restrooms with showers for visiting mariners. U.S. Customs is located in the yacht club building half a block to the west. During daytime hours in summer, customs officers can also be found at a shed on the outer breakwater, and boaters can register for moorage at a booth at the head of the dock.

Even nonsailors will enjoy a stroll down the floats to admire, and perhaps envy, the many boats, some from exotic hailing ports. The commercial fishing fleet ties up on the larger docks—gillnetters and purse-seiners with huge stern-mounted metal spools rolled fat with nets.

In the water, like ghostly Mary Poppinses, hundreds upon hundreds of hydroid jellyfish rise and descend and drift around the pilings. Researchers at the University of Washington's Friday Harbor Laboratories harvest thousands of these jellyfish each year to be processed into Aequorin, an important substance with bioluminescent properties that is used in medical research.

At low tide, dock pilings reveal underwater coatings of fluffy sea anemones, feather duster worms, opalescent nudibranchs, and spidery decorator crabs who glue bits of seaweed to their bodies as protective

Netting shrimp at the Friday Harbor docks

camouflage. Youngsters also enjoy dipping nets for shrimp from along the edges of the floats.

If the nautical scene of Friday Harbor palls, the rest of the island awaits. For persons arriving by boat or on foot via the ferry, various forms of transportation are available—some of them quite unique. Cars, bicycles, or mopeds are available for rent, tour buses make regular guided circuits of the island in summer (one is an old-fashioned double-decker bus), or planes can be chartered for aerial views.

WHALE MUSEUM

Where can you go to get a fish's-eye view of the 20-foot underbelly of an orca, stare into the jaws of a minke whale, or listen to whales conversing? In Friday Harbor, where the country's only museum devoted exclusively to the study of whales is located!

This outstanding facility features interesting displays on these great mammals. Models (some of them life-size) and actual whale skeletons fill the rooms, while murals, videos, and other exhibits give further information on the evolution of whales, kinds of whales and their anatomical differences, how they communicate, and how to identify local whales. One room has activities especially designed for children.

The Whale Museum is not an attic for storing old bones, but a vital, ongoing research and educational facility dedicated to the living whale. It conducts cruises, workshops, and classes, and its volunteers man whale observation posts at various sites on the island. The museum, which is part

Exhibit at the Whale Museum

of the Moclips Cetological Society, also publishes its own scientific magazine, *Cetus*, as well as a quarterly newsletter.

A "Whale Hotline", maintained here, catalogs calls of sightings, to better understand the habits and movements of local pods of orcas. Researchers have identified over a hundred different orcas by means of their size, sex, distinctive fin shapes, and scars. Each individual identified is given a number and, in some cases, an affectionate name. Some are known as Jelly Roll, Ewok, Victoria, Sparky, Chinook, Squirty, and Granny.

The Orca Adoption program is a unique service that was instituted by the Whale Museum. Persons who make a contribution ranging from $20 to $35 receive an adoption certificate, photo, and biography of the whale of their choice, along with a quarterly newsletter and membership benefits in the museum. Money raised by this program is used for research to help protect the future of the Puget Sound orca.

The Whale Museum is located in Friday Harbor at 62 First Street North, at the intersection of First and Court streets, three blocks from the ferry terminal. To find it, go south on Spring Street to First, then right two blocks to Court. From the boat dock it can be reached via a short trail that leaves Front Street just across from the road leading to the dock.

The facility, which is housed on the second floor of the Odd Fellows Hall, is open daily from 10 a.m. to 5 p.m. June through September, and 11 a.m. to 4 p.m. October through May.

Once you've absorbed all you can about whales, head for Lime Kiln Point State Park, on the west shore of the Island. Here visitors have a good chance of actually seeing whales as they pass by in Haro Strait. The park is described later in this chapter.

SAN JUAN ISLAND HISTORICAL MUSEUM

It has been claimed that San Juan County has more museums per capita than any other county in the country. Whether this is true or not, there's no disputing their quality. The fine San Juan Island Historical Museum is housed in a two-story white clapboard farmhouse in Friday Harbor, on Price Street north of the intersection of Spring Street, about ½ mile from the ferry dock. Park in the lot shared by the Saint Francis Catholic Church.

The house is furnished in the style of a gracious home during the turn of the century, and contains memorabilia from pioneer times and the Pig War. The museum is open during the summer on Wednesday and Saturday, 2 p.m. to 4 p.m., or by appointment.

UNIVERSITY OF WASHINGTON FRIDAY HARBOR LABORATORIES

With shorelines ranging from quiet bays and saltwater lagoons to rocky shelves swept by swift-flowing tides, the San Juan archipelago provides an exceptional opportunity for marine research. Tidal fluctuations of nearly 12 feet expose vast tidelands harboring specimens of many diverse marine plant and invertebrate species.

Recognizing the unique character of the archipelago, the University of Washington established a marine biology research center on San Juan Island in 1904. When land from a former military reserve at Point Caution just north of Friday Harbor became available, the Laboratories moved onto the 484-acre tract, there growing to become a fine educational and research facility, attracting visiting scientists from all over the world.

Ferries arriving at Friday Harbor pass the attractive campus on the north shore of the outer harbor. A modern-day aqueduct can be seen snaking along the bank; fashioned of polyethelene, the pipe delivers contaminant-free seawater to the laboratory aquaria.

In the past, guided tours of the facility were available; unfortunately funding constraints have caused these popular tours to be discontinued. At present the labs are open only to those involved in research.

The University of Washington also administers biological preserves at several other areas in the San Juans. These lands have been donated, purchased, or leased to protect them in a nearly natural state for research and educational purposes. The largest of these holdings is on Shaw Island, and includes most of the land and shoreline extending from Point George to Squaw Bay; others are at Argyle Lagoon and False Bay on San Juan Island and Iceberg Point and Point Colville on the southern end of Lopez Island.

In order to protect marine lands, all of the seashores and seabed of San Juan County and around Cypress Island in Skagit County are designated a marine biological preserve. Areas with this status are open for public recreation, but Washington state law prohibits the taking or destruction of any living specimen, except for food use, without written permission of the Director of the Friday Harbor Laboratories.

Intertidal lands are vast displays of marine life, where the competition and predation of these animals and their peculiar adaptations for survival can be observed. Delicate interrelationships are easily disrupted by public misuse, and overcollecting of any particular species, even natural predators such as starfish, can have far-reaching effects on the overall marine balance (in addition to being unlawful).

Especially sensitive are very slow-growing species that must not be harvested in quantity due to their long replacement cycle. While the edible mussel is fast-growing and readily replaces itself, the California mussel— larger, with a rougher ribbed shell—is much slower to replace itself in chilly Northwest waters. Goose barnacles, which sometimes are gathered for food, are also slow-growing in the San Juans.

Abalone were once rare here, but recently have become quite abundant; overharvesting of this popular food item could seriously deplete their numbers. Scuba divers and fishermen often take rockfish on rocky bottoms near pilings. A rockfish two feet long needs thirty years to grow that large, compared to a salmon, which will grow to an equal size in three to four years. It makes a lot of sense to protect large rockfish, since they contribute

Display pool at Friday Harbor Laboratories

relatively enormous numbers of young fish to the population annually, in addition to taking a long time to achieve their large size. Taking smaller individuals, *e.g.,* one to three pounds, has a lesser impact on future generations.

With an increasing scarcity of choice butter clams, oysters, and Dungeness crabs, human beach-foragers are displaying a greater interest in adding to their gastronomic fare the more bizarre marine forms: leathery chitons, limpets and moon snails, and grotesque sea cucumbers and goose barnacles.

The taking for food use of nearly every form of marine life in Washington is controlled by state law. The Department of Fisheries sport fishing pamphlet, available at most sporting goods stores, lists bag limits and other restrictions.

Even the removal of nonliving things such as driftwood or shells from the beaches can have negative effects. For example, at Lime Kiln Lighthouse hermit crabs have severe competition for shells. People removing shells that could serve as shelters can cause these invertebrates to become exposed to predators or the environment.

TURN ISLAND

Park area: 35 acres; 1,510 feet of shoreline
Access: Boat
Facilities: 10 campsites, picnic tables, stoves, pit toilets, mooring buoys, *no water*
Attractions: Beachcombing, hiking, clams, crabs, mussels, tidepools, scuba diving, paddling

Situated so near the boating throngs at Friday Harbor, Turn Island receives considerable use, especially by boaters with small craft that can be beached on the island's inviting shores. In summer the few campsites

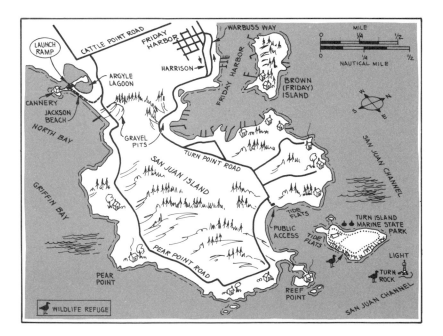

Deer swimming between islands (photo by Bob and Ira Spring)

arc frequently full, although the lack of drinking water precludes an extended stay.

In good weather even rowboats can manage an excursion through Friday Harbor and along the shores of San Juan Island to the park. En route, view the many gracious homes lining the shores on San Juan and Brown islands. Total distance is less than 2 nautical miles, all of it near land. Small boats may also be put in at the boat launch just ¼ mile across the channel. Directions to it are described below.

Turn Island is under joint jurisdiction; it is owned by the federal government as a part of the San Juan Islands National Wildlife Refuge, and also is managed cooperatively by the state for public recreational use as a marine state park.

The best anchorages are found on the west side of the island, where there are three buoys. Moorages here are only slightly sheltered by the landmasses and can be quite uncomfortable in a stiff northerly or with the slosh of heavy boat traffic on San Juan Channel; at other times they promise a pleasant night's stay.

At low tide the southwest end of the island becomes a big tideflat, with clams and mussels awaiting harvesting. Tidepools are exposed at low,

low water, or they can be observed by floating in a dinghy just offshore and gazing down into the water at the dazzling undersea world of marine life: brilliant purples, oranges, and reds; pastel pinks, greens, and lavenders— the color range is limitless. Polarized sunglasses reduce glare on the water and make viewing easier. The shallow water is excellent for snorkeling.

Camping and picnicking is concentrated on the southwest end of the island; the balance of the land is a wildlife refuge. Six campsites and pit toilets are sequestered in the open timber at the main campsite above the west beach, and another four sites and toilets are found above the gravel beach of the next cove to the south.

A 300-yard path cuts across the middle of the island, connecting the main camping area with a pretty 500-foot-long gravel beach on the far side. Encircling the island, another connecting trail invites a pleasant 1-mile tramp through light timber, looking out over busy San Juan Channel.

Near the northeast end, Turn Rock, with its navigational beacon, can be seen just offshore. The island and rock are so named because they mark the point where vessels must turn in the channel. The rock is another of the bird sanctuaries of the San Juan Islands National Wildlife Refuge, and is usually covered with chattering, busybody gulls.

The northeast side of the island is quite precipitous, with no beach access; beaches around the rest of the island are easily reached from the trail above. Near the east end of the island the trail passes an enormous 10-foot-high rock erratic, silent testimony to the geological forces that shaped this region.

Rabbits, raccoons, and other small mammals inhabit Turn Island, along with black-tailed deer. These deer, which can be found throughout the San Juans, swim from island to island, sometimes across extremely broad and swift-flowing channels.

Turn Island at one time held a huge bald eagle nest; however, the tree supporting it broke in a storm, destroying it. Reported to have been in continuous use by several generations of eagles for over seventy years, the nest had been abandoned at the time of its destruction. Frequent disturbances by humans can cause the birds to abandon a nesting site, or they may be driven out by infestations of vermin brought to the nest on captured rodents. There are other eagle nesting sites in the vicinity.

TURN POINT ROAD ACCESS

Hand-carried boats can be put in at a public access area on San Juan Island just spitting distance from Turn Island. To reach it by car, follow Harrison, a one-way street heading east along the shore of Friday Harbor. In a few blocks Harrison joins Warbuss Way and then becomes Turn Point Road. The road winds around Turn Point, and eventually arrives at the signed public access and a large dirt parking lot, about 2 miles from Friday Harbor. Turn Island can be seen ¼ mile across the channel.

JACKSON BEACH

Park area: 10 acres
Access: Ferry to San Juan Island, boat
Facilities: Boat launch (ramp)
Attractions: Boating, paddling, beachcombing

The only launch for trailered boats in the vicinity of Friday Harbor is found at Jackson Beach. To reach it drive south out of Friday Harbor on Argyle Ave. In ¾ mile turn east on Pear Point Road. Just before a large sand and gravel operation is reached Jackson Beach Road branches south and heads downhill to the launch ramp.

The road along the spit enclosing Argyle Lagoon ends at a cannery. With the exception of this commercial property and the lagoon itself, the remainder of the spit is a public day-use area. On the inside of the spit, between the lagoon and the cannery, a single-lane concrete ramp with adjacent float drops into a small, protected cove.

More than just a boat launch, this narrow strand also includes one of the nicest beaches on this end of the island, sloping and with a jumble of driftwood logs at the high tide level. Three pull-outs above the beach provide ample parking. The north end of the beach is wide, flat sand, inviting volleyball matches, kite flying, Frisbee games, or other beach recreation.

Jackson Beach

Argyle Lagoon, on the inside of the spit, is a research area for the Friday Harbor Laboratories; one condition for public use of the beach is that the lagoon will be protected and restricted from any public access. The lagoon is used primarily for short-term research projects, as it functions as a "mini-ocean." In such a controlled environment distinct populations can be followed, or small plots can be manipulated in order to observe the effects.

The North End

SPORTSMAN AND EGG LAKES

Area: Sportsman Lake—87 acres; Egg Lake—6.6 acres
Facilities: Sportsman Lake—boat launch (ramp); Egg Lake—dock
Attractions: Fishing, birdwatching, paddling

Bird heaven! Cattails and bogs edge the open water of two lakes only a few minutes' drive from Friday Harbor. Red-winged blackbirds perch sidesaddle on cattails; an array of wild migratory waterfowl coexist with plump domestic ducks and geese from neighboring farms. During spring mating season, marsh birds loudly advertise their territorial boundaries. All this and fish too!

Sportsman Lake lies to the left of the Roche Harbor Road, 4 miles northwest of Friday Harbor. A short spur road on the northeast side of the lake leads to a gravel boat ramp.

Sportsman Lake boat launch

Open to fishing the year around, the shallow 87-acre lake contains largemouth bass and spiny ray. All surrounding lands are private, but no matter, for the beauty lies in the bogs and the birds and the tranquil water. Drop in a boat for fishing, birdwatching, or just for a paddle around the lake.

Sportsman's tiny counterpart, Egg Lake, lies just 300 yards to the west. To reach the lake, continue west on the Roche Harbor Road for less than ½ mile to the intersection with Egg Lake Road. Turn left and follow the gravel road for ¾ mile; through the trees on the left the lake and a small floating dock can be seen. This is the only public access.

Egg Lake is regularly planted with rainbow trout. Fishing is permitted from April 16 through October 31; gasoline motors are not legal. Aside from the public dock, all bordering lands are private.

LAKEDALE CAMPGROUND

Facilities: Campsites, restrooms, showers, drinking water, trailer hookups *(no sewer or dump)*, picnic tables, fireplaces, boat and fishing gear rental, fishing docks, groceries

The overburdened little county campground at Smallpox Bay is the only public facility for campers on San Juan Island; however, a 200-acre commercial campground and recreation area located just north of Egg and Sportsman lakes offers everything a camper might wish—and then some. Here, former marshes have been dammed to form a network of private ponds for fishing, swimming, rowing, and canoeing, and shorelands are available for camping or daytime picnics

Nearly a hundred campsites are scattered along the shores of the lakes, some in timber, others in open, grassy areas. Since the lakes are private, fishing licenses are not required; but a fee is charged.

The entrance to the campground is on Roche Harbor Road, ¼ mile north of the Egg Lake Road intersection.

REUBEN TARTE PICNIC AREA

Park area: 6 acres; 600 feet of shoreline
Attractions: Scuba diving, birdwatching, picnicking

This out-of-the-way corner offers absolutely no facilities, and drivers may not care to attempt the road, but it's an interesting little nook that has a certain appeal.

Reuben Tarte Picnic Area is located on a small rocky prominence southeast of Limestone Point, on the north end of San Juan Island. To reach it, follow Roche Harbor Road for 8 miles from Friday Harbor, and turn right (north) onto Rouleau Road. In another mile turn right again (east) at the intersection with Limestone Point Road. At a T intersection in just under 1 mile, turn right, now heading south, on San Juan Drive.

In about ⅓ mile a gravel road, which may be unmarked, goes left down to the beach. The route is signed only "No Camping, County Ordinance," and may be difficult to find. The road to the picnic area borders on requiring four-wheel drive, as it is narrow, rutted, extremely steep, and gets slippery when wet. At road's end is parking for a couple of cars.

A grassy rock knoll pokes into San Juan Channel, between two tiny coves. The underwater rock formations of the point and offshore reefs are home for copious amounts of marine life, making the area a favorite with scuba divers, who explore along the channel and northwest to Limestone Point.

Colonies of coral and other sedentary marine animals, growing in the warm waters of an ancient sea, created the typical beds of white limestone that distinctively mark the 80-foot-high knob of Limestone Point.

Roche Harbor

Access: Ferry to San Juan Island, boat, or airplane
Facilities: Guest moorage, dock with water and electrical hookups,
    mooring buoys (fee), boat launch (ramp), boat rental, gas, diesel,
    restrooms, showers, laundry, groceries, hotel, restaurant, swimming
    pool, tennis courts, moped rental, U.S. Customs
Attractions: Boating, paddling, fishing, hiking, scuba diving,
    sightseeing, historical landmarks

Relics of an earlier, much different time mingle easily with the trappings of a modern-day vacation resort. A hundred-year-old log cabin

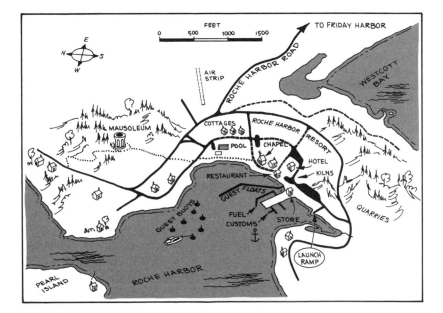

Roche Harbor Marina

stands within a few feet of busy tennis courts and an Olympic-size swimming pool. Skeletons of a tug and a ferry, reminders of the industrial heyday of the town, moulder on the beach overlooking the posh fiberglass cruisers bobbing at their moorings. Visitors register at the hotel, which in the 1850s saw duty as a Hudson's Bay trading post and which later hosted presidents Teddy Roosevelt and William Howard Taft.

To reach Roche Harbor from the Friday Harbor ferry landing, drive west on Spring Street, turning right on Second Street. In 3 blocks turn left on Guard and after one more block, right on Tucker. At a Y in the road, bear left on Roche Harbor Road, which continues to the resort, 10¼ miles from the ferry landing.

The harbor is 11 nautical miles by boat from Friday Harbor and 22 nautical miles from Victoria Harbor on Vancouver Island. In summer the busy docks are a happy mingling of Canadian and Yankee boaters checking in at Customs and stocking up on provisions and fuel before moving on to more remote islands. Rows of buoys in the harbor are filled by early evening, and courtesy boats from the resort, like large water bugs, ferry boaters from their buoys to the shore and back. Old friends are met, new ones are made, and sea stories are swapped.

On the week of Dominion Day (July 1) and the Fourth of July, the harbor is jammed with upwards of 500 boats and is even more festive, with fireworks and special events. The evening flag-lowering ceremony, which takes place throughout the summer months, holds special meaning at this time when Canadians and Americans join together in friendship to honor their countries.

Trailered boats may be launched at a surfaced ramp just south of the resort parking area, for a fee. Boat trailer parking is back up on the hill south of the quarries. The resort may also be reached by private plane, and San Juan Airlines provides regular service to the airfield near the resort.

The historic old hotel and restaurant, graced with a prize-winning formal flower garden, are the center of harbor activity. A display in the lobby of the Hotel de Haro tells of Roche Harbor's history. A young Indiana lawyer, John McMillin, built the largest lime-producing company west of the Mississippi, and for fifty years "ruled" the town. He became one of the richest and most influential men in the state, ran (unsuccessfully) for the U.S. Senate, and even entertained hopes of becoming one of Washington's governors.

After McMillin's death in 1936 his son operated the family business until the lime deposits began to play out. In 1956 the town was sold, the lime kilns were shut down shortly thereafter. Subsequent owners have restored the deteriorated buildings and developed the property into a modern resort that offers fine vacation and boating facilities to visitors.

AFTERGLOW VISTA MAUSOLEUM

Forsake the activity of Roche Harbor for a stroll through quiet woods to rub elbows with McMillin family ghosts. From the Hotel de Haro follow the path northwest past the church toward the swimming pool. On the left is a one-room log cabin, believed to have been the home of the Scurr brothers, who lived here in the mid-1880s and who sold the property to John S. McMillin.

Continue on the path until it joins Roche Harbor Road in ¼ mile. Turn left (north) and follow the blacktopped road past a small cemetery that sits just above the road and in ¼ mile find a dirt side road on the right; this side road is barred to vehicles, although it is often used by horseback riders and bicyclists. In 200 yards the path reaches the gateway arch of the mausoleum.

Several tiers of stairs lead to a platform encircled with Doric columns. In the center is a round stone table surrounded by six stone chairs. The encroaching forest adds to the eerie calm of the spot. It is a privilege to be permitted to visit this unique shrine; please treat it with respect.

John S. McMillin chose this spot for his final resting place because he enjoyed the splendid sunset afterglow on Spieden Channel; however today second-growth timber obscures the view he so prized. The significance of the construction of the tomb is based on the family history and on the Masonic Order, of which McMillin was a member. The intentionally broken column represents life broken by death, while the ring supporting the remaining columns represents the eternal life after death.

The table and chairs are placed just as they were in the family dining

Afterglow Vista Mausoleum

room, with McMillin at the head of the table and an open space at the foot facing westward, so that all could enjoy the sunset. The bases of the chairs hold the ashes of the deceased members of the family, who rest here for eternity, their spirits watching the sunset just as they did in life.

Beyond the road to the mausoleum, the main road drops downhill to end at private drives. The one to the left can be walked southward; near the swimming-pool/tennis-court complex watch for trails dropping through timber to the beach. Here are more antique log cabins, still in use as storage sheds, and the debris of two long-ago wrecked boats. From here walk the beach back to Roche Harbor; total distance of the loop hike is 1 mile.

LIME QUARRY

A row of abandoned lime kilns overlooks the waters of Roche Harbor. For a closer inspection of the kilns and the quarries that were the lifeblood of the town, take a loop hike along the road, pausing to inspect the rusted railroad tracks and machinery, visualizing the quarries at the height of their productivity, when 15,000 barrels of lime per day were turned out.

From the grocery store walk southwest along the road at the water's edge. Immediately to the left are the lime kilns, with their gracefully arching brickwork still intact. Continue uphill, following the road left when it turns sharply at the first intersecton. Pass gaping quarries where undergrowth is creeping back to gentle the harsh outlines.

Near the top of the hill stop and enjoy a sweeping view of Roche Harbor, Spieden Channel, Mosquito Pass, and Henry Island before the road ducks into timber, briefly losing sight of the harbor. Turn left at the intersection with a blacktopped road, then left again at a driveway that drops steeply downhill past some private homes, headed back to the bay. The driveway dead-ends at a path that brings the hiker back to the plaza between the hotel and the restaurant, a short distance from the grocery store. Total round-trip distance is 1¼ miles.

POSEY ISLAND MARINE STATE PARK

Park area: 1 acre
Access: Boat
Facilities: 1 campsite, picnic tables, pit toilet, *no water*
Attractions: Beachcombing, fishing, paddling, scuba diving, snorkeling, tidepools

A dot of an island just outside Roche Harbor provides a lovely afternoon picnic spot, or in fair weather a campsite with a superb sunset. The accommodations at Posey Island are meager, with a couple of scruffy picnic tables and space for a single tent, but its proximity to Roche Harbor makes this a popular site.

The island lies less than a nautical mile northeast of Roche Harbor, the nearest place where boats may be launched. Boaters in small craft can take a shorter route through the channel at the east end of Pearl Island, while deeper draft vessels are better advised to stay in the main channel at the west end of Pearl, and anchor well out, as the water surrounding Posey Island is quite shallow and reefs extend out on the north and east. The protected, shallow water makes this an ideal voyage for a canoe or kayak.

Due to the fact that the sun goes down in the rainy district of Vancouver Island, the San Juans have exceptionally vivid sunsets. The crimson and gold colors, intensified by the black masses of the islands, linger in the sky and sea long after the sun has disappeared. Posey Island, with its open views of Haro Strait and Canadian islands, is a prime spot for savoring the afterglow.

The West Side

MOSQUITO PASS

Mosquito Pass, a skinny, 1½-mile long waterway separating Henry and San Juan islands, connects Roche Harbor and Westcott, Garrison, and Mitchell bays. The pass and the three shallow bays are ideal for small boat exploration, although tidal currents can be strong and unpredictable in Mosquito Pass itself, where unpowered boats should use great care.

Deep-keel vessels should not attempt the channel without the aid of charts, as there are many rocks and shoals where the unwary can find

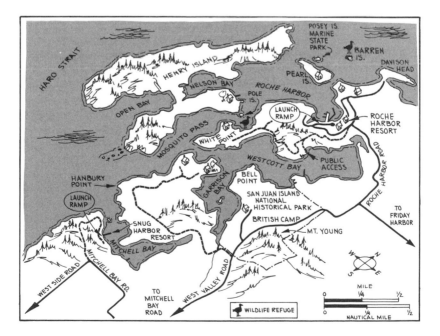

themselves embarrassingly aground. A phalanx of reefs and shoals marks the south end of the channel. Pay close attention to navigational markers—they know what they are talking about!

HENRY ISLAND

Resembling a letter H crudely scrawled in the water to the west of Mosquito Pass, Henry Island shelters the San Juan bays from waves off Haro Strait. The island rests on the protruding edge of an underwater shelf, and bluffs on the west side plunge steeply downward to a depth of 120 fathoms. The edges of this shelf, especially areas off Kellett Bluff, provide fine fishing and scuba diving.

Open Bay, indenting the bottom of the H, and a small bight north of Nelson Bay, at its top, give anchorage to boaters escaping the summertime bustle of Roche Harbor. Do not go ashore, for the entire island is privately owned. Approximately 80 acres at Kellett Bluff on the tip of the southwest lobe of the island are a lighthouse reservation; however, the steepness of

Snug Harbor, Mitchell Bay

the shore makes landing there impractical.

One mile due north of Henry Island, chunky Battleship Island, with "smokestacks" of three trees, surely does resemble its namesake in both size and shape. Battleship, along with Barren Island (lying to the east of the entrance to Roche Harbor near Davidson Head) and Pole Island (in the north entrance of Mosquito Pass), are all part of the San Juan Islands National Wildlife Refuge.

WESTCOTT BAY

Although most boaters visiting the British Camp portion of San Juan Island National Historical Park drop anchor in Garrison Bay, some choose to stop in Westcott Bay and walk the short trail along Bell Point. For descriptions of adjacent Garrison Bay and British Camp, see the following chapter.

Two protruding points on either shore divide Westcott Bay into two areas. The best anchorage is in the southwest portion of the bay; the northeast end becomes quite shallow. An extensive aquaculture operation on the southeast shore raises oysters, mussels, and clams for sale to restaurants. Give the underwater pens a wide berth.

One small public road end on the west side of Westcott Bay is the only public shoreline on the bay. To reach it by land, turn off Roche Harbor Road just past the resort entrance and airstrip, onto the first dirt road to the left. In about ½ mile a gravel spur drops left downhill to end at a grassy head; here a lunchtime sandwich can be spiced up with salty views across the bay.

MITCHELL BAY

Access: Ferry to San Juan Island, boat
Facilities (at Snug Harbor): Guest moorage, gas, outboard mix, boat launch (ramp), cabins, campground, restrooms, groceries, boat rental and charter, marine repair and supplies, fishing tackle, scuba air
Attractions: Boating, fishing, scuba diving, crabs

The small marina on the south shore of Mitchell Bay is well named, as the entrance to the harbor is, indeed, very snug. However, once inside this cozy little haven the water is adequately deep for most small craft in all but extremely low tides. At the entrance a shoal marked by a small island extends from the south side of the bay; stay well to the north of this rock. All beaches and docks are private, except for the marina on the south shore.

To reach Mitchell Bay by land, head south from Roche Harbor Road on West Valley Road, and in 3¼ miles turn west on Mitchell Bay Road. In ¾ mile the road winds downhill to the marina and resort. On the hillside behind the resort are 10 campsites on a series of graded platforms overlooking the bay.

Haro Strait

SAN JUAN COUNTY PARK

Park area: 15 acres
Access: Ferry to San Juan Island, boat
Facilities: 11 campsites, picnic tables, fireplaces, restrooms, groceries,
    boat launching (ramp), group camp, *no water*
Attractions: Boating, scuba diving, snorkeling, beachcombing, tidepools

The story is told that long ago a number of Indians stricken with smallpox plunged into the icy San Juan waters to rid themselves of their burning fever; as a result they subsequently died of pneumonia. The tiny bay on the west side of San Juan Island where the tragedy occurred has since that time been called Smallpox Bay.

Despite its unfortunate history, today the bay is of more pleasant significance, for it is the site of popular San Juan County Park. Located on the West Side Road, 3½ miles south of the West Valley Road intersection, the park occupies land at the head of the bay and an abandoned orchard on a bluff. Although the park officially has only 12 campsites, and a group camp by the office/store, over a hundred people may be crammed into its 12 acres on summer weekends. To be assured of a site in summer, make reservations well ahead of time.

San Juan County Park

The pressure of such numbers is beginning to show, in the pollution of the water system, deterioration of the flora, and irascibility of the local residents who are unable to find a place to camp in their own park. To better enjoy the area, and be appreciated by the San Juan Islanders, visit off-season. It is possible that in the future this will become a day-use park and a campground will be established elsewhere on the island. At present, campers must bring their own water or purchase it in jugs at the campground store.

In winter, when it is uncrowded, it is a relaxing spot with exquisite nighttime views across Haro Strait to the lights of Vancouver Island. Explore the shores of the bay or saunter through twisted madronas to the top of the bluff, but even the healthy risk pneumonia by attempting to swim in the bay.

With dive spots within walking distance of campsites, the park is a favorite among scuba divers. Easy snorkeling is found in the bay, while the rocky bottom that plunges steeply to 80 feet just offshore is a challenge to more experienced divers. In addition to the usual bright palette of anemone, urchins, and starfish, look for abalone clinging to rocks and octopus hiding in crevices.

Gulls, and sometimes seals, congregate on Low Island, 100 yards offshore—another of the bird refuges of the San Juan Islands National Wildlife Refuge.

The tiny log cabin in the campground was built at the turn of the century as a home for a widowed homesteader and his daughter. While the building was under construction, the pair lived in a cave that he dug in the side of a nearby hill. The cabin once had an outside stairway to provide access to the daughter's bedroom on the second floor.

LIME KILN POINT STATE PARK

Park area: 39 acres; 2550 feet of shoreline
Access: Ferry to San Juan Island
Facilities: Restrooms, picnic tables, interpretive displays, drinking water
Attractions: Whale watching, birdwatching, lighthouse

Just past San Juan County Park, West Side Road turns from blacktop to gravel and continues southward through sparse timber. In 3 miles it curves around a hill and bursts suddenly into open marine views. To the right, at the bend of the hairpin curve, a single-lane dirt road leads to Lime Kiln Point State Park.

Recognizing the unique location of the park on a rocky point overlooking Haro Strait, the state has developed it as a whale-watching site, complete with interpretive signs. A ranger is usually on duty in the summer to answer questions.

A hundred yards down the road is a small loop with parking for a dozen cars. When crowded, park at the road head instead, being careful not

Watching for whales at Lime Kiln Point State Park

to block either road, and walk the gravel road or scramble along the rocky shoreline to the interpretive site and to the lighthouse north of it.

From the parking lot a short trail leads to grass-covered rocks above Haro Strait, dotted with picnic tables for resting while awaiting the arrival of whales. A set of interpretive signs here explains identification of minke whales, orcas, Dall's porpoises, and harbor porpoises, and describes characteristics of their behavior.

June through September is prime whale-watching season as these mammals search Haro Strait for runs of salmon returning to Fraser River spawning grounds. There's no guarantee that whales will appear on cue; come armed with binoculars and a lot of patience; in summer whales may pass by here several times during the day, usually within ¾ mile of the shore, and at times much closer. While waiting for the whales to appear, focus binoculars on the variety of waterfowl that gather to feed in offshore tide rips, explore tidepools along the shore, or have a picnic.

The whales most commonly seen in the San Juan Islands are the "killer whale," *Orcinis orca*, or orca as it is more correctly called, and minke (*mink-ee*) whales. Northwest Indians considered the orca, a toothed whale, to be the ''wolf of the sea,'' for working in highly organized packs or ''pods'' of up to thirty individuals, they are swift, efficient predators of schools of fish, dolphins, and even larger whales. Bad press to the contrary, however, authenticated reports of attacks by orcas on humans are quite rare, and when captured by man they display gentle, friendly, intelligent behavior.

Unlike orcas, minke whales usually travel alone or in pairs. They are baleen whales, having comblike structures in their jaws that are used to strain food from seawater. Minkes, the smallest of the baleen whales, are similar in size to orcas, but do not have as high a dorsal fin, and their bodies are slimmer. Gray whales (also baleen whales) are sometimes seen in Puget Sound, but are more rare.

Smaller harbor porpoises, and Dall's porpoises (both of which, like orcas, are toothed whales) are also frequently spotted in the San Juan Islands. Dall's porpoises are black with white markings, but only orcas display the striking white underbelly reaching from the jaw to near the tail, the great fin ranging from three to five feet tall, and the awesome 20- to 30-foot-long body.

Beyond the parking area for the park the road is gated, but it continues as a footpath past ranger residences to Lime Kiln Lighthouse. Poised on a rocky outcropping where it balefully hoots its presence to passing ships, it is one of the most scenic in the state. Built in 1919, the lighthouse, now automated, has been in continuous operation since that time, and is listed on the National Register of Historic Places. In 1984 the State Parks Commission took over maintenance of the surrounding property for public use.

At this site was one of the earliest lime kiln operations in the San Juans; excavations and remnants of some of the old structures can still be seen north of the lighthouse.

SPOTTING WHALES

Whale sightings are certainly one of the most thrilling experiences of the San Juans, and one that is not reserved for boaters alone, for pods of whales have been seen from land at many places in addition to Lime Kiln Point State Park, and even from the ferry. At such times ferry captains have been known to slow their engines and alert passengers who want to take in the sight.

A spotting may consist of only a momentary revelation—a fish flinging itself out of the grayness of the sea, twisting frantically, then dropping back into the water, to be followed by a pursuing boat-sized curving back, displaying a five-foot-high triangular fin that is gone as quickly as the small fish.

At other times a ruffling on the surface of the water is noticed; then suddenly the water is filled with several great black bodies slashed with white, surfacing and blowing for several minutes, which may then disappear and reappear a quarter of a mile away. Porpoises have been known to playfully escort passing boats, swimming alongside or even diving back and forth beneath the keel for minutes at a time.

At the turn of the century settlers reported regular sightings of great pods of whales containing more than a hundred individuals. Although these reports perhaps were exaggerated, there is no doubt that there once were far more whales than there are today. It is believed that there are three pods, totaling about eighty individuals, now residents of the inland waters. Other pods of itinerant whales pass through here regularly.

While whale sightings are not commonplace in the San Juans, neither are they rare. The Moclips Cetological Society, under contract with the U.S. National Marine Fisheries Service, is engaged in cataloging all whale sightings in the islands, Strait of Juan de Fuca, and Puget Sound, in order to attempt to identify them and chart their movements.

Any whale sightings should be reported to the Orca Survey at 1-800-562-8832. Information on sightings should include the time and location, direction of movement of the whales, numbers sighted, and, if possible, the type of whale and any identifying characteristics of the individuals, such as notches in fins or bent fins.

It is illegal to harass or pursue with a boat any marine mammal. If whales are sighted, they should be observed at a slow speed. Federal law prohibits approaching whales closer than 100 yards, and deliberately positioning boats in their path. Boaters are far more likely to be able to observe a pod for a length of time if they stay at a distance and do not appear to be a threat. Frequently whales will come quite close to boats if they do not perceive them as a threat; the mammals seem totally aware of even small boats, and there has been no incident reported in the San Juans of even a canoe being overturned by a whale surfacing under it.

Orcas off San Juan Island

WEST SIDE ROAD

Deadman Bay, just south of the Lime Kiln Road intersection, is a popular scuba diving spot. It is said to be named for a sensational murder that occurred here in the late 1800s. Land surrounding the bay is private property. There is parking beside the road for a few cars; a jeep road leads down to the beach for easy access for swimming, picnicking, or launching hand-carried boats.

South of Lime Kiln Lighthouse the 2-mile stretch of West Side Road is one of the most spectacular in the islands, well worth the drive in itself. Twisting high on rocky bluffs, it offers views outward across the glittering expanse of Haro Strait and steeply downward to waves beating against the rugged toes of San Juan Island. In spring masses of California poppies flame between rocky outcrops. The recently paved road makes the route more attractive for bicyclers.

FALSE BAY

More than 200 acres of strange creatures to investigate — skittery purple shore crabs; two-foot, flame-colored ribbon worms; shoe-shaped chitons; prehistoric-appearing clingfish; barnacles and rock oysters (jingle shells) fated to spend life fastened to but one rock, with never a change of scenery.

Shallow, nearly circular False Bay is located on the southern end of San Juan Island, with its narrow mouth opening onto Haro Strait. The shores provide a pleasant beach walk at moderate to high tides, but the real fun comes at low water, when the entire bay nearly dries. Don rubber boots and wander through the muck to observe seashore life.

To reach False Bay from Friday Harbor drive west out of town on Spring Street. At an intersection 1½ mile from town turn left (south) onto False Bay Road, which can be followed 3½ more miles to the bay. Small pull-outs for parking are adjacent the road at both the south and north ends. Overnight camping or beach fires are not permitted.

The bay is owned and carefully monitored as a biological study area for the University of Washington. Several scientific theses have been written on the ecological systems found here. The contained environment, sheltered from the disturbing action of large waves, allows the study of discrete marine populations. Do not disturb rods, sticks, tubes, or anything that looks peculiar; these usually mark a research project in progress. Avoid any such staked-out areas, and do not dig in the vicinity. Look all you wish, but *do not kill or collect any specimens anywhere in the bay*. Walk carefully to avoid damaging any of the marine life.

A good seashore guide such as *Seashore Life of Puget Sound, the Strait of Georgia and the San Juan Archipelago*, by Eugene Kozloff, or *Living Shores of the Pacific Northwest*, by Lynnwood S. Smith, helps immeasurably in the identification and understanding of these invertebrates.

False Bay

A magnifying glass is also useful. A clear glass jar filled with fresh seawater aids in studying the delicate animals; slip the specimen carefully into the jar to observe it, then quickly return it to its home. If the water becomes too warm it may die. Handle shell-less creatures with damp hands to avoid damaging their protective slime coating.

When walking this or any beach, avoid dislocating stones harboring marine life. Certain marine specimens live only on the exposed tops of rocks, while others seek protection of the bottom; eggs are often attached to the undersides of beach rocks. If a stone is lifted and then replaced upside down, the invertebrates formerly on the top will suffocate on the bottom, while the others die of exposure on top.

Study a single rock to see the many kinds of life it supports. Pick up a piece of seaweed and check it out for "hitchhikers." Pools hold tiny fish waiting to be released by the next incoming tide.

PEDAL INN BICYCLE CAMP

The only campground on the south end of San Juan Island, a commercial facility restricted to bicycles, offers a pleasant respite after a long pedal down-island. To reach the camp turn west off Cattle Point Road onto False Bay Drive just a mile north of the American Camp boundary. In 1 mile arrive at the campground. The last stretch of road leading to the campground is gravel, although well graded and level.

The campground's 10 campsites lie in trees along the shores of a serene little pond edged with lily pads and cattails. A resident bald eagle that nests on the property preys on waterfowl frequenting the pond.

Future plans for the campground include showers, laundry, a small store, and additional campsites. The camp can also be reached from the West Side Road via Bailer Hill and False Bay roads.

EAGLE COVE PUBLIC ACCESS

Park area: 0.3 acre; 100 feet of shoreline

Just outside San Juan Island National Historical Park's American Camp is a small public cove fronting on the Strait of Juan de Fuca. This rock-rimmed cove is surrounded by a high bank that protects its beautiful sandy beach from much of the wind that whips the shoreline to the eastward. In addition to being popular with San Juan residents for beachcombing, swimming, and sunbathing, the cove is also a favorite scuba diving area, with underwater forests of kelp hiding rockfish, lingcod, abalone, and other marine life.

To reach the Eagle Cove access, turn south on Eagle Cove Road, just west of the American Camp boundary. In ½ mile there is a blacktopped parking area for a few cars with a sign stating "Public Access. No Overnight Camping." A 100-yard-long path descends through a tall, cool arch of underbrush alongside a creek drainage; muddy and slippery when wet.

At low tide the shore can be walked south to American Camp and all the way to Cattle Point, 3½ miles distant. Be careful not to get forced up onto the bluffs by incoming tides.

San Juan Channel

GRIFFIN BAY CAMPGROUND

Park area: 15 acres; 330 feet of shoreline
Access: Boat
Facilities: Campsites, picnic tables, fireplaces, pit toilets, mooring buoys, drinking water
Attractions: Beachcombing, boating

One of the beauties of this remote little park is that few people stop here, so one is almost assured of getting away from the noisy hordes. For a number of years the Department of Natural Resources tried to establish a park at this location. After some resistance from nearby property owners who feared the hazard of untended campfires at such a remote spot, the park was finally opened in 1984, but was limited to a boat-in site with no upland public access.

The park lies about ½ nautical mile south of Low Point, due west of Halftide Rocks. Approach from the south side of Halftide Rock in order to avoid shoals and a row of rotting pilings that may be submerged at high water. Skippers of deep keeled boats may find the vicinity of the park a bit scary, as the depth sounder begins to drop off some distance from shore. At low tide the buoys may be in water too shallow for some boats.

Picnic tables are on the low bank above the water, but campsites and fireplaces are 400 yards back from the shore. Water is available from a hand pump that will delight the kids.

FISH CREEK

Why it holds this name is a wonder, for it's not a creek at all, but a slotlike saltwater cove at the extreme end of San Juan Island. The "fish" part of the name is more understandable—during the 1850s the Hudson's Bay Company had a fish packing station here.

All the shoreland around Fish Creek is private, so there is no way to reach the water by land, but for boaters it is an enchanting little corner, and a handy little anchorage for waiting out fog or bad weather in the straits.

CATTLE BEACH PICNIC AREA

Access: Ferry to San Juan Island, boat
Facilities: Picnic tables, pit toilets
Attractions: Beachcombing, hiking

Two small gravel and driftwood beaches, separated by a glacier-scoured rock promontory, face on the entrance to San Juan Channel. Beach life is scarce here, but water-smoothed agates are often turned up among the pebbles.

This Department of Natural Resources picnic area is located ¾ mile east of the American Camp boundary, along Cattle Point Road. Several picnic tables on top of the bluff provide sweeping views of the channel and Lopez Island. Nearby, a concrete building, which was built in 1927 as a Coast Guard radio station, has been converted to use as a picnic shelter, complete with fireplace, well protected from the prevailing winds.

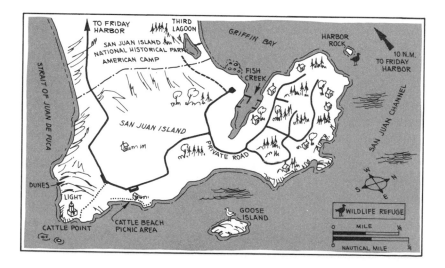

Beach at Cattle Beach Picnic Area

Interpretive signs near the picnic area tell of the geological history of the point, the centuries of use by Salish Indians, British and American settlers, and the history of the Coast Guard radiocompass facility that was located here. A steep trail descends earthen steps in the bank to the small southern bay; the northern bay requires steeper slippery scrambles down from bluff top to beach.

Small boats may be landed on either beach, but there is no offshore anchorage. Use great care in small boats on this end of the island; tide rips can be quite strong.

GOOSE ISLAND

Just 400 yards off Cattle Beach is Goose Rock, which is owned by The Nature Conservancy and administered by the Friday Harbor Laboratories as a biological preserve. It is one of few such islands in the San Juans to have nearly natural vegetation.

During pioneer times it was the practice to row sheep to grassy islands for summer grazing. (It was also necessary to frequently row barrels of fresh water to the flocks.) As a result, some plant species were completely wiped out on the islands, and other, tougher species took over. For some reason Goose Island escaped this fate, making it a unique botanical study

Cattle Point Lighthouse

area today. Its only current inhabitants are the hordes of squawking gulls and harbor seals and sea lions that sun here.

CATTLE POINT

The white concrete tower of Cattle Point Light has long been a welcome sight to boaters emerging from fog banks of the Strait of Juan de Fuca. Perched on sand dunes 80 feet above the beach, it can be reached by land by a 300-yard trail from the parking lot just south of American Camp, at the "toe" of San Juan Island, or by walking the beach at low tide east from South Beach for 2 miles. Vehicles of any type are prohibited beyond the parking lot, as the dune area is quite fragile.

The dunes are a rarity in the San Juans. Winds sweeping off the strait pile the sand in great, smooth mounds that are inviting to walk on and explore. Farther back from the beach, the sand has been stabilized by tough grass and bramble bushes. Here the ubiquitous San Juan rabbit digs burrows and peers insolently at visitors from the safety of the thicket, and in summer and fall a myriad of yellow-and-black American goldfinches flit and forage among the Canadian thistles along the trail.

British Camp and Garrison Bay

5. San Juan Island National Historical Park

Perhaps it was the kindly hand of Fate that determined that the United States and Great Britain be brought to the brink of war over a pig. With tempers as testy as they were, the deceased party could easily have been a man instead of a recalcitrant porker. As it was, the military authorities felt foolish being at loggerheads over the honor of a pig, permitting more rational minds to prevail and avert a serious war.

The Treaty of 1846 caused it all. When British and American negoti-

ators signed the document establishing the Oregon Territory boundary, they chose to overlook the vague language defining the boundary through a cluster of "worthless islands" lying between the mainland and Vancouver Island. Hudson's Bay Company, however, was well aware of the value of the timber, fur, fish, and grazing lands of the San Juan Islands. They claimed the territory for Queen Victoria by establishing an outpost overlooking the Strait of Juan de Fuca on the southern end of "Bellevue" Island, as San Juan Island was then called. Meanwhile the American westward expansion brought to this paradise Yankee settlers who scraped out homesteads, disregarding the property claims and, perhaps more important, the tax collectors of the British.

Lyman Cutlar chose as his farmsite a few acres in the middle of a Hudson's Bay sheep pasture. There he built a shack and planted potatoes. Cutlar was mighty attached to his crop, for that spring of 1859 he had rowed 40 miles round trip across the Strait of Juan de Fuca to purchase the seed potatoes. Thus, when a Hudson's Bay pig proceeded to willfully and regularly trespass into his potato patch, he violently objected. After registering a complaint with the unsympathetic Hudson's Bay agent, Cutlar solved the problem by dispatching the offending pig with his rifle.

Tempers flared and Cutlar was threatened with arrest. In somewhat pithy language he questioned the jurisdiction of the Crown, and appealed to American authorities. James Douglas, Governor of British Columbia, who had long been rankled by the incursion of American settlers, saw an opportunity to settle the matter of British sovereignty in the islands, and ordered a ship to San Juan Island to support the Hudson's Bay position.

American and British militarists who scouted the waters in the years following the Treaty of 1846 had noted that San Juan Island strategically guarded the Strait of Juan de Fuca, Haro Strait, and the mouth of the Fraser River. They were determined the territory should not fall into the hands of a potential foe. Soon both sides were massing ships, men, and armaments. At times they were only a bullet away from all-out war. The superior British flotilla could easily have leveled American fortifications with their heavy guns; however, if battle had really begun, all American settlers in the area would enter into the fracas and the British would be outnumbered. Moreover, the fight was sure to spread to Vancouver Island, where there were nearly four American "foreigners" to every British subject. Leaders on both sides realized that any serious war would bathe the islands in the blood of hundreds of American and British citizens.

Lieutenant General Winfield Scott was dispatched by President James Buchanan to take command of American matters in the San Juan archipelago. Arriving in October of 1859, and finding the battle had fortunately not yet begun, he proposed to Douglas that the island be jointly occupied by equal forces of the two factions until arbitration could settle the boundary dispute.

The British eventually accepted this plan, and American Camp was established on the southern tip of the island on barren slopes near the Hud-

Early morning at Garrison Bay

son's Bay trading post. Meanwhile the British marines landed on the shores of a protected harbor on the northwest side of the island, which they named Garrison Bay.

Once the threat of all-out war in the San Juans was assuaged, the U.S. government turned its attentions to more urgent internal problems in the southern states. With the beginning of the Civil War in April of 1861, the San Juan dispute was relegated to a diplomatic back burner. Britain, too, was embroiled in domestic problems and did not press for settlement of the dispute. Time wore on and the hastily erected tents at British and American Camps were replaced by permanent barracks, hospitals, and social halls. Timber was cleared for parade grounds and gardens. Duty was good on San Juan Island.

Finally, with the boundary commission at an impasse, the question was submitted to an impartial arbitrator, Kaiser Wilhelm I of Germany, who in October of 1872 decided in favor of the United States. The dispute was finally settled—thirteen years after a British boar filled his jowls with American potatoes and thus stepped into history.

Several excellent books on the complete history of the war are available. Keith Murray's *The Pig War* and *The San Juan Water Boundary Question*, by James McCabe, are both quite authoritative.

Following withdrawal of armed forces, the lands of American Camp and British Camp were privately owned. In 1966 Congress commemorated the peaceful settlement of the dispute by designating the two areas as San Juan Island National Historical Park, and parcels of land on Griffin and

Garrison bays were purchased. Numerous interpretive displays and signs have been installed to help visitors understand the historical significance of the park. More are planned for the future. The park's primary function is historical, not recreational, but in such a beautiful setting, with beaches, forests, and grasslands, even those who care not a whit for our heritage cannot help but love the park.

The park grounds are open during daylight hours year-round, although buildings at British Camp are closed off-season. Information is available at the park office in Friday Harbor. During summer weekends historical programs are presented by park rangers and volunteers wearing dashing replicas of British and American military uniforms or other costumes appropriate to the time.

ARCHAEOLOGICAL FINDS

Archaeological digs completed by park personnel in 1977 searched for Indian and pioneer artifacts. Additional annual digs have been conducted since 1983, sponsored by the University of Washington, to explore Indian use of the area over the past 4000 to 7000 years. A number of the items found by archaeologists are on display at British Camp.

Occasionally visitors walking over the grounds of either camp may discover artifacts. It is imperative that these discoveries are not disturbed, and are left exactly where found, as the location and surrounding soil are of as much archaeological importance as the artifact itself. Note the location and report it to a ranger, who will contact a trained archaeologist to ensure proper examination and removal of the find.

British Camp

Park area: 529 acres; 7920 feet of shoreline
Access: Ferry to San Juan Island, boat
Facilities: Dinghy dock, picnic tables, pit toilets, *no water*, hiking trails,
    no overnight camping
Attractions: Historical displays, hiking, boating, paddling, clam digging
    (observe posted regulations for clam digging)

The most interesting of the Pig War relics are found at British Camp. Three of the original buildings from the old garrison have been restored; one houses artifacts, an interpretive display, and a self-operated slide show on the history of the park. A fourth building, believed to have been the hospital or surgeon's quarters, was sold and moved to another location on the island after the British left. When found it was returned to its original site and restored.

The blockhouse near the beach was built to protect the marines from marauding Indians, rather than from warring Yankees, and also served as a guard house. A traditional formal garden, fenced against deer and rabbits, is typical of those planted during the time. Near the barracks grows a spreading big-leaf maple tree; once it was the largest of its kind in the world, but it is now slightly outranked by one in Oregon.

An interpretive trail leads uphill from the formal garden to a grassy bench overlooking the bay where the officers' quarters were located. On a second, higher bench quarters were built for the commanding officer of the Royal Marines and his family. The small stone obelisk found here was erected on October 12, 1904, to commemorate the thirty-second anniversary of the resolution of the boundary dispute.

To reach British Camp from Friday Harbor, follow Roche Harbor Road, which curves around the north end of San Juan Island. At a major intersection 8½ miles from Friday Harbor turn left (south) from Roche Harbor Road onto West Valley Road. Entrance to British Camp is on the right in 1½ miles. From the parking area a 200-yard path, edged by a picturesque split rail fence, leads to the military site on Garrison Bay.

The 1½ mile boat excursion from Roche Harbor to British Camp winds through lovely Mosquito Pass and the narrow entrance to Westcott Bay. Consult a good chart for the location of numerous shoals along the way; Garrison Bay is quite shallow throughout and deep keeled vessels should enter with care. The two protected bays are ideal for kayak or dinghy exploration.

Tiny, wooded Guss Island, which lies only 300 yards offshore in Garrison Bay, was named for a San Juan storekeeper during British occupation. Although it is also part of the park, it has been designated as an archaeological preserve, and is closed to the public.

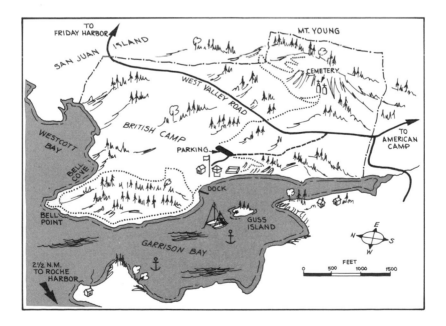

Historical display at British Camp

Vague remnants of one of the old docks are still visible near the block-house. A small dock with space for a few dinghies is now located farther north along the beach. In summer the bay is often filled with boats anchored and rafted together. Skippers may also anchor at Westcott Bay, then dinghy to Bell Point and walk the trail to British Camp.

This section of the historical park was formerly known as English Camp. Scottish, Welsh, and Irish visitors pointed out that the Royal Marines stationed at Garrison Bay had representatives of these countries as well as England, thus the name was recently changed to the more historically correct British Camp.

BELL POINT

A level, ½-mile hike through madrona and fir leads to pretty Bell Cove on Westcott Bay. Rusted spikes and planks still scarring old trees along the way give evidence of pioneer use of the area. The signed trail starts on the north side of the British Camp clearing near the shore.

The beaches of Bell Point may be closed to clam digging during certain seasons, although Bell Cove is normally open year-round. Observe posted signs. Dig clams only if you intend to use them, and observe limits; heavy public use of the clam beds could exhaust them, causing the beaches to be closed in order to let them reestablish. Tides permitting, Bell Cove can also be reached by walking the beach.

For an alternative return to British Camp, follow the old wagon track heading east from Bell Point, skirting Westcott Bay. In about ¼ mile the route reaches a clearing. Turn right (south), following the grassy track between the old-growth timber of Bell Point and a thick stand of recent-growth firs. Listen here for the distinctive trilling song of the chipping sparrow, which nests in the area. The track eventually emerges at the north corner of the British Camp clearing. Total distance of the loop trail is about 1 mile.

A larger, more distinctive bird that sometimes startles visitors by its presence at British Camp is the wild turkey. These nearly domestic fowl were introduced on San Juan Island nearly a decade ago, and have become well established. Even occasional poaching by Thanksgiving-minded hunters has failed to make a dent in the population.

BRITISH MILITARY CEMETERY

A small plot on the slopes of Mt. Young holds the graves of seven marines who died during the British occupation of San Juan Island. Locate the trailhead to the cemetery at the picnic area that is at the northeast corner of the parking lot at British Camp. The signed trail wends steadily uphill along an old overgrown wagon track.

Tombstones at the British Military Cemetery

Sun filters through second-growth alder, fir, and madrona. Walk quietly and perhaps you will be rewarded with glimpses of black-tailed deer, or occasionally great horned owls, blinking sleepily in the trees. An owl's favorite perching spot can sometimes be located by watching for piles of droppings beneath the tree. The owls take large numbers of rodents, and are responsible, even more than eagles and hawks, for controlling the island's rabbit population. The winter wren nests here—listen for its lovely sustained warbling song as you hike.

Although the route crosses the West Valley Road in ¼ mile, hikers must begin the trip at the parking lot, as there is no parking space along the road. Above the highway the trail continues.

The cemetery, in a grassy clearing, is reached in another ¼ mile, just beyond the Mt. Young trailhead. A neat white picket fence encloses four tombstones for servicemen who died in accidents while serving at British Camp. The stones tell the story of each mishap; note that one commemorates two marines who were drowned at sea. Two other graves are unmarked. Gravestone inscriptions have been duplicated on interpretive signs along the fence to prevent people from going inside the fence to read them.

Total distance from the British Camp parking lot is less than ½ mile; elevation gain is 250 feet. A short spur trail leaving the northeast corner of the cemetery clearing shortly joins the trail that goes to the top of Mt. Young.

Several of the trees in the clearing were killed or badly scarred by a 1972 fire. Take heed of the havoc a cigarette ash accidentally dropped in dry grass can cause.

MT. YOUNG

Probably the most spectacular viewpoint on San Juan Island is reached by hiking a little more than ½ mile beyond the British Military Cemetery. The trip is well worth the effort on a clear day. From a trail branch just before reaching the cemetery the path heads north, circling the west side of Mt. Young. A former path going straight uphill from the cemetery was steep and dangerous and caused erosion problems; don't use it.

The trail climbs steadily to round a north-facing rib of Mt. Young, then heads south on a path cut through high arching brush. At a bench 100 feet below the summit the trail forks: switchbacks to the left lead to the top of the mountain; at the end of the path to the right is an interpretive display on an open, grassy rock platform. The British marines maintained an observation post on the summit of the mountain during the Pig War.

Views, views, views. Henry Island, White Point, Bazelgette Point, Mosquito Pass, Westcott Bay, and Garrison Bay all merge in a mosaic of land and water. Mitchell Bay, whose entrance is obscured by land, looks like a small lake—but with a fleet of large pleasure boats bobbing in it! Southward can be seen the snowy peaks of the Olympic Mountains, while

Garrison Bay and Mosquito Pass from Mt. Young

to the north are the Canadian Gulf Islands, marked by the imposing profile of Saltspring Island. Across Haro Strait lies Vancouver Island where, over 100 years ago, British frigates sailed forth to uphold the sovereignty of the Crown. The display at the lower viewpoint identifies all major landmarks.

Stroll to the east side of the hill for views of Mt. Baker. Looking southeast from the summit, immediately above the silhouette of Mt. Eric on Fidalgo Island, on a very clear day Sloan Peak can be seen; ranging southward are the misty outlines of Mt. Baring, Mt. Index, and other Stevens Pass peaks more than 90 miles distant.

Elevation gain from the parking area is 590 feet; from the cemetery trailhead, 370 feet. Round trip from the parking lot to the top is 2½ miles.

American Camp

Park area: 1,223 acres; 22,440 feet of shoreline
Access: Ferry to San Juan Island, boat
Facilities: Picnic tables, restrooms, drinking water, fire pits, *no beach fires, no overnight camping*
Attractions: Historical display, hiking, boating, paddling, fishing, beachcombing, birdwatching, nature trail

American Camp is a marked contrast to British Camp. Instead of the protected harbor and wooded enclave, here are vast marine panoramas and miles of surf-swept beach. First-time visitors may be struck by the austerity of the park, but those who linger discover its diversity, ranging from the subtle beauty of rippling grass on the slopes of Mt. Finlayson to the exhilarating rage of winter storms pounding on South Beach.

To reach American Camp from British Camp, continue south on West Valley Road and in 3¾ miles turn right (south) onto Boyce Road. In 1 mile turn left (east) on San Juan Valley Road and in 2¾ miles right (south) on Douglas Road. In 1½ miles turn left (east) on Little Road, which ends shortly at a T intersection with Cattle Point Road. Here head right (south) and in 2¾ miles reach the American Camp entrance. Total distance from British Camp, 12 miles.

To travel directly to American Camp from Friday Harbor, at the Y intersection on the south side of town, bear left (south) on Argyle Avenue. Follow the arterial south and then west to its intersection with Cattle Point Road. The route is well signed. Total distance to the park, 5 miles. Bicyclers making the long, dry trek from Friday Harbor should note that the only drinking water in the park is at the headquarters just inside the park entrance. There are restrooms here as well; other locations have pit toilets.

For visitors traveling by boat, there are no docking facilities at American Camp; however, in calm weather small boats can be beached on gentle shores on either side of the park. Griffin Bay provides the only semi-protected anchorage; when entering the bay carefully check nautical charts

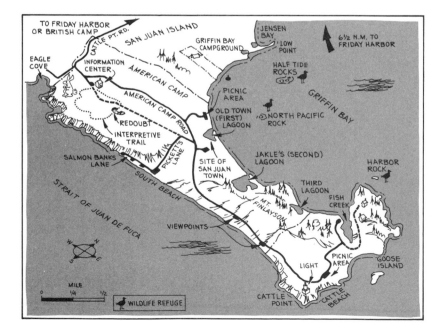

and depth finders for the location of numerous submerged rocks. The north beach of the park is about 6½ nautical miles from either Friday Harbor or Fisherman Bay.

Kayaking or canoeing around the park is interesting, especially along the southern shore; however it is recommended only for experienced paddlers. Great care must be used in small boats as the wind and current can be extremely strong; attempting to maneuver an underpowered boat under such conditions can be a frightening experience. Shark Reef, lying to the east immediately across San Juan Channel along the shore of Lopez Island, is an inviting destination for those skilled enough to attempt it.

PARK HISTORY PROGRAMS

On summer weekends and holidays the national park presents at British Camp an outstanding series of programs and special events that attract both tourists and local residents. The programs are designed to make history come alive—in some presentations parks personnel and volunteers wearing period costumes re-create the daily lives of the soldiers, laundresses, and settlers during the time of the Pig War. Authentic props such as a Sibley tent and laundry tubs fashioned from whiskey barrels complete the scene. For other programs employees and visitors take part in songfests, square dances, and games reminiscent of the 1860s.

At American Camp ranger-guided tours are held daily throughout the summer. These walks, which begin at 11 a.m., leave from the park headquarters and information center, and cover the areas of Pickett's Redoubt

Pickett's Redoubt at American Camp

Interpretive trail sign at American Camp

and the Hudson's Bay farm. Large groups planning to visit the park can request a guided tour with a ranger in costume.

INTERPRETIVE TRAIL

For those who miss the excellent guided tour, or who would rather walk at their own pace, a ¾-mile-long self-guided interpretive trail covers the historical section of the park. The starting point for the tour is at the picnic area east of the park information center. Signs at numerous points along the walk narrate Pig War history and interesting features of the park. At the top of the ridge, Pickett's Redoubt commands views of American Camp and waters stretching west to Victoria. Still in evidence are the earthworks (redoubt) thrown up by American troops, where five cannons were mounted.

RABBITS

The long arm of San Juan Island is largely covered by soft glacial till deposited centuries ago by retreating ice. The loose mixture of sand, stone, and boulders, ideal for tunnelling, made American Camp a "Watership Downs West" for San Juan rabbits. It is believed that the rabbits are descendents of domestic animals brought here during the 1880s by settlers. They either escaped from captivity or were turned loose and, finding local conditions to their liking, multiplied—and multiplied—and multiplied! It has been estimated that by the late 1970s some 250,000 bunnies (give or take a few) populated San Juan Island. Their evidence was everywhere at American Camp—droppings covered the ground to the extent that in many places more dung than dirt was visible.

In the mid 1980s, for reasons not entirely understood, the rabbit population decreased dramatically. One plausible theory is that plants such as vetches, when subjected to overgrazing by large numbers of rabbits, produce a chemical that acts as a birth-control agent. When grazing returns to normal, this chemical is no longer produced. Whatever the reason, the rabbits seem to be making a slight comeback in recent years. Hunting or trapping has not been permitted since the park was established in 1966, which allows useful data to be gathered on population cycles.

The rabbits are a major food source for eagles, great horned owls, and other predatory birds living on the island. Fluctuations in the rabbit population can also be reflected in the natural balance established between the predators and their food supply. When the rabbits are abundant, tunnel entrances make the ground in places look like a bombed battlefield.

SOUTH SHORE WALK

Leave the interpretive trail and wander open slopes above the water to enjoy the austere beauty of the park. No formal trails. In late summer the inland section of the slope is covered with patches of nettles and Canadian thistles. Long pants are advised.

Near the edge of the cliff the harsh environment causes the vegetation to be miniaturized. Many species of plants are so tiny that novice botanists can identify them only when they bloom. Collinsia grow less than an inch tall, showing quarter-inch blue-purple blossoms in late May. Lupine, whose distinctive leaf whorls grow over four inches across on the alpine slopes of Mt. Rainier, here have ground-hugging leaves smaller than a thumbnail.

Bays along this section of the island are unlike those found anywhere else in the San Juans. The soft glacial till, scooped out by winds from the Strait of Juan de Fuca, form perfect, grassy amphitheaters dropping steeply to beaches jammed with huge driftwood logs. Explore the small coves if you wish, but bear in mind the stiff, 50-foot scramble back up to the top.

The rounded bay to the west was the site of the original Hudson's Bay Company settlement. Artifacts can sometimes be found in the vicinity—rabbits dig them out occasionally and toss them aside, with total disregard for their historical significance. Unauthorized digging for artifacts (by humans) is prohibited, and any that are on the surface must be left where they are found and their location reported to a park ranger.

If hiking legs need further exercise, traverse the bank eastward, staying well above the shore. Do not walk too near the edge, as the earth is soft on the high bank, and footing may be insecure. When the slope gentles, drop down to South Beach near the parking lot. Return to the information center via the road. Total distance of the loop hike is about 3 miles.

South Beach

SOUTH BEACH

For road access to 2 miles of unbroken beach edging the Strait of Juan de Fuca, turn right off American Camp Road onto Pickett's Lane. In ½ mile is the first parking lot, where there are picnic tables, fire pits, and pit toilets; Salmon Banks Lane leads west to three more parking areas and more picnic tables. Beach fires are permitted only in the fire pits. Lightweight boats may be carried the short distance from the parking areas for launching, surf permitting.

When storms kick up in the straits, heavy wave action along the beach is exciting to watch. Drift logs are dangerous at these times—stay well away from moving logs. Such storms toss flotsam and jetsam onto the beach, making this the prime area on the island for finding beach treasures.

With calm weather and favorable tides the beach can be walked all the way east to Cattle Point, 2 miles from the parking lot. Very little marine life is found on the gravel beach; constant movement of the surf-tumbled sand and gravel lets nothing survive for long. Low tide exposes rocky shelves to the west, and tidepools filled with fascinating critters. During the summer and fall salmon runs, numbers of commercial fishing trawlers are frequently seen tending their nets just offshore.

EURASIAN SKYLARK

The vicinity of American Camp is the only known nesting area in the continental United States of the Eurasian skylark, although the bird has been sighted recently on Whidbey Island and the Olympic Peninsula. Introduced to Vancouver Island by the British, who brought several pairs from Europe in 1903, some individual birds winged their way to San Juan Island, where they took up residency.

Skylarks frequent open grassy fields where they forage for seeds and insects and build their nests. Its drab brown-streaked plumage appears similar to that of a female house sparrow; however, it can be distinguished from the sparrow by its larger size (7−7½ inches) and its distinctly marked white stomach, wingtips, and outer tail feathers.

The Eurasian skylark's popularity arises from its melodious song in flight—a high-pitched, sustained torrent of runs and trills as it hovers 200 feet in the air. Listen for it as you roam the park, especially in the area of South Beach and Pickett's Lane.

SAN JUAN TOWN

When American troops built their stronghold on San Juan Island, a shanty town sprang up nearby just outside the military camp boundary on the shore of Griffin Bay. Shopkeepers in San Juan Town sold a few supplies to the soldiers, settlers, and Indians, but it was soon apparent that liquor was the commodity in greatest demand. Other enterprising merchants brought in Indian women for "nefarious purposes." Robberies, assaults, and sometimes murders took place, with open defiance of civil and military officers. Authorities were able to tame the town a bit, but it always remained a center for booze, brothels, and brawls.

In 1873, when San Juan County was established, the new commissioners felt that San Juan Town, with its rowdy reputation, was unsuitable for a county seat. Instead they selected a few acres at Friday Harbor on the north end of the island. In time businesses drifted away from Old San Juan Town (especially when Friday Harbor also acquired a saloon), and by the late 1800s the once thriving village was a ghost town. The deserted buildings were accidently burned to the ground in 1890, bringing to a close the career of the colorful, if somewhat tarnished village.

The saltwater lagoon visible on the north side of American Camp Road is just west of the old townsite. A few footings of the original buildings have been excavated and can be found by searching the grassy fields. Halfway down the hill the track of an old road is still visible.

GRIFFIN BAY

Early sailing ships hove to in Griffin Bay waiting out westerlies whipping the Strait of Juan de Fuca. Today fast-moving powerboats whiz by in San Juan Channel, rarely stopping to enjoy the languid pleasures of the bay.

Even though the water of the bay is inviting when seas are calm, boaters should be aware that a number of rocks are scattered at or near the water's surface. Consult a good large-scale chart and approach with care. Barren Half Tide Rocks lie northeast of the park boundary, near a row of rotting pilings. About ½ nautical mile south of these rocks is North Pacific Rock; it is unnamed on most charts, but is shown as a rock baring at a -2 foot tide. Harbor Rock lies farther east, just off the tip of Cape San Juan. Nesting grounds for marine birds, these three groups of rocks are part of the San Juan Islands National Wildlife Refuge.

Between North Pacific Rock and Harbor Rock the approach to the beach is clear, except for rocks lying quite close to shore. Some good anchorages can be found in this section of the bay, although those to the west are exposed when winds are stiff—which is most of the time. The best spot to drop a hook is to the east, in or near Fish Creek.

The gentle shore of Fourth of July Beach, which extends west for ½ mile from the San Juan Town Lagoon (First Lagoon) to the park boundary, holds driftwood and some interesting marine life. The park has a picnic area here with a parking lot, picnic tables, and a large grassy field ideal for kite flying or tossing Frisbees. A path leads past pit toilets to the beach. Carry a small boat or kayak the short distance to the beach and you'll be rewarded with a leisurely paddle the length of the park.

To reach Fourth of July Beach turn north off Cattle Point Road at a signed intersection 1 mile east of the park entrance.

JAKLE'S LAGOON

While American Camp is impressive, it can at times seem bleak. Jakle's Lagoon, a secluded nook of the park, offers a pleasing contrast, with ferns, rich moss carpet, and tall firs. At the urging of The Nature Conservancy the road to the lagoon is closed to vehicles to protect eagle nesting areas and the delicate lagoon.

The lagoon itself has been set aside as a natural environmental study area. It is used by the University of Washington's Friday Harbor Laboratories as a collecting site for marine specimens and has been the subject of several studies and Ph.D. theses.

Jakle's Lagoon

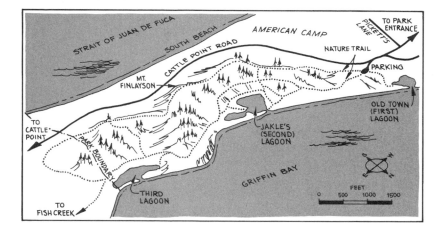

The trailhead to the lagoon is located a few hundred feet east of the Pickett's Lane intersection on Cattle Point Road, where a side road branches north, ending in a short distance at a gate. All vehicles are prohibited beyond this point. There is parking space for a few cars; use care not to block the gate in case of emergency. Hike the abandoned road downhill, dipping into the forest.

This is also the start of the Jakle's Farm Nature Trail, which is a fine destination in itself for those not wanting to hike all the way to the lagoon. The nature loop, which is marked, follows an uphill fork for ¼ mile, then wanders over very gentle terrain; total distance is slightly less than a mile. A brochure available at the park office describes the flora found at numbered stakes along the trail. This, the first such guided nature trail on San Juan Island, was developed jointly by the park and the San Juan Horticultural Society.

Those continuing on to Jakle's Lagoon will find a confusing network of old roads crisscrossing the hillside; keep bearing downhill and eastward to reach the lagoon. When the only four-way intersection is reached, turn left—the lagoon is about 200 feet farther. A grassy point protruding into the southwest side of the lagoon is a fit spot for a Hobbit home. In winter, when the forest drips with San Juan mist and fog lies heavily over the lagoon, one can easily imagine magical creatures scurrying in the undergrowth.

Signs posted along the trail warn hikers not to smoke while on the trail. Campfires are also forbidden in the forest and on the beaches. In the dry summer the fire hazard here is extreme and a spark could start a blaze that would destroy the entire wooded area, bringing death to the birds and animals living here.

With moderate to low tides the Griffin Bay beach can be walked be-

Twinflower (left) and calypso (right), found near Jakle's Lagoon; calypsos are an endangered flower species (photos by Bob and Ira Spring)

tween the site of San Juan Town and Jakle's Lagoon for a loop trip with an opportunity to beachcomb. Round trip is 1½ miles.

THIRD LAGOON

Another, smaller lagoon lies ½ mile farther east. San Juan Town Lagoon is first, Jakle's is the second, and this, appropriately, is simply known as Third Lagoon. It may be reached one of several ways; the easiest route, tide permitting, is to walk the gravel beach east from Jakle's Lagoon.

For an inland route, return to the abandoned road from Jakle's Lagoon and continue east. The beauty of the forest makes this route well worthwhile. In spring, find calypso, twinflower, and bleeding heart popping through the carpet of rich moss.

The road climbs to the top of a ridge, then descends again; where it levels off at the bottom, watch for a faint road on the left leading to the lagoon. If the side road is missed, continue until the lagoon is clearly in sight through open timber and head cross-country. A hundred yards east of this side road, a trail heads to the right (south) next to a marsh. This path climbs uphill through thick timber, emerges at a meadow, and joins the Mt. Finlayson trail.

Just beyond the lagoon the road is gated at the eastern park boundary; from here it crosses state and private property to Fish Creek. Round trip from the parking lot is about 2½ miles. Elevation gain (on return), 130 feet.

MT. FINLAYSON

The rolling hill of Mt. Finlayson is the highest point on this end of the island. A trail that is actually a mowed firebreak leaves the Jakle's Lagoon parking area and wends through the meadow near the edge of the forest. Magnificent examples of wind-shredded Douglas fir tower beside the way. Along the way two faint trails head north into the forest; the westernmost one is the return loop of the nature trail, the one farthest east leads down to Third Lagoon.

From the mountaintop look north to Griffin Bay, east to Lopez Island and the Cascades, and south across the Strait of Juan de Fuca to white Olympic peaks. Ocean freighters ply the strait, bearing cargoes from exotic lands headed for Puget Sound ports. Once they carried silk, tea, and spices; today they are laden with plywood and Hondas. Distance from the upper parking lot to the summit is 1 mile; elevation gain, 200 feet.

From the top of Mt. Finlayson the trail continues east out of the park and onto state-owned land, then drops steeply down the eastern ridge line to an abandoned gravel pit near Cattle Point Road. A faint trail leads northeast across a boulder-strewn meadow to an old overgrown road heading northwest into the trees and back into the park. Watch in the open old-growth timber for woodpeckers and brightly colored Western tanagers. The road fades to a trail and ultimately joins an old road from Fish Creek near the east end of Third Lagoon.

CATTLE POINT ROAD VIEWS

East of Pickett's Lane, Cattle Point Road traverses the open lower slopes of Mt. Finlayson, providing sweeping views south across the Strait of Juan de Fuca, east to the Cattle Point Light on the end of San Juan Island, and beyond that to the rocky southern end of Lopez Island. Within the sweep of the view are more public lands than can be seen from any other viewpoint in the U.S. From the North Cascades to Mt. Rainier, from the national forests spanning the Cascades to the once forts, now parks, of Admiralty Inlet and then to the heights of the Olympics are national wilderness treasures set aside for recreation and preservation.

Two pull-outs along the road are accompanied by interpretive plaques identifying these areas and paying credit to the legislative accomplishments of Senator Henry "Scoop" Jackson, who helped make these reserves possible.

Reid Harbor

6. North from Spieden Channel and President Channel

Traveling north from the busy thoroughfares of Spieden Channel and President Channel, boaters encounter Spieden, Waldron, and Stuart islands and their associated smaller islands. These landfalls, which are similar geologically to the Sucia Islands group to the north, are composed of folded, eroded sedimentary beds with long ridges extending underwater as a network of reefs and shoals that make boat pilots wary, but beckon to fishermen and scuba divers. Lying deep in the rain shadow of Vancouver

Island, their climate is dry enough that the Cactus Islands do, indeed, support cactus.

These are islands to enjoy from the deck of your boat, for aside from the state parks on Stuart Island, all shore land is privately owned or held as a wildlife refuge, and there are no commercial developments.

Spieden and Sentinel Islands

The most striking in appearance of this northwestern group, 480-acre Spieden Island, with its long northern slope neatly forested and its southern side barren except for tawny grass, appears as if a prankish barber had been at work. Lying alongside to the south, 15-acre Sentinel Island is a miniature duplicate of its neighbor.

Spieden, which is the only large San Juan Island without a bay or harbor of any sort, has not been commercially developed, and until recent years its life was pleasantly bucolic. In the early 1970s an abortive attempt was made to capitalize on its dry climate and open rangeland by transforming it into an African game farm and renaming it "Safari Island." The island was stocked with ungulates such as Corsican mouflon sheep, Japanese sika deer, European fallow deer, Indian blackbuck antelope, and wild goats. No predators were brought, assuming that sportsmen who paid to come to the island would adequately keep the herds under control.

Immediately there was a loud outcry from conservationists protesting this "sitting duck" type of sportsmanship. Whether it was because of the voice of the conservationists, or because the project was ill conceived, the business went broke and the land was sold to other interests . . . but some of the wildlife remained.

Without any natural controls these animals have increased to the point that they now number over 350 individuals, and are seriously overgrazing

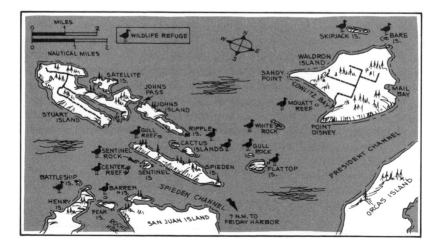

the island's vegetation. A couple of attempts to round them up and relocate them have been unsuccessful, and thus far, despite all human efforts, these strange visitors from foreign lands remain. Passing boaters with binoculars can sometimes spot these exotic creatures.

Spieden Island is currently owned by Alaska Airlines, which has a small vacation resort here for its employees.

Sentinel Island, Spieden's small companion, was acquired by The Nature Conservancy in 1979 as a nature preserve. It is an active eagle nesting area, holds a nesting community of pigeon guillemots, and its rocky shores are used by harbor seals for resting and sunning. Unlike nearby Yellow Island, which is also owned by The Nature Conservancy, going ashore on Sentinel Island is permitted only in the fall, after nesting season, and then only with permission.

Flattop Island and Other Bird Refuges

Sentinel Rock and Center Reef (both southwest of Spieden Island), Ripple Island and Flattop Island (both northeast of Spieden Island), and White Rock (between Flattop and Waldron islands) are all part of the San Juan Islands National Wildlife Refuge. They are nesting sites for glaucous-winged gulls, pelagic cormorants, black oystercatchers, and pigeon guillemots. Large flocks of harlequin ducks and occasionally some loons can be seen here in the summer.

Although in the past boaters have stopped at Flattop Island, the largest of these bird refuges, public recreational use of Flattop, as well as the less

Common murres

hospitable rocks, is now prohibited in order to protect the bird nesting areas.

Disturbance of nesting birds by humans has a detrimental effect on the survival of the young, for when nests are abandoned, even for a short period of time, the unattended eggs may be broken by predatory birds or competing birds of the same species, or the eggs may chill and fail to hatch.

Nesting gulls are extremely territorial during this time and will viciously defend their foot-square domain against intrusion by other birds; if a parent gull is chased from her nest, the frightened chicks often scatter into foreign territory and are killed by rival birds. Boaters must recognize that it is imperative for the survival of the chicks that they stay away from the nesting grounds.

Stuart Island

Island area: 1,786 acres; 5,130 feet of shoreline
Park areas: Reid Harbor, 44 acres; Prevost Harbor, 40 acres; Turn Point, 67.3 acres
Access: Boat
Facilities (at Reid and Prevost harbors): Floats, mooring buoys, campsites, picnic tables, stoves, drinking water, pit toilets, marine pump-out station
Attractions: Clam digging, crabbing, fishing, paddling, hiking

Here are not one, but two marine state parks, back to back, spanning a slim neck of land, and a third "walk-to" state park at Turn Point, a former lighthouse reserve.

Stuart Island thrusts deeply toward the Canadian border, only 3 miles from several of the Gulf Islands, making the harbors popular stops for B.C.-bound vacationers. Indeed, the outline of the island itself, ignoring its deep harbors, suggests a boat headed for Canadian waters, and Johns Island is its dinghy in tow.

Reid Harbor and Prevost Marine State Parks, often collectively referred to as Stuart Island State Park, provide fine facilities for overnight boaters. Those who stay a while longer enjoy the fishing, the beaches, and the shellfish, while the more energetic might even sample the forest hikes and pastoral road walks revealing the serene inner beauty of the island.

Stuart Island lies 3½ nautical miles north-northwest of Roche Harbor on San Juan Island. When planning a trip from Roche Harbor to Stuart Island in a small boat, consider strong tidal currents and shoal areas in Spieden Channel. The entrance to Reid Harbor is constricted by submerged rocks and shoals. Stay in the middle of the channel or slightly to the west to avoid running aground.

Boats cruising the north side of the island via Johns Pass should use care at the south entrance to the channel. Kelp marks several rocks and a

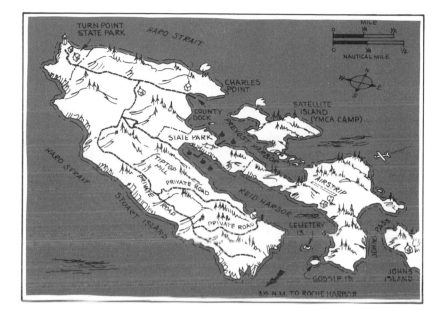

½-fathom shoal extending well out from the eastern tip of Stuart Island. Give all obstructions a wide berth. Check a good navigational chart for exact position of hazards.

Stuart Island is a fine destination for kayakers, with enough nooks and crannies to fill several days' worth of exploration; however, the distance and the strength of tidal currents encountered en route to the island make this a trip only for experienced paddlers.

The ½-mile recess of Reid Harbor is one of the best anchorages in the San Juans. The enclosing arms of the island drop off sharply to 5 fathoms, giving good anchorages almost up to the shoreline, while the gravel beach at the head of the bay is gradual enough for small craft to land easily.

A dock and float on the north shore, two floats anchored near the head of the bay, and fifteen mooring buoys spaced about the harbor provide easy tie-ups for about forty boats. The large blue-striped buoy in the center of the harbor is for use of Coast Guard vessels when stationed in the vicinity.

Prevost Harbor, on the north side, with its broader beaches, offers a different perspective of the island. The only safe entrance to the harbor is by Charles Point, west of Satellite Island; do not attempt the channel on the east with boats of any draft as it is dangerously rocky and shallow.

The state park contains a dock with float, six buoys, and good anchorages, although there may be some difficulty getting hooks to dig through the thick eelgrass at the bottom of the harbor.

Boats opting to anchor in the superb little bay on the north side of the harbor at Satellite Island should be wary of a large rock, submerged at tides

Clamming at Reid Harbor

above 8 feet, lying near the center of the entrance. Satellite Island is owned by the YMCA, which maintains a summer camp there, and does not encourage visitors. The tideland below the mean high water level is a public Department of Natural Resources beach, however, and is open for clam digging during favorable tides.

On the north side of Prevost Harbor, tucked behind the protective wing of Charles Point, lie the county dock and a few homes. No facilities or provisions are available there, so visitors should limit their stops to the state park docks.

Stuart Island has a population of less than thirty permanent residents living in homes scattered about the island. A small private airfield on the northwest tip of the island serves these residents. Fishing and farming have provided a livelihood for islanders since the days of early homesteading. The reef netting site off the entrance to Reid Harbor has been fished continuously by Indians and their descendants for six generations.

The shores do not exhibit the sculptured sandstone cliffs so characteristic of the northern Sucia Islands group—instead the steep banks are heavily covered with vegetation almost down to the water line. The rounded, forested dome of Tiptop Hill, the highest point on the island, rises 640 feet above Reid Harbor.

REID AND PREVOST HARBOR STATE PARKS

Situated on the high bank above Prevost Harbor and on either side of the marsh at the head of Reid Harbor are nineteen state park campsites with fireplaces, all pleasantly shaded by light timber. Water faucets are conveniently located throughout the campgrounds.

The beaches of Prevost Harbor make for interesting low tide exploration. Walk carefully to avoid crushing Dungeness and rock crab that burrow in the eelgrass. Gentle (and cautious) probing of the grass may yield some of dinner-table size. Any crabs left stranded in the sun may dry out and die; undersized and female Dungeness crabs should be returned to a protected, damp spot or put into the water.

The park's gravel beaches, especially the one at the head of Reid Harbor, provide first-rate clamming for littlenecks and butter clams. Those with the stamina to dig deep enough may claim some geoducks. Tidelands on Reid and Prevost harbors lying outside the park are privately owned and are posted.

A ½-mile trail connects the Prevost Harbor dock with the head of Reid Harbor. Catch the cross-island trail south from the dock, following it past the side trail to the toilets. Just before dropping down to the Reid Harbor dock, a trail branches right (west) along the top of the ridge. Twisted red-barked madronas frame pretty views of sleek boats bobbing at their moorings in Reid Harbor.

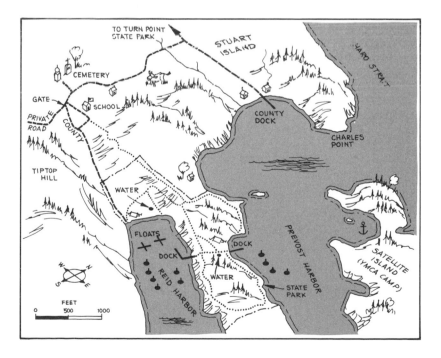

In about ½ mile the trail turns sharply downhill for a short but extremely steep section (slippery when wet). At the bottom, in a marshy flat, bear left at a trail fork and head east for 300 yards, emerging at the campground at the northwest corner of Reid Harbor.

CEMETERY AND GOSSIP ISLANDS

Lying on the east side of the Reid Harbor entrance are two undeveloped marine state park islands. The larger of the two, Gossip Island (also known as George Island), is about an acre of rock and grass and a few scruffy trees; at low tide it nearly joins the Stuart mainland. Smaller Cemetery Island, lying slightly farther into the harbor, is nearly barren.

Dinghy adventurers can paddle or putt out from their anchorages to walk the beaches, watch the boat traffic, and perhaps wave at an incoming friend, or just have an entire island to themselves for a day. Fires and overnight camping are not permitted.

The water surrounding the two islands is designated as an Underwater Marine Recreational Area for use by skin divers.

STUART ISLAND SCHOOL

An easy stretch of the legs gives visitors an opportunity to gain insight into the history and lives of the people who make this island their home.

Find the trail skirting the southern boundary of Reid Harbor State Park at the south end of the campground at the head of the bay. The route, along the country road, climbs gradually uphill. In about ½ mile watch for a fork on the right leading to the schoolyard in a clearing.

The clearing may also be reached from the park by following the bluff-top trail along the north side of Reid Harbor. On this route avoid branches in the trail descending steeply to the left, and continue straight ahead for ½ mile to the schoolyard. The trail follows along the south side of a wire fence marking the park boundary. On the edge of the clearing is the classic, one-room white clapboard schoolhouse that served generations of children living on Stuart, Johns and Spieden islands.

This is perhaps the most interesting school in the state; it has been featured on television. In early days the children from the nearby islands would row to Stuart daily, in all weather, and then hike overland to school. Later, outboard motors made the trip easier, although still somewhat hazardous at times.

One December day in 1961, while all of the school's youngsters were on a boat outing, the boat sank in bad weather and all aboard were drowned. The school remained closed for sixteen years following the tragedy, and local children commuted to San Juan Island. In the fall of 1977 it reopened with an enrollment of eight. Growing population dictated the need for a larger, more modern facility, and in 1980 the new school standing nearby was opened. Although it is more spacious and its modern design provides a flood of cheery light, the building is still one room, and is

Stuart Island Cemetery

heated with wood stoves. Student enrollment usually numbers around a dozen.

STUART ISLAND CEMETERY

To find the historic little Stuart Island Cemetery, continue west on the path past the school to its junction with a dirt road. Turn right, down the road signed to the lighthouse, and in 30 yards watch on the left for a seldom-used road leading to the cemetery.

Spanning almost a century of island time, the gravestones tell the story of many settlers who lived here for long years, and others who enjoyed this lovely, though sometimes harsh land for only a brief while.

Examine the gravestones, speculate about the lives of these people, but remember to treat the cemetery with respect.

Round trip from Reid Harbor to the cemetery is a little over 1 mile.

TURN POINT STATE PARK

Far on the western tip of Stuart Island, a lighthouse blinks warning to freighters, fishermen, and pleasure boats traveling through the waters of Haro Strait. Turn Point Lighthouse, so named because it marks the point where boats must turn in the channel, was established in 1893 on a tract of land high atop a rocky cape, with a sweeping 300-degree view of the surrounding sea. The current concrete tower housing the light and a diaphragm foghorn was built in 1936.

Originally the dramatically scenic point was the home of Indians who fished the nearby waters. After the construction of the lighthouse a succes-

143

Lighthouse at Turn Point State Park

sion of lighthouse keepers lived here, raised their families, and often left
their names imprinted on the history of the area. The fine, spacious home
and idyllic island were an ideal place to raise a family. One of the
lighthouse keepers was Edward Durgan.

In his book *Lighthouses of the Pacific*, Jim Gibbs describes an incident that earned Durgan a certificate of merit. One February night in 1897
the tug *Enterprise* ran aground near Turn Point and the barge under tow
was cast adrift with men still on its deck. With the exception of the captain,
the crew was inebriated to a man. As Durgan and his assistant, Peter Christiansen, were attempting to rescue both the men on the tug and those on the
barge, one of the drunken crew went berserk, attacking the lighthouse
keeper with a knife. He was subdued by Durgan and Christiansen and the
rescue was successfully carried out. By morning's light the crew was all
safe in the lighthouse, and the drunken assailant was chained in the chicken
house.

In recent years the lighthouse has become automated; it seems unfortunate at times that fine old traditions must give way to modern technol-
ogy. Today the 67 acres of land are leased by the Washington State Parks
and Recreation Commission as an undeveloped state park. The residence
has fallen into disrepair, although there have been attempts to find someone to use the property and care for it.

Turn Point is best reached by an overland hike from Reid or Prevost
harbors. The steep cliffs below the point and the treacherous water offshore
make landing by boat impractical. Catch either of the trails to the
schoolyard described above, then continue past the school to the junction
with a dirt road. Follow the dirt road north past several farmhouses.

Walking the quiet, tree-shaded road is like stepping into time suspended. The nautical bustle of the harbors seems a planet away, and rarely is anyone seen along the deserted track. Even if some farmhouses appear unoccupied, all the land is private property; do not trespass.

About 1½ miles from Reid Harbor the route intersects the Prevost road. Several homes can be seen down the road on the right, beyond Satellite Island, and on a clear day Mt. Baker hovers above. Turn left at the intersection and continue past rolling fields where cattle share pasturage with deer. At about 2½ miles Turn Point State Park is reached.

Views spread in all directions across Haro Strait to Canadian islands and down the 50-foot cliff to the sea churning against the flanks of the point. Walk with care as the footing at the edge of the cliff can be insecure.

Take the hike in the late afternoon to enjoy the fiery sunset behind Vancouver Island and the crimson afterglow, but pack along a flashlight for the return trip through the forest. Fires and overnight camping are not permitted at Turn Point. The round trip from Reid Harbor is about 5 miles.

Waldron Island

Waldron is a staunchly individualistic island, defying categorization, either physically or socially, with any other in the San Juans. Although it is located quite close to Orcas Island, lying only 2 nautical miles west of Orcas's West Beach, in reality it has little basic familial relationship.

The people of Waldron display this same individualism, along with a strong sense of self-sufficiency, for the island has no electricity, no water district, no telephones, stores, or regular ferry service, and most residents prefer it that way. This is not a totally primitive island, however, for many homes are modern, with either private gasoline generators or tanks of propane to power lights, radiotelephones, appliances, and furnaces.

The island is one of the more unusual pieces of topography to be found hereabouts. More than half the island is a marsh and meadow flatland covered with glacial drift, rarely more than 100 feet in elevation; however, at the southern tip the cliffs of Point Disney suddenly rush up to a height of over 600 feet. The imposing fortresslike walls of the point display beautiful banding of exposed layers of fossil-bearing sandstone and conglomerate.

Point Disney was the site of the island's only commercial enterprise—a sandstone quarry that operated here during the early 1900s. When concrete paving became favored over sandstone cobbles, the quarry closed. Some of the workmen departed, others remained to farm.

Waldron has less than a hundred year-round residents, with most homes located along the two broad bays of the northwest shore. The "village" of Waldron consists of a few abandoned buildings huddled around the county dock on Cowlitz Bay. There is a small float attached to the dock, but passing boaters rarely stop here as there are no onshore facilities and visitors are regarded with suspicion. The open bay is a marginal

anchorage, even in good weather. Mouatt Reef, which is exposed at low tide, lies at the entrance to the bay, 300 yards off the end of the dock.

The island's only other harbor is rockbound Mail Bay on the east side, which in early days was the local mail stop, and is sometimes still used today by the mail boat when the seas are too rough at Cowlitz Bay; obviously "neither rain, nor sleet, nor snow, nor towering seas. . . ." Mail Bay offers a few anchorages in 10 to 40 feet of water; skippers should be wary of submerged pilings, remnants of early docks, along the north side of the bay.

The Nature Conservancy has purchased 273 acres of beach, meadow, and marshland on the west side of Waldron Island, facing on Cowlitz Bay, in order to preserve it in its natural state. While the land is open to public use, it must be emphasized that this is a biological preserve, not a recreational area; camping and picnicking are not permitted. The area should be visited only by those seriously interested in viewing and studying the birds —and what a magnificent assortment of birds it is!

Douglas fir, oak, and madrona forests attract colorful goldfinches, Western tanagers, red crossbills and nuthatches, while red-winged blackbirds and long-billed marsh wrens and a myriad other marsh birds inhabit the wetlands. Ponds are resting grounds for migratory freshwater ducks and occasional groups of long-necked whistling swans. Eagles nest in the forested heights above the island, as well as across President Channel on Orcas Island. The nesting sites are carefully protected by island residents and conservation organizations.

EAGLES

A black silhouette with six-foot wingspan, soaring, wheeling in the summer sky, its white head glinting in the sun, then suddenly swooping downward to alight in a skeletal tree snag—a bald eagle is one of the most spectacular sights in the San Juans. At times they seem so common that tourists become blase about them, but those who understand the significance of their presence can never fail to be thrilled by sightings of those elegant raptors.

The San Juan Islands have the largest and healthiest concentration of nesting bald eagles in the continental U.S., with about fifty pairs that are known to breed here. The local population thins briefly in the fall when spawning salmon lure them up inland rivers, although a few prefer their local diet and remain year-round. Other migratory bald eagles summer in the islands after nesting in Alaska and coastal British Columbia.

About 10 percent of the eagles found in the San Juans are golden eagles. Some of these also nest here, although they prefer more protected sites inland in trees and cliffs away from the water to the seaside snags that bald eagles often choose. The two birds are not closely related—golden eagles are considered true eagles, while bald eagles are sea eagles, as are osprey.

Immature bald eagles are often mistaken for golden eagles, since they

Point Disney, Waldron Island

Bald eagle in the San Juans (photo by Bob and Ira Spring)

do not display their characteristic dark body and snowy head until their third or fourth year. Young bald eagles are evenly brown-colored with some white mottling as they mature, while golden eagles display distinctive patches or bands of light-colored feathers at the base of the tail and in the wing linings at the base of the primaries.

It is remarkable to find such a concentration of these strongly territorial birds in one area, along with large numbers of hawks, vultures, owls, and other predators with competitive feeding requirements. With the bountiful supply of rabbits, fish, and other favorite tidbits, coupled with the isolation of the islands and the current protective attitude of the residents, the eagles have modified their behavior to a more social existence. While golden eagles take large numbers of live rabbits, and thus are valuable to the islands in the control of these prolific rodents, bald eagles prefer fish, waterfowl, and carrion. They frequently will steal captured prey from other birds.

Eagles, which may be seen almost anyplace in the San Juans in spring and summer, sometimes even near such busy places as Roche Harbor or Sucia Island, can be spotted in snags of forested areas, gliding low over quiet bays, or rising in concentric circles in the thermals above mountains.

A number of San Juan residents, assisted by The Nature Conservancy, have attempted to locate all bald eagle nesting sites in the islands, and have taken steps to protect them by obtaining conservation easements of 20 to 40 acres as a "buffer zone" around each nest tree, to prevent logging or public disturbance of the site. The trees are surveyed by air and boat each year to determine activity. About fifty chicks are believed to be successfully raised in San Juan nests each year.

In addition to the serious threat of loss of nesting sites by human enchroachment, the birds also succumb to such natural hazards as storms, disease, and predatory raccoons, crows, and hawks. Although they are placed on the list of endangered animal species and are protected from being killed (except in Alaska), they are occasionally shot by irresponsible hunters. Stiff penalties can result from killing or disturbing the birds. In the 1980s some persons who deliberately cut down a tree containing a golden eagle nest subsequently paid $10,000 in fines.

Still another threat to these majestic birds is the poisons in the environment. Since they have exceptional longevity, being known to live up to thirty years in the wild, all the while absorbing agricultural and industrial toxins in air, plants, and water, and in addition eating large quantities of carrion that may itself have died as a result of such poisoning, the eagles' bodies become storehouses of DDT, dieldrin, PCBs, and mercury. These poisons, if they do not kill the bird outright, can cause sterility, thinning of eggshells, failure of eggs to hatch, and weakened chicks, ending the reproductive capabilities of the adult.

The bald eagle is so perilously close to extinction, it is imperative that it be given every possible protection if the species is to survive. Visitors to the San Juans should stay well away from nesting sites, enjoying these birds from a distance with field glasses.

Bald eagle nesting sites are selected with a definite goal of overseeing territory. The tallest tree is chosen, and a platform of sticks, moss, shredded bark, and mud is constructed. Nests are reused from year to year, and eventually are used by the eagles' offspring. Each year the nest is redecorated and expanded with additions of sticks and mud until, over a period of decades, it can become many feet across and weigh more than a ton. Such huge nests have been known to have come crashing down during storms, or to fall from their own sheer weight.

One to three eggs are laid in the nest, and in early April the downy chicks appear, although usually only one will survive. While the female may desert her nest if disturbed during the incubation period, she rarely will abandon it once the eggs are hatched. In about twelve weeks (about mid-July), the young have feathered out and are ready to leave home. Just prior to this time they can be seen teetering awkwardly on the edge of the nest, exercising their wings.

Nesting eagles in the San Juans have been known to be quite accustomed to island residents, but agitated by the presence of strangers. The best means of viewing them is from inside a car or boat, with binoculars.

Harbor seal near Bare Island

Skipjack and Bare Islands

Lying only 4½ miles from the northwest shore of Orcas Island, Skipjack Island has in the past been a popular destination for small boat adventurers. The island, however, along with Bare Island, ¾ nautical mile to the east, is one of the wildlife preserves of the San Juan Islands National Wildlife Refuge and now is closed to any public use. Landing on the islands is prohibited, except by special permit.

The islands, which lie due north of Waldron Island, support large rookeries of glaucous-winged gulls, pigeon guillemots, black oyster-catchers, auklets, and other pelagic birds. As man's use of the other San Juan Islands increases, it is vitally important that some of these lands be reserved exclusively as refuges. *Any* intrusion by man, no matter how cautiously done or well-intentioned, can frighten birds from their nests, leaving their eggs and young open for predation by rival birds. Even after the nesting season, it is important that the birds have rocks on which to rest undisturbed.

The waters south and east of the islands are popular salmon fishing grounds, and the long underwater reefs nearby are popular with scuba divers. Boaters engaged in these activities should stay well away from the bird refuges.

Olga community dock

7. Orcas Island

Orcas Island is unique among the San Juans, with its three long inlets thrusting deep into the interior of the land, giving it more shoreline and more protected waters than any of its neighboring islands. In addition, it has taller mountains and more surface area than any of the others; however it only exceeds San Juan Island by a mere one and a half square miles.

Proud residents can certainly boast that it has more of everything, including the largest park, Moran State Park; but with all this bounty Orcas Island has only limited saltwater lands open to public use. With the exception of the hike-in park at Obstruction Pass, public waterfront is limited to

a few meager road ends at Cormorant Bay, Buck Bay, West Beach, and near Smuggler's Villa on the north shore.

Although some persons believe that Orcas Island was named for the whale that is so abundant in the surrounding waters, it was in fact named by Franciso Eliza in 1792 for the viceroy of Mexico. It is doubtful this early Spanish explorer deliberately chose the name for its double meaning, for major landfalls such as this were always named after important political figures, not for any wildlife, which at the time was taken quite for granted.

Islanders today, however, care little for Don Juan Vincente de Guemes Pacheco y Padilla Orcasitees y Aguayo Conde de Revilla Gigedo (yes, all that was his title), and generally prefer to relate the island to the magnificent mammal. Eliza further honored his patron by giving the name Isla y Archipielago de San Juan (islands and archipelago of Saint John) to this entire group of rocks.

While San Juan and Lopez islands have, since the time of early settlement, had a history of bustling industry and agriculture, Orcas holds a long tradition as a vacation land. Ever since the 1890s, when ferries first made runs to the San Juans, mainlanders have flocked here to summer at gracious inns, or to rough it in canvas tents set up at beaches around the island. Several of the original inns have been modernized and are still in

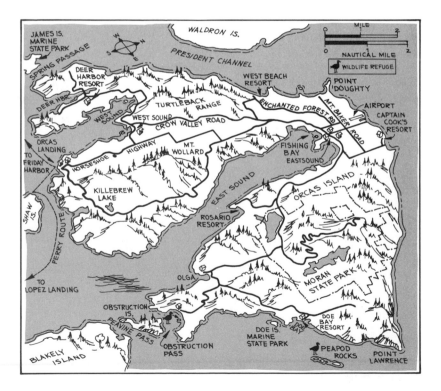

operation today, while newer resorts have accommodations ranging from rustic beach cabins to modern apartments.

Today Orcas Island is served by the Washington state ferry from Anacortes (about a one hour trip), or from Sidney, B.C., on Vancouver Island (about two hours away). The Orcas Island Airport, which is 1 mile north of Eastsound, is a daily stop on the schedule of San Juan Airlines. Charter air services also provide flights to the island.

Hamlets at Orcas Landing, Eastsound, West Sound, and Deer Harbor have groceries, general stores, and interesting little shops, while outstanding meals can be had at a number of restaurants. Daily or weekly lodging is available at resorts, inns, and bed-and-breakfast establishments ranging from rustic to posh; in summer reservations are a must.

The only public camping areas are at Moran State Park and a small hike-in campground at Obstruction Pass. Private resorts at Doe Bay and West Beach also have some camping space. In summer campsites fill rapidly; be sure of overnight accommodations before planning to camp on the island. Most campgrounds make reservations.

The major marinas are at Deer Harbor and West Sound. Orcas Landing, West Beach, and Captain Cook's Resort also have some boating facilities, although of a more limited nature.

Bicycling is a favorite mode of travel on Orcas Island, as anyone can testify who has witnessed the droves of bicycles exiting from a ferry in summer. Orcas roads, however, are two-lane affairs with limited shoulders and plenty of ups and downs and curves. Although auto traffic often is light, cyclists should use both care and courtesy when traveling here.

Don't let traffic back up behind a slow moving party of cyclists pull over at a safe place and let cars go by. Travel single-file and make yourself visible with a bike flag, reflectors, lights, and colored clothing.

Nearly all island roads are blacktopped and wind through forest and farmland, at times edging some of the many miles of shoreline. Visitors trying to find their way around the island will be struck by the fact that few of the roads carry road signs, and those that do change their names seemingly at random. Locals giving directions refer to landmarks and names that do not appear on either maps or signs, such as "OPALCO Road" (which, incidently means the road where the Orcas Power and Light Company is, and is signed as Mt. Baker Road).

The signs that are seen are generally directional ones at intersections, pointing to one destination or another. The one reassuring thing is that one cannot get seriously lost on the island, and even if you do end up wandering a bit, you will probably discover a pretty corner of the island that you might not have seen otherwise.

Waterfowl are sure to be seen; their numbers are far greater during the winter migratory season. A startled deer may dash across the road, then pause to stare back curiously at passersby. The greatest scenic sight of all, whether by bicycle, foot, or car, is the road to the top of Mt. Constitution in Moran State Park, with the culminating view out to a sea full of islands.

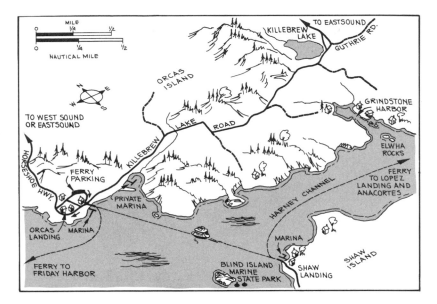

Orcas Landing

Access: Ferry to Orcas Island, boat
Facilities: Float, guest moorage, gas, diesel, water, groceries, fishing
tackle, bait, marine supplies, shops, restaurant, hotel

A small collection of stores clustered near the ferry landing caters to
tourists waiting for the ferry and transient boats stopping to fuel up and
resupply ship's stores. The marina adjacent to the west side of the ferry
landing is equipped to meet most boating needs, while the grocery store
has provisions for land or water visitors. The marina has some limited
overnight moorage along its 300-foot-long float in the summer.

A number of gift shops and snack bars line the road on the slope above
the ferry ramp, offering tourists pleasant places to browse and while away
their time while their cars sit in line, and to purchase a few remembrances
of the island.

Most interesting of the buildings at Orcas is the three-story, Victorian-
era Orcas Hotel, overlooking the bay, that attests to the long-time role of
the island as a resort center. Constructed in 1900, it began accommodating
vacationers in 1904 and did a flourishing business for many years. Ex-
tensively restored in 1985, the Orcas Hotel has guest rooms furnished in
the style of the original hotel, as well as a restaurant and bar. The hotel is
now on the National Register of Historical Places.

The meager parking space at the ferry landing, with which residents
and tourists used to struggle during hectic summer months, was replaced in
1981 by a spacious new facility with ample parking for cars awaiting the

Ferry unloading at Orcas Landing

ferry, plus restrooms and revamped traffic patterns. Parking at the shops and hotel can still be quite constricted, however. An open grassy area adjacent to the stairs that lead from the lot to the terminal has a few picnic tables for open-air relaxation. In summer the wait for the ferry may still be long, but at least it is more enjoyable.

KILLEBREW LAKE

Area: 13 acres
Facilities: Public float
Attractions: Fishing, paddling, birdwatching

A lily pad lake, its quiet waters reflecting cattails, skunk cabbage, pussy willows, and fir trees along its margins. Although land bordering the lake is owned by the state Department of Wildlife, there are no developed public use facilities. A short float on the northeast shore, patched and somewhat the worse for wear, provides the only access; the marshy nature of the shoreline limits any approach from other sides.

To reach Killebrew Lake, turn right immediately after leaving the ferry and follow Killebrew Lake Road east on a road that first parallels the shore, then winds through thick forest, arriving in 2¾ miles at a Y intersection where White Beach Road continues on the right, and the lake and a small pull-off loop are to the left. The south end of the loop is quite overgrown, and it is better accessed from the north. There is parking space for a number of cars along the pull-off; RV camping is permitted, although there are no toilets or drinking water.

Boats must be hand carried for launching. Spend some time paddling about the lake, floating and watching the array of birds that visit the marsh

Killebrew Lake

and the dragonflies darting among the lily pads, or fish for the cutthroat trout that the lake is stocked with. Boats with gasoline motors are not permitted.

GRINDSTONE HARBOR

No public facilities from either land or sea, but a secure anchorage worth mentioning. Lying on the north side of Harney Channel, 2 nautical miles east of the Orcas ferry landing, the small, deeply indented cove has space for just a few boats to drop a hook.

A wicked reef just below the surface in all but minus tides lies in the center of the entrance 300 yards offshore. Its slightly more obvious companion lies just inside the entrance on the east. A slow and cautious approach, somewhat favoring the west side of the harbor, leads past a channel-pinching point to the pleasant inner harbor and anchorages in 10 to 15 feet of water. Respect the privacy of the shoreline.

The harbor received its name because Paul Hubbs, an early settler who lived there, owned a grindstone. He was often called upon to sharpen the axes, knives, and other tools of the pioneers.

More recently Grindstone Harbor achieved notoriety when the (then) captain of the ferry *Elwha* attempted to steer the 382-foot vessel into the entrance to the harbor while showing a lady friend the sights, and hung it up on a reef. The event has since been immortalized in story, song, and a local bar drink called "*Elwha* on the Rocks." The reef has now been officially named Elwha Rock.

Deer Harbor

Access: Ferry to Orcas Island, boat
Facilities (at the marina and resort): Guest moorage, power, water, diesel, gas, marine supplies, restrooms, showers, laundry, inn, cabins, swimming pool, groceries, stores, restaurant, kayak rental
Attractions: Boating, fishing, paddling, crabbing

Smallest of the Orcas Island inlets, Deer Harbor indents the western lobe of the island for merely a mile. The marina and resort at the head of the bay is a handy stop for boaters seeking to avoid the long trek into Eastsound for supplies, and is a tourist attraction for both mariners and landbound visitors.

Deer Harbor lies 6 nautical miles north of Friday Harbor, along a route threading through the interesting "rock pile" of the Wasp Islands. Good anchorages can be had in the bay, although its extreme head is quite shallow. A little wooded islet, appropriately named Fawn Island, lies near the entrance; passage can safely be made on either side of it, although a shoal extends from its southern end.

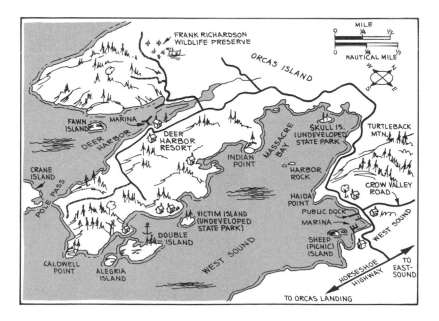

To reach Deer Harbor by land, drive 2½ miles north from the ferry landing to the West Sound intersection. Turn left here and follow the road as it curves around West Sound, then heads south to Deer Harbor, 4 miles from the settlement of West Sound.

Landlubbers and seafarers mingle in the shops and restaurants of the charming little resort. Several of the neat clapboard buildings date from the 1890s, when it was first established. Adding to the atmosphere, all types of interesting boats tie up at the docks, ranging from shiny plastic runabouts to beautiful old classic sailing vessels.

All of the Deer Harbor Resort is private property and is restricted to the use of patrons. The owners have a right to charge people for putting in boats, parking, or other use of the facilities. The resort has its own water supply, and during the rare advent of a dry summer, water shortages may develop, curtailing its availability for all but essential needs.

The general store at Deer Harbor

At one time a launch ramp on the northwest corner of the bay, opposite the resort, provided access to the waters of Deer Harbor, but it is now privately owned and closed. Hand-carried boats can be put in at the resort for a fee.

Kayakers with experience in handling tidal currents can paddle 2 nautical miles west from Deer Harbor to Jones Island Marine State Park, investigating Fawn Island en route, or can head southeast for 1¼ nautical miles to Pole Pass, then on around Caldwell Point into the expanse of West Sound. The current can be strong in Pole Pass; refer to a tidal current chart for the best time to attempt the channel.

FRANK RICHARDSON WILDLIFE PRESERVE

The Frank Richardson Wildlife Preserve encompasses portions of a 20-acre marsh on top of the hill west of Deer Harbor. Year around the marshland teems with birdlife. In spring look for hooded mergansers, cinnamon teals, mallards, and American coots with their broods. Marsh wrens and red-winged blackbirds call from the rushes.

To reach the preserve, take the road west at the head of Deer Harbor. The road curves around the bay, then heads steeply uphill. In 1¼ miles from the Deer Harbor Road intersection the marshland lies on the right. The narrow road has no shoulders and no parking alongside the preserve; find pull-offs at either end of the marsh and walk the road to observe the birds.

Frank Richardson Wildlife Preserve

Frank Richardson was a professor of zoology at the University of Washington. He resided on Orcas Island from shortly after the time of his retirement until his death in 1985. The preserve was established to honor him and his important contributions to the study of wildlife.

West Sound

Access: Ferry to Orcas Island, boat
Facilities (at West Sound Marina): Guest moorage with power, water, diesel, gas, restrooms, showers, marine supplies and repair, groceries, boat launch (sling)
Attractions: Boating, paddling, shrimping

The "middle" of Orcas Island's three main inlets, West Sound is both middle in size and middle in location, located between East Sound and Deer Harbor, and running north for 3 miles to the base of Turtleback Range. Prevailing northerly or southerly winds make the waterway a favorite with sailors who happily leave the busy traffic of Harney Channel for brisk sails up the sound.

The remarkable outline of Turtleback Range, with the "shell" formed by 1,500-foot Turtleback Mountain and the "head" created by Orcas Knob, is quite easily seen from the waters of West Sound. Another good view of the turtle can be had from the north end of President Channel, on the northwest side of Orcas Island.

A long rock at the entrance to Massacre Bay, midway between Haida Point and Indian Point, is marked by a daybeacon. At high tide considerable portions of the rock are submerged—give it wide berth.

On the eastern "thumb" of West Sound is the village of West Sound, where there is a marina, yacht club, store, and country dock. The southernmost dock at West Sound is the property of the yacht club. Immediately north of this private dock is the country dock with a 50-foot float, which is accessible to the public for day use only. A concrete staircase at the head of the dock provides access to the beach.

The marina, tucked behind Sheep Island, is the best on Orcas Island, with both permanent and transient moorage, fuel, repair and maintenance services, haul-out, chandlery and a grocery/deli.

Boats planning to drop a hook for the night will find Massacre Bay quite shallow and open to southerly winds; the most protected anchorage is on the northwest side of Double Island, near the entrance to the sound.

To reach West Sound by land from the ferry landing, follow the Horseshoe Highway north for 2½ miles to the first major intersection and turn left. The village is reached in one more mile.

The inlet offers little to the land-bound visitor aside from the very scenic drive around Haida Point. Pretty little Skull Island is visible from the road near the head of Massacre Bay, but once the road rounds the head of West Sound it ducks into timber and all marine views are lost. In winter Massacre Bay fills with great rafts of all kinds of migratory waterfowl—buffleheads, scaups, goldeneyes, grebes, and scooters—squawking and

Migratory ducks on Massacre Bay

skittering about uneasily at every imagined menace from shore. When startled by the sight of a human or a stopping car, they depart in huge flocks of whirring wings, to alight farther down the sound.

INDIAN HISTORY

Lummi Indians claimed the San Juan Islands as their tribal territory and large numbers of them summered here, gathering berries, bird eggs, and roots of camas and other plants, then returning to the protection of mainland longhouses to wait out the dreary rains of fall and winter. Permanent villages were established on San Juan Island at Friday Harbor, Fisherman Bay on Lopez Island, and West Sound on Orcas Island. The West Sound village, located at the head of the bay, is reported to have been named Elelung, and included a large permanent longhouse. Temporary shelters were wooden frameworks covered with woven mats that were removed when the tribe moved elsewhere.

The bounty of the islands provided the Indians with all they required —fish, shellfish, deer, birds, and other small animals for meat; berries and a wide variety of other plants for food (some nutritionists believe that the Coast Indians had a diet superior in vitamins to that which modern man has today); animal skins for clothing; and an abundant supply of cedar trees that were utilized for nearly every purpose from homes and canoes, made from the wood of the trees, to clothing and baby diapers made from shredded bark.

With only the most basic of materials the Indians developed ingenious

161

means of harvesting food. Nets and fishing lines were fashioned from incredibly thin strips of bark and plant fibers that were braided for strength. Fishhooks had hinged barbs or gates to prevent the escape of the catch. At Pole Pass, between Crane and Orcas islands at the mouth of Deer Harbor, the Indians were known to stretch nets across the 200-foot channel, supported by tall poles (hence the name), to knock down low-flying flocks of birds. Reef netting, invented by ancestors of the Lummis, is still effective as a commercial fishing method today.

These Indians practiced the unusual custom of binding flat boards to the foreheads of their babies to permanently shape them with a broad, flat forehead and high crown, considered at the time to be quite beautiful. It is believed that a group of Coast Indians, traveling in the eastern prairies, were the ones that Lewis and Clark sighted, causing them to erroneously name the local Indians the Flathead Tribe—the native Montana Indians were never known to practice the custom.

The local Lummis were generally peaceful people, content with the abundance of their land; nevertheless they occasionally suffered at the hands of war parties from the fierce tribes of the north, and would retaliate. Territorial acquisition was not the intent—such raids were primarily for the purpose of taking slaves who were usually used later for ceremonial sacrifices, or killed at the whim of their captors.

The most vicious of these raids in recorded history occurred in 1856, when a party of Haida Indians from the north swept down on the West Sound village and slaughtered most of the inhabitants, taking the rest for slaves and completely destroying the settlement. More than a hundred Indians were reported to have been killed in the raid—and since that time Massacre Bay has borne its lurid name.

SKULL AND VICTIM ISLANDS MARINE STATE PARKS

Park area: Skull Island, 2½ acres; Victim Island, 3 acres
Access: Boat
Attractions: Picnicking, paddling, crabbing

Skull and Victim islands may be grisly names for such innocuous bits of land, but rather than any recent problem, they, along with Massacre Bay, recall the area's past history of bloody Indian raids.

Located only 400 feet off the shore of West Sound, Victim Island lies a third of the way up the sound, just north of Double Island, while Skull Island is near the head of Massacre Bay. Although they lie within arm's length of the nearby shore, there is no access to the parks from land.

The islands are small ("intimate" if you prefer) and rocky, with a few picturesquely scrubby trees. After a day of paddle exploration of the shore of West Sound either is a fine spot to pause for a snack or a snooze. These are undeveloped parks, thus there are no amenities such as water, toilets, or garbage cans. Fires or overnight camping are not permitted; please take all garbage home with you.

The shoreline of West Sound wanders in and out, forming coves and bays ideal for small boat perusal. The only public tidelands in West Sound are those surrounding Sheep (Picnic), Skull, Victim, Double, and Oak islands. Uplands are private except for Skull, Victim, and Oak islands and a small rock north of Sheep Island.

Obstruction and Peavine Passes

Among an entire album of scenic treasures, Obstruction and Peavine passes rank as sublime. On clear days ferry travelers in Harney Channel are treated to the sight of the ethereal cone of Mt. Baker floating above the twin passes, with blue-gray layers of islands and hills stretching between.

Lying near the end of Rosario Strait, this doorway in the eastern wall of the San Juans serves boaters approaching the islands from Bellingham, which is 18 nautical miles northeast, and Vancouver, B.C. Obstruction Pass doglegs around Obstruction Island and has submerged rocks lying near the edge of the channel; Peavine Pass on the south, although narrower, is easier to navigate.

A county boat-launching ramp on Obstruction Pass provides the closest put-in for trailered boats seeking access to the east side of Orcas Island. To reach it, follow the road to Olga, turning east ¼ mile before reaching Olga onto a road signed to Doe Bay. Follow this road, turning south in another ½ mile on a road marked to Obstruction Pass.

The road meanders down valleys and around hills, finally reaching Obstruction Pass about 1½ miles from the Doe Bay Road intersection. A 125-foot-wide parking lot adjacent to the fire station has a concrete ramp at

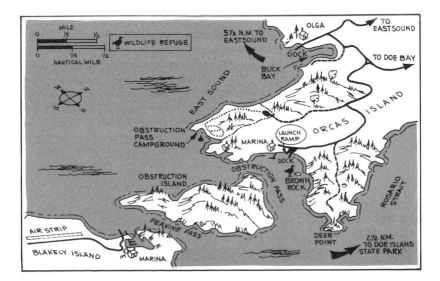

its west side, and a county dock and float at its east side. The dock is for loading and unloading only—no overnight moorage. Property on either side of the launching facility is private, although that to the west contains a marina, resort, small grocery store, and other businesses associated with the marina.

Boats put in here can explore westward to the DNR campground at the point, and on into Buck Bay and East Sound. Eastward and north are Doe Island State Park and Peapod Rocks. Brown Rock, lying in Obstruction Pass, is a bird sanctuary of the San Juan Islands National Wildlife Refuge.

Currents in Obstruction and Peavine passes can run in excess of 4 knots, and heavy tide rips occur east of Obstruction Island. Use care in small boats.

OBSTRUCTION PASS CAMPGROUND

Park area: 80 acres; 400 feet of public tidelands
Access: Ferry to Orcas Island, boat
Facilities: 9 campsites, picnic tables, fireplaces, latrines, mooring buoys,
    no water
Attractions: Boating, paddling, fishing, shrimping, hiking,
    beachcombing

A forested point of land facing on Obstruction Pass gives backpackers and boaters alike an opportunity to camp in seclusion above a quiet beach. This Department of Natural Resources facility has four campsites, five picnic sites, and two group picnic areas scattered about a timbered flat, some within view of the water. If hikers wish further exercise after the walk in, a loop trail circles the area, through lush ferns and undergrowth.

To reach the trailhead to the campground, turn east off the Olga Road about ¼ mile before reaching the town of Olga, onto a road signed to Doe Bay. In ½ mile turn south on the Obstruction Pass Road, which winds around an open valley, then circles a wooded hillside and heads south. As it curves east again, about 1 mile from the Doe Bay intersection, a gravel road branching right is signed to the Obstruction Pass DNR Recreation Site. Turn on this rough, narrow road and follow it for 1 more mile to the parking area at the trailhead (space here for about thirty cars). Overnight camping at the trailhead is not permitted.

Before reaching the campground the nearly level trail wanders for ½ mile through timber and along steep bluffs above East Sound, with occasional short side spurs to rocky outlooks on cliffs above the water.

By water, the park lies 1 nautical mile south of Olga on East Sound, and ½ nautical mile west of the boat ramp on Obstruction Pass. There are two mooring buoys in the bay, and space for several more boats to drop anchor in the gravel bottom. It's a pleasant spot, with a nighttime view of brightly lit ferries in Harney Channel; however, during a strong southerly it might be a little rough. The pebbled beach slopes sharply into the bay, but

Kayaks beached at Obstruction Pass Recreation Site

offers a fine place to draw up small boats. It is a favorite kayaking destination. At low water explore tidepools along the rocky beach on either side of the bay.

DOE ISLAND MARINE STATE PARK

Park area: 6 acres; 2050 feet of shoreline
Access: Boat
Facilities: 5 campsites, picnic tables, pit toilet, dock with float, *no water, no garbage collection*
Attractions: Hiking, fishing, beachcombing, scuba diving

Compared to the more spacious facilities of Sucia, Stuart, or Jones island, Doe Island is a "minipark," but it is a delight nonetheless. The nearest boat launch is at Obstruction Pass, 2½ nautical miles to the south.

Deep draft boats should approach the island from the east, as a tideflat extends out from Orcas Island toward the west end of Doe Island. A dock with a 30-foot float lying on the north shore of the island is restricted to thirty-minutes' use from 8 a.m. to 3 p.m. Water depth at the dock is 8 feet at mean low water, adequate for most craft except at very low tide. Buoys placed in the channel between Doe and Orcas islands are private, not for public use; however, there is space to anchor. Small boats and kayaks may easily be landed behind the east point and on the gentle beaches of the park's south side, but be wary of rocks just offshore.

Campsites with fireplaces are spaced about the island—three in the timber and two in sunny clearings just above the south shore with views across Rosario Strait to Cypress Island. A latrine is located near the dock.

A trail circling the island on the bank above the beach leads to a rocky point that is festooned with flowers in spring. On the south side the bluff has been undercut by waves, forming an interesting cave to explore. Gulls and other seabirds often gather on the wave-washed beach rocks, flying in startled flocks when approached too closely.

DOE BAY

Access: Ferry to Orcas Island, boat
Facilities: Cabins, mineral springs, sauna, meeting halls, campsites, store, kayak rentals, guided kayak tours
Attractions: Mineral baths, sunbathing, kayaking, beachcombing

Doe Bay Resort has for years been an on-again, off-again operation, sometimes public, sometimes private, always marching to its own drummer. At present the resort is open to the public, in its own laid-back style. It still retains a flavor from the days when it belonged to the Polarity Institute, which was concerned with esoteric meditation, natural foods and purgatives, and merging the opposing positive and negative forces within the body.

The resort has tent camping on a large bluff to the north, mineral spring baths and a sauna near the office, cabins above the beach, and a willingness to cram overflow campers into whatever flat space is left. Part of the resort's ambiance is a "clothing optional" attitude in the more secluded areas.

For visitors arriving by boat, a few good anchorages and one lone mooring buoy can be found in the bay.

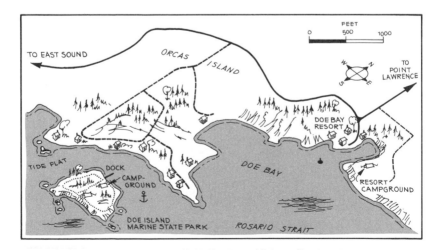

Camping at Doe Island Marine State Park

PEAPOD ROCKS

This mile-long chain of islets serves two "levels" of interest. Below the sea is a State Parks Underwater Recreation Area, frequently used by scuba divers, while the grassy rocks protruding above the water are part of the San Juan Islands National Wildlife Refuge, attracting flocks of seabirds who congregate and nest here.

The underwater area from Doe Bay to Peapod Rocks is highly rated among scuba divers for its wide range of terrain and difficulty, from the protected waters of the bay to the deep current-swept walls of the rocks.

The largest of the islands is North Peapod, which has a navigational beacon. At the far end of the chain is, appropriately, South Peapod Rock, while stretching in-between is an assortment of rocks that appear and disappear with the tide.

Landing boats on the rocks is prohibited, since such intrusion is disturbing to nesting birds. This is a favorite haul-out area for seals and sea lions, which can often be spotted sunning on the rocks or in the water

Doe Bay Resort

nearby. Again, too close observation by man can startle the animals and cause them to leave their resting and warming grounds.

East Sound

More than 7 miles long and a mile in width, the long, blunt inlet of East Sound nearly carves Orcas Island in two. Fjordlike hills rise steeply along the sides, and then suddenly drop down to the flat at the head of the bay. This is a small inland sea in itself, with three diminutive ports-of-call, on which sailors can spend hours cruising about. East Sound is so large that it can "make its own weather"—when winds funnel down the mountain-rimmed channel it can be quite choppy here, even when it is calm in outside waters.

With a smooth shoreline and beaches dropping off steeply, anchorages are few. Only at Buck Bay, Cascade Bay, and the head of the sound are the waters shallow and protected enough to permit an overnight stay.

OLGA

Access: Ferry to Orcas Island, boat
Facilities: Float, guest moorage, restaurant, water

This small settlement on Buck Bay, near the mouth of East Sound, has a dock and float providing some space for visiting boaters. Although it is owned by the Washington State Parks Commission, the dock is operated and maintained by the Olga Community Club, which charges a small fee for overnight stays. The log breakwater that once protected the dock was damaged by a storm and has not been replaced.

The dock has no power outlets: water is available from a faucet at the gazebo near the head of the dock. The Olga grocery store is a popular sustenance stop for touring bicyclists. It occasionally falls victim to the harsh economic realities of the island and closes; as of the summer of 1988 it was open. An excellent restaurant is nearby.

In calm weather some anchorages are possible along the shore to the south. The lagoon at the head of the bay dries at low tide. Be cautious of a large rock in the center of the bay that is submerged at high tide.

To reach Olga by land, follow the Horseshoe Highway north from the ferry landing through the town of Eastsound, then continue on the Olga Road through Moran State Park and south to the village. Total distance is about 17 miles.

ROSARIO

Access: Ferry or airplane to Orcas Island, boat
Facilities: Docks, guest moorage with electrical and water hookups, mooring buoys (fee), restrooms, showers, laundromat, diesel, gas, groceries, fishing tackle and bait, boat launch (ramp), hotel, restaurant, coffee shop, convention center, swimming pools, moped rental, boat rental, car rental
Attractions: Boating, fishing, hiking, swimming (pools), sightseeing, historical landmarks, beachcombing, tennis

Unquestionably the most outstanding historical landmark of the San Juans, Rosario has gained nationwide recognition as a fine resort and convention center. It effectively combines the quiet grandeur of a turn-of-the-century estate with the slick posh of a modern marine resort.

The Rosario estate was built in 1904 by Robert Moran, a Seattle mayor who was a shipbuilder, millionaire, and man of unlimited talents and energy. Personal illness had forced Moran to sell his shipbuilding enterprises in Seattle and retire to Orcas Island, where he purchased land enclosing Cascade Bay on East Sound, and designed and supervised the building of his mansion, Rosario.

Moran built his mansion as solidly as he had built his ships, anchoring it on solid bedrock with concrete walls and inch-thick plate glass windows. The fifty-four-room main building required six years to complete; it is claimed that two years alone were consumed laying the wooden parquet floor of the interior.

The care lavished on the structure was also extended to the home's furnishings and to the grounds of the estate. An organ with 1,972 pipes, installed by Moran, is still used regularly, and visitors still admire an imported stained glass window. A figurehead salvaged from an old clipper ship that was wrecked in the San Juans was set up on the grounds and re-

Materials salvaged from ships decorate Rosario Resort: left, figurehead from the America; *right, fence from anchor chain*

mains there today, a symbol for this elegant resort. Carved in 1874 from a solid pine log for the sailing ship *America*, the figure uses the motif of the Liberty silver dollar used during this period.

Moran left his mark not only on this quiet bay, but on all of Orcas Island. He purchased large quantities of property on the island, and eventually donated 3,600 acres of mountainous land, clothed with forests and lakes, to the state of Washington to be used as the park that today bears his name. In addition he helped build roads, develop water systems, and provide much-needed jobs for the islanders during the Depression years of the 1930s.

Following the death of his wife, Moran sold Rosario in 1938. Another local ex-mayor, Gilbert Geiser, formerly of Mountlake Terrace, purchased the property in 1960 with the dream of turning it into a resort. With energy and expertise possibly matching that of Moran, he has transformed the unique estate into a modern facility that attracts vacationers, seminars, and conventions year-round.

All of the original buildings of Rosario were named to the National Register of Historical Places in 1979, assuring their preservation in their original state, with only necessary modernization.

To reach Rosario by land, follow the Horseshoe Highway east from Eastsound, bearing right at an intersection 1 mile east of town. In 3¼ more miles, a prominent sign points down the road to the right to Rosario Resort, 1¾ miles away.

By boat, Rosario lies on Cascade Bay, halfway into East Sound, along the eastern shore. Rosario Point reaches out to enclose the broadly curving bay, with a jetty-created moorage basin. Buoys placed in the bay are for use by guests of the resort. Nearly any time of the year it is necessary to have reservations for an overnight stay at the floats or in the hotel. Boats unable to secure moorage can usually find space to anchor in the bay.

Since this is private property, a landing fee is charged for use of the buoys or coming ashore from anchored boats. The fee also covers the water taxi to the resort and use of selected resort facilities, including the restaurant. A meal in the resort's outstanding dining room makes a stop at the resort a vacation highlight for any galley slave.

ROSARIO LAGOON TRAIL

If guests at Rosario become sated with the multitude of attractions the resort offers and feel the urge to stretch their legs, a path leads up the steep hillside to the tennis courts beside Rosario Lagoon, where a trail can be followed to Cascade Lake in Moran State Park.

Walk past the concrete lagoon and generator building of the Rosario

Rosario Lagoon

estate to find the trailhead opposite Discovery House—and what a trail-head! Every bit in keeping with the elegance of the resort, the rustic path is planked at its start, and protected by a roof of cedar shakes. It zigzags briefly up the hillside through shadowed woods, stopping at a tiny pavilion, an ideal spot for resting, picnicking, or a romantic tryst.

From the pavilion the path follows a road between resort villas to the Satellite Hall. Here follow the dirt road on the uphill side of the hall to its intersection with a higher paved road near the Cascade Creek drainage. Turn left, and in 100 feet find the signed trailhead next to the steel aqueduct carrying water to the Rosario power generators. From here the trail climbs steadily—rising 350 feet in about a mile, keeping close to the aqueduct. Fragments of an older aqueduct can be seen below the trail, along with the cascading stream that gives Cascade Bay its name.

Finally the trail crosses two bridges and emerges on a road at an un-marked trailhead opposite the sluice gate of the Rosario Lagoon dam; tennis courts are to the left. Trails at either side of the dam circle the shores of the lagoon, reaching Cascade Lake and the Moran State Park boundary in about ¼ mile. See chapter 8 for further descriptions of the state park.

EASTSOUND

Access: Ferry to Orcas Island, boat
Facilities: Groceries, stores, fuel, hotel, restaurants
Attractions: Shopping, sightseeing, museum

Since the 1880s Eastsound has served as the business district for Orcas Island. At that time the few stores located here sold axes, seeds, flour, blankets, and horse collars to settlers, a blacksmith shod their horses, and a gracious inn provided meals and lodging to vacationing mainlanders. The town hasn't grown up much since that time—in fact some of the original buildings are still there—but today there is a service

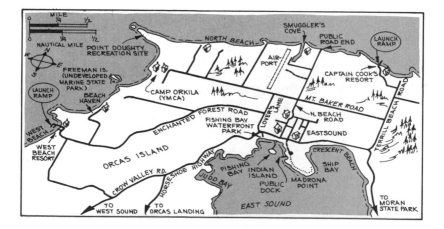

station instead of a blacksmith shop and the general store has a deli and is stocked like any modern grocery store. The beautiful little Emmanuel Episcopal Church, built in 1886, still opens its doors on Sunday morning to worshippers.

As in early times, stores along Main Street and North Beach Road are interspersed with private residences, although some of these homes have been converted to shops selling antiques, arts, crafts, and gift items to visitors. Outlook Inn, which still provides overnight accommodations and fine meals, advertises that it has been in operation since 1883, making it one of the earliest such establishments in the San Juan Islands.

By land, the town is reached from the ferry landing by following the main road, Horseshoe Highway, north to the head of the sound, a distance of 9 miles. The Orcas Island airport is less than a mile due north of the town on the road to North Beach.

MADRONA POINT

The last unspoiled peninsula on East Sound, Madrona Point, was scheduled for condominium development in 1989. The land, however, was a sacred burial ground of the Lummi tribe, which lobbied heavily for federal funds to purchase the land and preserve it from desecration. In late 1989, as bulldozers pressed at the boundaries, Congress approved a bill that authorized purchase of the point and its transfer to the Indians as a preservation area.

Today the area is open to public day use, courtesy of the Lummi tribe. The rocky madrona-clad headlands offer spectacular views of Fishing and Ship bays, and occasional rock-rib accesses to stony beaches. Enjoy the beauty, and respect and revere this solemn point as much as the original inhabitants did.

The county plans to place a dock and day-use float at the north end of Madrona Point on Fishing Bay in 1991 to provide Eastbound access to visiting boats anchored offshore. The dock will be located at the end of the first street heading south onto Madrona Point from the east side of the Eastbound business district.

ORCAS ISLAND HISTORICAL MUSEUM

A major highlight of a visit to Eastsound is its interesting Historical Museum, located two blocks north of Main Street on North Beach Road. Four old log cabins, originally built elsewhere on the island, were brought to Eastsound and reassembled into the structure housing the museum. Displaying a variety of construction methods from massive hand-hewn, dovetailed boards to the traditional "round log" style, the building is nearly as interesting outside as the collection inside.

The museum has an outstanding display of Indian and pioneer artifacts and mementos from early island days. Many of the Indian objects were collected by Ethan Allen, a Waldron Island resident who was the

Fishing Bay and Indian Island

county superintendent of schools during the early 1900s. The Allen collection, which is so valuable that it is housed in a fireproof vault, includes about 20 glass-framed wall displays containing countless Indian arrowheads.

Also on display is Allen's handmade boat, in which he rowed from island to island visiting the one-room schools in his district. In 1898 there were 27 such schools scattered around the San Juan Islands.

Behind the main structure is a shed housing an interesting collection of antique farm machinery. The museum, operated by the Orcas Island Historical Society, is open from 1 p.m. to 4 p.m. Monday through Saturday, summers only.

North of the museum is an antique water tower and the Orcas Visitor Information Center.

FISHING BAY WATERFRONT PARK

Although Eastsound faces on Fishing Bay, it has in the past lacked a real orientation to the water. Current plans are to change this by putting patio decks on the waterfront side of some of the businesses, and developing a pedestrian walkway along the shore.

Plans are for the footpath to go west a short distance, ending at what is presently an undeveloped county park. The park property sits on a low bank above the bay. A few gigantic old Douglas firs provide shade to the grassy meadow. At present the park consists of only a few primitive picnic tables and an open swath of grass. There is no vehicle access to the site, and precious little parking in the vicinity. Even with rustic amenities, it's still a lovely site to have a beach picnic, with its unobstructed views all the way down the long fjord of East Sound.

Just 200 yards offshore lies inviting little Indian Island, which is owned by the state and open to the public. At minus tide a sandbar links the islet to the mainland.

The Northwest Shore

On the "outer shore" of Orcas Island, the gentle uplands roll smoothly into the sea, interrupted only by small rocky points and the long finger of Point Doughty. Broad sandy beaches provide some of the best recreation on Orcas Island; however, there are no public accesses, aside from a few road ends.

Several commercial resorts along this shore of the island have varying facilities, and also have varying reactions to the wander-in public, depending on the nature of the resort. Since this shoreline provides the closest access to the popular marine state parks lying to the north, there are frequent demands on these businesses to launch boats and put in kayaks. Even though they are commercial businesses offering services to the public, they have every right to limit use of their land and facilities to paying customers.

Resorts along the shore are reached by land from roads branching from the East Sound and Crow Valley Road. All are well signed. By boat, West Beach is 10 nautical miles northeast of Roche Harbor, while North Beach is about 3 nautical miles farther.

Small boats or canoes launched from this side of Orcas Island can spend hours investigating the shoreline, stopping at Freeman Island and Point Doughty. Sucia Island is a tempting destination, lying only 4 nautical miles to the northeast, but is recommended only for those experienced with open water hazards, for there are reefs and tide rips along the way.

These same reefs and tide rips make this a popular salmon fishing grounds, where many anglers troll during the summer months. The offshore reefs attract scuba divers who dive from boats at Parker Reef, Point Doughty, and throughout President Channel, finding abalone, swimming scallops, and exceptionally large lingcod and cabazon. Free diving and snorkeling are good near the docks and bays of the resorts, and on a series of rocky ledges between Freeman Island and the Orcas Island shore.

NORTH SHORE RESORTS

Access: Ferry to Orcas Island, boat
Facilities (at Captain Cook's): Restrooms, boat launch (ramp), gas, groceries, restaurant
Attractions: Boating, fishing, beachcombing, scuba diving, kayaking

The only resort on the north side that has boat launching is Captain Cook's. To reach it drive east out of Eastsound on the Horseshoe Highway, and in about 1 mile turn north on the road signed to Terrill Beach. As it nears the north side of the island, the unpaved road to the resort takes off to the west. After 1991, cabins and RV campsites will no longer be available, as most of the property will be converted to residential development. The

Turtleback Range and Orcas' north shore from President Channel

resort plans to continue operating the dock, ramp, fuel supply, store, and restaurant.

Two other resorts, Smuggler's Villa and North Beach, lie to the west along the north shore. At both of these resorts the facilities are only for registered guests.

NORTH SHORE ROAD ENDS

North Beach Road End. A public road end lies just east of the Orcas Island airport and Smuggler's Villa Resort. To reach it, take North Beach Road north from Eastsound; ¼ mile from its intersection with Mt. Baker Road, the road ends at a sand and cobble beach signed "Public shore. No overnight parking or camping." There is room here to park a half-dozen cars. The gentle beach is suitable for launching hand-carried boats to explore the northern shoreline.

For the more skilled and adventurous, cross to Sucia Island, a scant 2 nautical miles away, beyond the menace of Parker Reef. Unfortunately, since cars cannot park overnight by the roadside, kayakers must make plans to park elsewhere if they plan extended trips. The beach on either side of the road end is private.

Terrill Beach Road End. Although the very end of Terrill Beach Road, ½ mile east of Captain Cook's, is nominally public, there is only a trail through brush to a high bank, with no beach access. Neighboring property and beaches are private—please respect them.

WEST SHORE RESORTS

Access: Ferry to Orcas Island, boat
Facilities (at West Beach): Dock with float, boat launch (ramp),
    groceries, gas, fishing tackle and bait, guest moorage, cabins,
    campground, RV hookups, restrooms, showers, laundromat, picnic
    tables, fireplaces, cabins, boat rental, scuba air
Attractions: Boating, fishing, paddling, scuba diving, beachcombing

A resort on the west side of Orcas Island provides facilities for boaters
headed for offshore fishing grounds, scuba diving sites, or a day's recreation
at Sucia Island and points beyond.

The resort is especially popular with scuba divers who dive north to
Point Doughty, and south along the shoreline to Lover's Cove. The small
moorage basin is protected by a log breakwater that gives some respite
from waves off President Channel.

A second resort to the north, Beach Haven, has facilities only for its
guests.

POINT DOUGHTY RECREATION SITE

Access: Boat only
Area: 60 acres; 8,260 feet of shoreline
Facilities: Picnic tables, fire rings, campsites, pit toilets, *no water*
Attractions: Fishing, scuba diving, tidepools, beachcombing

It's not an appealing anchorage, with kelp beds, tide rips, and submerged rocks in the vicinity, but for small boats that can be hauled up on

Freeman Island Marine State Park

the beach, Point Doughty offers go-ashore camping near some of the best scuba diving to be found in the Northwest.

The Department of Natural Resources area is accessible to the public only by boat. A public trail from above was proposed at one time, but the idea was abandoned for fear that the heavy public use of such a trail would disturb eagles that nest in the area. An overland path does reach the point from YMCA Camp Orkila, down the beach to the south, but that route is restricted to use by youngsters from the camp.

A few campsites perch on the grassy slope above the beach, with stunning views across President Channel out to Boundary Pass. Offshore rocks can make landing boats at the beach a bit tricky; be prepared to wade. Bluff erosion can also make the scramble uphill to the campsites difficult.

Several generations of Northwest youngsters have had their first taste of the San Juans at YMCA Camp Orkila, which is on the west shore, just south of Point Doughty. Since 1906, when the camp was founded, up to 3,000 children each year have fished, swum, beachcombed, sailed, canoed, hiked, and had wilderness camp-outs here, and have grown to love the islands.

FREEMAN ISLAND MARINE STATE PARK

Park area: Less than an acre
Access: Boat
Facilities: None
Attractions: Beachcombing, tidepools, scuba diving, fishing

This undeveloped state park is an eroded, narrow ridge of an island, with a fringe of gnarled old trees. Perhaps eventually it will all wash away, but for now enjoy the meager little island, made beautiful by the ravages of weather and time.

Freeman Island lies just 300 yards off the northwest shore of Orcas Island. Boaters frequently take day excursions to the island from West Beach Resort, Beach Haven, or Camp Orkila, all less than a mile away.

The shores are very rocky; boat landing is best on the south side and west end. Scuba divers often dive in the reef extending to the west.

Fires or overnight camping are not permitted. Please do not litter; if you picnic take your garbage home with you.

Entrance Mountain from the Mt. Constitution Road

Afoot & Afloat

8. Moran State Park

Park area: 4,934 acres; 1,800 feet of saltwater shoreline
Access: Ferry to Orcas Island, boat from Rosario Resort
Facilities: 166 campsites, picnic tables, stoves, kitchen shelters, drinking
    water, restrooms, showers, RV dump station, swimming beach, boat
    launch (freshwater), boat rentals, hiking trails
Attractions: Hiking, fishing (freshwater), swimming (freshwater),
    boating (gasoline motors not permitted), view tower, bird-watching

    Drive, bike, or hike—no matter how you get there, Moran State Park
is a "must-see" for anyone touring the San Juan Islands. Oddly, though,

on this water-oriented island there is no easy way for people arriving via private boat to reach the park. Unless they are willing to make the steep hike up from Rosario, or rent cars or motor scooters at the resort, they must be content with the many magnificent views of Mt. Constitution visible from the waterways.

From the northern reaches of Rosario Strait the lookout tower on the 2,407-foot-high summit is visible to the naked eye. Boaters can gaze up and admire the scenic mountain and realize that landlubbers in the tower are admiring *their* scenic craft cutting the blue waters.

By land the park is reached via ferry from Anacortes or Sidney, B.C., to Orcas Island. From Orcas Landing travel north on the Horseshoe Highway to the village of Eastsound, loop around the end of the sound, and head south again. The route is well signed. Distance to the park entrance is 13 miles. Access to the park from Rosario is described in chapter 7.

Moran is ranked as the fourth largest Washington state park. Thirty-six hundred acres of parkland was a gift to the state in 1920 by wealthy shipbuilder Robert Moran, who built his lavish estate, Rosario, on Cascade Bay, just below. Additional parkland was acquired over a period of time by

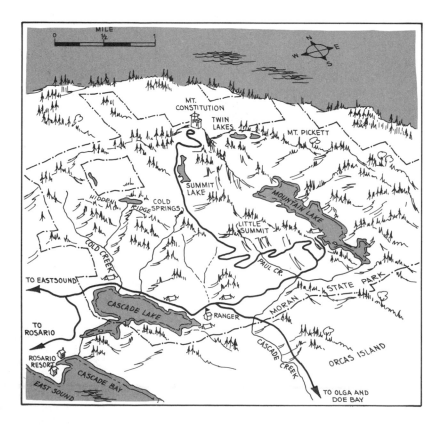

various means until today the park contains nearly 5,000 acres. Much of the park development, including the picturesqe old timber and stone picnic shelters, was done in the 1930s by the Depression-era Civilian Conservation Corps.

CAMPING

Located on Cascade and Mountain lakes are four pleasant car camping areas with a total of 151 campsites; an additional 15 sites are in a primitive camping area east of Cascade Lake.

Because of the ferry trip many visitors to the park stay several days, and campgrounds are usually filled every night throughout the summer. Reservations are accepted from Memorial Day to Labor Day. With over 60,000 campers per month in prime season, without a reservation chances of finding an empty campsite during this period are slim.

Information regarding state park reservations is published in many newspapers in spring and summer, or can be obtained by calling the state parks information number listed in appendix A in the back of this book. When park campgrounds are full, a notice is usually posted at the Anacortes ferry terminal. If this occurs, either go elsewhere on the mainland or telephone ahead from the ferry terminal to find accommodations at commercial campgrounds or motels on one of the islands. *Do not travel to the San Juans in summer unless you are sure of overnight lodging.*

A group camp, the Environmental Learning Center, near the south end of Cascade Lake, accommodates large organized parties (by reservation only). This camp can accommodate up to 155 persons; a fee is charged for its use. The ELC has a kitchen, dining hall, restrooms, showers, cabins with bunks, and its own stretch of beach on the lake.

Public areas in the park were completely renovated in 1978, ensuring a pleasant stay for park visitors. Campsites were leveled, new stoves and picnic tables were installed, water, sewer, and wiring systems were improved, and the rustic log buildings were refurbished.

BICYCLES IN THE PARK

Moran State Park is popular with bicyclists, and although the steep Mt. Constitution road would severely tax someone who's out of shape, many cyclists do make the trip to the top (some cheat a bit by having a truck tote the cycles to the summit). Brakes must be in good condition for the downhill run. Drinking water is available at Cascade Lake, Mountain Lake Landing, and the summit. Bicycles are permitted only on the Pickett Road and Southeast Boundary trails; all other trails are restricted to foot use.

PARK WILDLIFE

Over twenty different mammals and a hundred species of birds are found in the state park. On occasion rabbits, wild turkeys (which have been

Deer at Moran State Park

introduced), or raccoons can be seen near the roads, campgrounds, and along the lake shore. Shy black-tailed deer frequently cross roads—drive carefully to avoid hitting them.

For the best wildlife viewing take the trails and walk quietly, watching and listening for telltale movement, the chattering of squirrels, and the calls of birds. There are no bears or poisonous snakes. Lakeshore trails are excellent places to spot river otter, muskrat, and mink, especially in late evening. Watch for burrows, tunnels, and otter slides at the water's edge.

For the safety of wildlife and the convenience of other park visitors, pets must be on a leash no longer than 8 feet, and under control at all times while in the park, *including in the backcountry*. Pets illegally unleashed on trails have killed fawns and other wild animals. The best idea is to leave your pet at home and improve the outdoor experience for everyone.

HIKING TRAILS

Over 30 miles of trails lace Moran State Park. Most are enclosed by forest, but at times the timber opens and rocky, moss-covered bluffs protrude to give superb views north, west, or south—Matia, Barnes, Clark, Lummi, Cypress, Blakely, and Lopez islands lie below, and on clear days, the snowy mass of Mt. Baker rises above and beyond. All of the trails in the park are described in this chapter. Most are described the easy way—beginning at the top and hiking downhill. Many variations are possible, with side trails leading to alternate destinations. One nice advantage of trails in the park is that groups of hikers with varied stamina, such as families with several children, can hike together for a distance, then some can choose an easy exit back to civilization, while those with more endurance can continue on a more demanding route.

Trail maintenance at Moran State Park is done as crews are available from state and federally funded youth corps. Maintenance is sporadic on the less popular trails. In marshy areas, brush and nettles may overgrow the path and in some spots downed timber may be encountered. Severe winter storms in 1990 caused major trail damage. Before hiking the more remote trail segments check with park rangers.

Many trips are one-way, beginning at one point on the road and emerging farther along. Hikers who do not wish to retrace their route may be able to arrange transportation with a friend. The lower park road between the two park entrances also serves as a main Orcas Island county road, connecting Eastsound with Olga and Doe Bay. Traffic on the county road travels fast, even during busy summer times; use great care when walking alongside the road or crossing it.

Overnight camping is not permitted anywhere in the park except at established campgrounds. On long hikes carry water as there is no safe drinking water on any of the trails; stream and lake water may contain harmful bacteria. When nettles and brush beating are anticipated, wear long pants and carry a stick to push vegetation aside.

Fire hazard can be extreme, especially in open meadows; be sure all cigarettes are properly extinguished, don't smoke while moving on trails, and don't toss cigarettes from cars. During periods of severe fire danger the park may prohibit all open fires, and cooking in campgrounds is restricted to barbecues or campstoves.

Cascade Lake

Usually the busiest place in Moran State Park, Cascade Lake boasts the park's three largest campgrounds (North End, Midway, and South End) and a day-use recreation center. All the campgrounds have spacious, level campsites with fire grates and picnic tables. Restrooms and water faucets are centrally located; Midway and North End campgrounds have showers.

North End Campground, with 52 campsites, is ¼ mile inside the park's west entrance on a rise above the road and lake. Just beyond the campground is the park registration booth, manned during periods when reservations are accepted. At other times campers must self-register at Midway Campground.

A few hundred feet down the road from North End Campground, facing on Cascade Lake, are the picnic area and recreation center where there are picnic tables, children's play equipment, and rustic picnic shelters with stoves. A beach with roped-off sections for wading and swimming has a float and diving board, although there are no lifeguards. On hot summer days the swimming area is crowded, and parking in the vicinity is difficult.

Rowboats and foot-operated paddle boats are available for rent at Cascade Lake in the summer. Private boats may be launched at a ramp at lower Midway Campground—only electric motors are permitted. Visitors usually enjoy an exploratory paddle of the lake, peeking into tiny bays and gazing up at the heights of surrounding cliffs. Trout fishing is popular, either from boat or shore; the bridge across Rosario Lagoon, reached by trail from either end of Cascade Lake, is sometimes a successful spot. The lake is stocked with rainbows, cutthroats, and silvers every June. Observe state Department of Wildlife regulations on licenses, season, and limits.

Midway Campground, ¾ mile farther south along the lakeshore, has 49 campsites lining both sides of the road, with some along the lake shore. Smaller South End Campground, located on a spur road around the far end of the lake, has 17 campsites, some of them walk-ins for bicyclists and backpackers.

A primitive camp area with 15 informal sites for bicycle and walk-in camping is located away from the lake on the north side of the Mt. Constitution road, ⅛ mile east of the county road intersection. This campground has no drinking water, and has only pit toilets.

FOREST RECOVERY DISPLAY

On January 24, 1972, a violent storm with winds up to 100 mph wracked the San Juan Islands. At Moran State Park hundreds of trees were downed, some of them century-old patriarchs. Park personnel spent months in clean-up and repair of facilities and trails. Near Cascade Lake a 200-foot, 200-year-old Western red cedar toppled by the winds has been left undisturbed as a reminder of the storm and an illustration of forest recovery.

Find the interpretive exhibit behind the registration booth and north of a large picnic shelter. A billboard display describes the storm. The giant

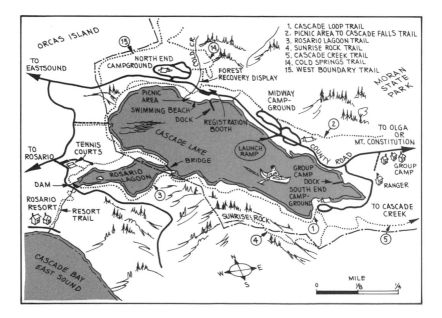

Cascade Lake

tree is a progressive exhibit; visit it from time to time over the years to witness how nature, the original "ecological recycler," reclaims its own products.

CASCADE LOOP TRAIL

This nearly level hike with ever-changing perspectives of the lake and mountain is enjoyable whether done only in part or walked as a 2½-mile trail and road circuit. The trail circles the southwest side of the lake on a bank 30 feet above the water, with very few accesses to the lake itself.

Begin the hike west of the picnic area at Cascade Lake, passing through a marshy area bordered by a picturesque split-rail fence. The trail splits, one path high and one low, then reconnects and wanders along a rocky bluff where weathered Douglas firs frame the lake views and droop low over the water. At a fork in a few hundred yards a spur heads west to the Rosario Resort road. At another fork less than ½ mile beyond, the right-hand trail, described in the following section, goes out of the park along the edge of Rosario Lagoon.

Another 300 yards down the lakeshore a rustic log bridge spans the mouth of the lagoon. Farther south along the lake are good views of the mountain summit. Belted kingfishers and shy, long-legged great blue herons may be spotted along the shore; watch also for signs of muskrat and otter. Muskrat burrows, which resemble those of beaver, can be seen in the water. A large snail found in abundance along the shores of Cascade Lake is a dietary staple for these muskrats—look for piles of empty shells.

South End Campground is reached 1½ miles from the trailhead. Follow the road past the group camp and service buildings to the junction with the paved county road. Turn left (west) and walk the shoulder of the road back to the picnic area. In the future a trail on the hillside above the road will eliminate the need for walking in traffic. Total distance around the lake is 2½ miles, with an elevation gain of 50 feet.

For a slightly longer loop hike, pick up the Cascade Creek trail by campsite 17 of South End Campground and follow it for about ¾ mile until it emerges at the county road. Cross the road and catch the trail that continues uphill for an additional ¼ mile to Cascade Falls. A left-hand fork leads to the Cascade Falls parking area.

At the parking area, cross the Mt. Constitution road and pick up the east end of the Picnic Area to Cascade Falls trail as it heads west, traverses a steep sidehill past the primitive camping area, and continues on to upper Midway Campground. From here the trail proceeds west to reach the road near the registration booth opposite the picnic area. Total round-trip distance of this hike, including the trail around the lake, is about 4 miles.

ROSARIO LAGOON

Detour from the Cascade Lake loop onto a path by a quiet arm of the lake. Most of the lagoon lies outside the park boundary; the trail, sometimes used by fishermen, is unmaintained, but easy to follow. Hike the Cascade Lake trail around the north end of the lake to an unmarked trail fork ¾ mile from the picnic area. Rosario Lagoon can be seen through the trees on the right.

The right-hand fork of the trail leads out of the park along the north edge of the lagoon. The quiet water is a popular stopover for migratory waterfowl; mergansers, goldeneyes, buffleheads, and ring-necked ducks are but a few of the many colorful birds that call at the lagoon in fall, winter, and spring.

As the trail nears the end of the lagoon, a jeep track goes straight ahead, terminating in a parking lot north of the Rosario Resort tennis courts. Continue left along the shore to a large concrete dam, ¼ mile from the Cascade Lake trail intersection. Many years ago Cascade Lake was only a large marshy area. Before the turn of the century the dam that created the lake was built to provide hydroelectric power for Rosario, below.

At the dam the trail reaches a paved road; walk down the road to the east side of the dam. On the right a trail can be seen dropping down the steep slope to Rosario before paralleling a steel aqueduct. A small sign on the left of the road points to the trail that continues around the lagoon back into the park. If the route is lost in the brush at the outlet of the lagoon, follow close to the water's edge until it again becomes clear.

Lake water laps at the hiker's boots; salal and swordfern crowd the trail. The Cascade Lake trail is rejoined at the log bridge. Total distance of the detour loop around the lagoon is about ¾ mile.

SUNRISE ROCK

A short but steep climb leads to views down to the shimmering water of Cascade Lake and across to the lookout tower of Little Summit. In recent years this trail has received little maintenance and may require some route-finding; check with the ranger regarding its condition before attempting it.

Follow the Cascade Creek trail out of South End Campground as previously described. In ¼ mile the Sunrise Rock trail branches right, drops slightly downhill, then begins the climb to the viewpoint, gaining 350 feet in ¼ mile. In cool, virgin forest the trail passes several ancient Douglas firs nearly six feet in diameter showing the ravages of forest fires, lightning, and woodpeckers.

Where the trail becomes sketchy, look for an apparent clearing in the trees around the hill on the right. A mossy ledge provides views of the lake and mountain. Distance from South End Campground to the viewpoint is about ½ mile; total elevation gain is 500 feet.

Cascade Creek

Flowing between Cascade and Mountain lakes, Cascade Creek offers scenic waterfalls, woodland flowers, and perhaps wildlife just a short distance from the road. Even novice hikers can negotiate the easy trails, although they are often muddy; sturdy shoes should be worn. The stream is closed to fishing.

The odd little American dipper or "water ouzel" may be seen here

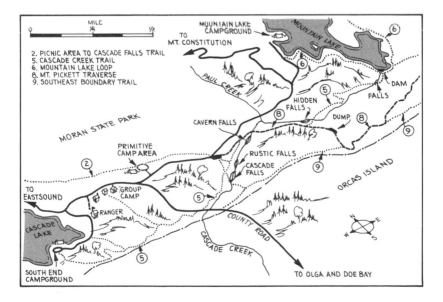

from September through April along the banks of the stream. The plump, slate gray bird, slightly larger than a wren, dives into the swift-flowing water and walks along the creek bottom to catch aquatic insects, invertebrates, and small fish. A unique adaptation—flaps covering its nostrils—enable it to survive underwater.

CASCADE FALLS

A chain of waterfalls on Cascade Creek can be reached by a short spur trail from the road, or may be viewed as part of a longer scenic jaunt from Mountain Lake to Cascade Lake. For the shorter trip, park at the trailhead on the south side of the road, ½ mile from the Olga-Mt. Constitution road intersection. Be careful not to block the service road that goes straight ahead. The trail sign on the right directs hikers first to Rustic Falls; however the unmarked abandoned road to the right of the trail sign can be followed directly to Cascade Falls in ½ mile.

Although the hike is worthwhile any time of the year, the waterfalls are at their best in winter and spring when rainfall swells the lakes and streams. By late summer of a dry year the falls may be reduced to a narrow trickle. At Cascade Falls, the most spectacular of the four, the water fans widely across a 100-foot cliff, dropping into a tiny pool at its base. For a head-on view of the cataract cross the stream on slanting (and slippery) downed logs.

The trail switchbacks to the top of the falls, then levels out in the brushy valley of Cascade Creek, where salal and salmonberry overhang the stream. In spring you may find mushrooms and wildflowers along the trail, but by summer dense patches of nettles discourage off-trail wandering.

The upper falls are much smaller than Cascade Falls, but lovely nonetheless. Rustic Falls is about 500 feet from Cascade Falls, and ¼ mile farther is the narrow plume of Cavern Falls. Just beyond Cavern Falls, the trail merges with the dirt service road; continue on for ¼ mile to Hidden Falls, located below the footbridge at the Mountain Lake trail intersection.

The service road can be followed back to the parking area on the return trip. Total distance of the loop hike is slightly over 1 mile; elevation gain, 200 feet.

CASCADE CREEK TRAIL

For the longer hike from Mountain Lake to Cascade Lake, find the signed trailhead at Mountain Lake Landing, across from the ranger's cabin. The path heads south along the lakeshore and passes a spur trail from Mountain Lake Road.

The concrete dam at the lake outlet is reached ½ mile from the trailhead; drop down the side of the dam to the wooden footbridge crossing Cascade Creek and turn right at a signed trail intersection at the end of the bridge. Downstream 200 yards is a pretty spot where the water cascades in foamy white rivulets and an unusual L-shaped bridge crosses the creek.

From here the trail occasionally leaves the creek for short distances only to switchback steeply down the drainage and rejoin the creek. At a third bridge at Hidden Falls, 1½ miles from Mountain Lake Landing, the Mt. Pickett service road is joined, then is abandoned again in another ½ mile where the main trail branches left.

Pause to enjoy scenic Cavern, Rustic, and Cascade falls tumbling down the slope. Sections of an old wooden aqueduct still in evidence at spots along the trail are part of the park's original water system. The route crosses the county road near the south park entrance, 2 miles' trail distance from Mountain Lake Landing. Find the continuation of the trail, which may be unsigned, slightly up the road to the west.

Cascade Creek heads south out of the park, paralleling the county road, but the trail continues west through a timbered flat, passing giant century-old Douglas firs. Walk quietly and watch for Douglas squirrels, pileated woodpeckers, and black-tailed deer in the open forest.

Avoid an unmarked spur trail to the right leading to the group camp and continue on the left fork through brush and, in spring, colorful displays of wildflowers. A short distance before reaching the lake signs at another trail intersection point left to Sunrise Rock, straight ahead to the Around-the-Lake trail, and right to South End Campground. By taking the right-hand spur the inviting blue water of Cascade Lake can soon be seen, and shortly the campground is reached, 2¾ miles from the start and 550 feet of elevation loss.

Energetic hikers may wish to extend the hike by continuing straight ahead at the last intersection and following the trail on the south side of Cascade Lake, arriving at the picnic area at the north end of the lake in another 1½ miles.

Mountain Lake Landing

Lying a bit off the main thoroughfare, Mountain Lake does not receive as much tourist attention as does popular Cascade Lake. It therefore offers more solitude to those who are willing to leave their cars to enjoy its crystal waters and level, tree-cloaked shoreline.

To reach the lake, drive east in the park on the county road to the Olga-Mt. Constitution road intersection. Continue toward Mt. Constitution, and 2 miles from the intersection a right-hand fork is signed to Mountain Lake Landing. The road ends in ½ mile at a small parking lot. A vehicle-accessible campground with 7 campsites lies in a hollow immediately west of the parking area; 11 additional walk-in sites are a short distance from the road on a small peninsula overlooking the lake.

The long lake fills a narrow green valley trough between Mt. Pickett and Mt. Constitution. Rainbow, cutthroat, silver, and Eastern brook trout stocked in the lake each spring make this a popular fishing spot. The best fishing is from boats; they may be rented at a boat dock below the parking area. Or bring your own for fishing—or just for a tranquil paddle and magnificent views of Mt. Constitution. Launch boats on the north side of the peninsula at Mountain Lake Campground; gasoline motors are not permit-

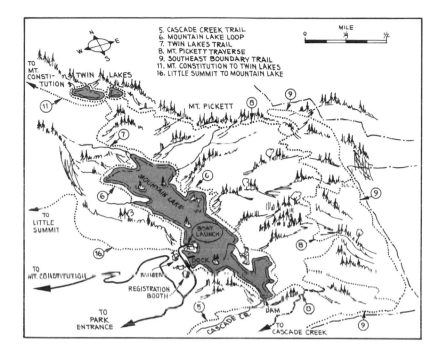

ted. Pack a lunch and go ashore on one of four miniature islands in the lake to spend some time with your thoughts.

MOUNTAIN LAKE LOOP

A nearly level hike circles the shore of Mountain Lake, highlighted by a unique view of the summit of Mt. Constitution. A counterclockwise route around the lake is recommended so the prime views of the mountain lie ahead rather than at the hiker's back.

The trail begins south of Mountain Lake Campground, contours the lakeside, and in ½ mile crosses the outlet of the lake on a bridge below a concrete dam. Just beyond the dam a right-hand fork of the trail turns down Cascade Creek, while the main trail continues straight ahead along the shore. Avoid a spur branching to the right a few hundred feet east of the dam that joins the Mt. Pickett trail.

The long summit ridge of Mt. Constitution rises above the lake. Little Summit can be seen on the left and the stone observation tower of the main summit far on the right. Below the summit precipitous 1,000-foot cliffs show their dramatic profile.

Look for bald and golden eagles, hawks, and osprey soaring in the updrafts near the mountain. Four pairs of osprey are believed to nest in the vicinity, although others summer here. The same factors of population, pollution, and pesticides that threaten bald eagles have severely reduced

Mountain Lake

the osprey population. In addition, bald eagles frequently steal fish they
have caught and generally harass them, at times causing them to leave.
Ospreys, which resemble small white-breasted eagles, favor the heights of
Mt. Constitution, with its remote nesting sites and fish-filled lakes.

At the north end of Mountain Lake, 2¼ miles from the trailhead, a
trail branch goes right to Twin Lakes. Continue along the lakeshore, with
views across the lake to wooded Mt. Pickett, named for the commander of
U.S. forces in the San Juans during the "Pig War" boundary dispute of
1859 to 1872.

Trail's end is reached at the parking lot at Mountain Lake Landing,
1¼ miles from the Twin Lakes trail intersection. Total distance of the trip
is 3½ miles. The only appreciable elevation gain of the hike is midway
around the lake where the trail climbs 50 feet above the water to skirt a
rocky cliff.

TWIN LAKES

Tucked away on a timbered shoulder of Mt. Constitution, a pair of
small lakes are the destination for one of the park's most pleasant hikes.
During fishing season anglers will want to take along a fly rod to try for
rainbow and cutthroat trout in the chilly spring-fed waters of the larger of
the two lakes. The smaller lake is not stocked, and the stream joining the
two lakes is too small for trout.

This trail and its continuation from Twin Lakes to the summit of Mt.

Constitution have been designated as the Bonnie Sliger Memorial Trail to honor a young woman who died in 1977 in a tragic fall at Doe Bay. She was a popular Youth Conservation Corps supervisor who had spent much time working with youngsters on trail maintenance in the park.

From the trailhead by the ranger's cabin north of Mountain Lake Campground, the wide level path meanders along the lakeshore for 1¼ miles to the north end of the lake.

Leave the lake at a signed trail junction, following the Twin Lakes trail along a brook. In a stand of alder are scattered remnants of an ancient log cabin, possibly built by Civil War draft dodgers who are said to have lived in the area. Big Twin Lake is reached just short of a mile from the trail intersection. Total distance from Mountain Lake Landing to Big Twin Lake is 2½ miles; elevation gain is 200 feet.

Trails circle the shores of both lakes. The edges of the lakes are fairly overgrown with trees to the waterline, with only a few spots where the lakeshore itself is easily accessible. Breaks in the enclosing timber permit glimpses of the summit of Mt. Constitution. Distance around Big Twin Lake is about ½ mile, slightly less around Little Twin Lake.

MT. PICKETT TRAVERSE

A long trek combining a trail and an abandoned road may be used as part of an ambitious around-the-park excursion. Check with park rangers for information on current trail conditions.

Begin the hike at the Cascade Falls pull-out on the Mt. Constitution road, ½ mile east of the Olga road intersection. Follow the dirt service road east past Hidden Falls and the intersection of the trail to Mountain Lake. The road first climbs gradually but steadily, then levels a bit at a flat near Mountain Lake, where a spur heads left to the Mountain Lake trail. Here the road begins to climb again in earnest, switchbacking up a steep arm of the mountain. Tall second-growth timber limits views to a few tantalizing glimpses between the trees of distant blue water.

The road again levels somewhat at 1600-feet elevation, and near a large marsh on the left a spur of the Southeast Boundary trail heads right (east). The road continues steeply upward through dense stands of pine. At a switchback just below the summit the trailhead for the Southeast Boundary trail branches to the east.

The 1,750-foot summit of Mt. Pickett is finally reached 3½ miles from its start at the Cascade Falls trailhead. Now the road continues steadily downhill to the northwest for another mile before narrowing into a footpath. The trail continues for ½ mile farther to the shore of Little Twin Lake.

The nature of the forest changes dramatically upon crossing the Mt. Pickett summit. The south slope consists mainly of second-growth fir and cedar with typical Cascades-type underbrush. North of the summit a verdant carpet of moss coats the open ground between huge trunks of towering old-growth cedar, with stands of alder around marshy areas.

Total distance from Cascade Falls to Twin Lakes is 5 miles; elevation

Foxglove along the Mt. Pickett trail

gain from the falls to the summit is 1,250 feet, with 650 feet lost on the descent to Twin Lakes. From Twin Lakes hikers may return to the road via the short but very steep trail to the summit of Mt. Constitution (1½ miles), or the gentle but somewhat longer Mountain Lake trail (2¼ miles). For those who prefer downhill to uphill, hike the trail in the reverse direction, starting at either Mountain Lake or the summit of Mt. Constitution.

SOUTHEAST BOUNDARY TRAIL

One of the longest and most strenuous trails in the park lay overgrown for years. It was originally built during the 1930s by the CCC, but after many years of disuse was reclaimed by trail crews in 1987.

The upper trailhead for the Southeast Boundary trail heads east from the Mt. Pickett trail at a switchback a hundred yards south of the top of Mt. Pickett, as described previously. The path swings around the east side of the mountain summit, dropping through a forest of open old-growth cedar.

In ½ mile the route swings to the southeast and begins a long traverse south, descending gradually at first then more abruptly as it crosses steep sidehills supporting thick stands of Western hemlock. Splendid views north and east at a few outcroppings reveal a scattering of islands below and Mt. Baker towering in the distance.

In a clearing at the head of a drainage, 1¾ miles from the trailhead, the trail meets a short spur descending from the Mt. Pickett road. This spur leaves the Mt. Pickett road near a large marsh on the lower shoulder south of the summit, and then picks its way down a precipitous hillside to join the main Southeast Boundary trail. Total length of the spur trail is ½ mile; elevation difference, 600 feet.

From this junction the Southeast Boundary trail continues south, through a series of ups and downs (mainly downs) to arrive at the park's southeast boundary, 1¼ miles from the spur trail intersection. Here is a choice, as the trail offers two forks—unfortunately both climb relentlessly uphill. The right hand fork ascends 550 feet in a little over a mile to join the Mt. Pickett road a hundred yards uphill from its intersection with the Mountain Lake spur trail.

The left fork climbs westward along the southern boundary of the park. At 1¾ miles from the trail fork a junction is reached with a path leading north to the Cascade Falls parking area. In another ¼ mile the trail reaches its southern terminus at the county road at the park's east boundary.

Total distance of the longest trail choice is 5 miles, not including the 3½ mile hike up the Mt. Pickett trail to reach the Southeast Boundary trailhead. Elevation difference is 1,300 feet, with much more elevation gained and lost en route.

Mt. Constitution

Rising nearly half a mile above the surrounding sea, Mt. Constitution is a dramatic landmark recognizable from many points throughout the San Juan Islands. The expansive view from the summit and the fascinating old stone tower make Mt. Constitution the culmination of most tourists' visit to the San Juans.

The U.S. Exploration Expedition of 1838-1842, commanded by Charles Wilkes, named the mountain after the famous American frigate. In a fit of patriotism Wilkes chose to name all of the San Juan Islands "the Navy Archipelago," and began flinging names commemorating the officers and ships of the War of 1812 at every bit of land and water in sight. It may have been that he was unaware of the Spanish and British names already given to many of the landmarks, or (more likely) he felt American names were more suitable, since the U.S. was attempting to establish its claim in this region.

In Wilkes's scheme, Lopez and Orcas islands were named Chauncy and Hull islands in honor of two U.S. Navy commodores. East Sound was designated as Old Ironside Inlet after the ship Hull commanded, and West Sound was Guerrier Bay, for the British warship that Hull defeated.

Five years later British Captain Henry Kellett in his surveying expedition restored many of the original Spanish and British names. A number of Wilkes's names were retained, however, including Blakely, Decatur, James, Jones, Frost, Shaw, Clark, and Watmough (all honoring U.S. naval officers)—and also, of course, Mt. Constitution. Old Ironside inlet, fortunately, did not persist.

From October to April the road to the top of the mountain is gated at the Olga road intersection at 5 p.m., except during fishing season, when it is blocked above Mountain Lake, allowing early-morning access to the lake for anglers. From June through August the road is kept open until 10 p.m. to accommodate late-day hikers and tourists who stay on the mountain to enjoy spectacular sunsets from the summit.

The Mt. Constitution road leaves the county road 1¼ miles east of the main park entrance; in another mile it begins the upward climb to the top of the mountain. Narrow, with steep switchbacks and hairpin curves, it is not recommended for trailers, buses, or large mobile homes. Halfway up, at the end of a switchback, is a small pull-out space with dramatic views down to Cascade Lake, the twin summits of Entrance Mountain, East Sound, and Spencer Spit on Lopez Island.

At Little Summit the road levels out and traverses the long plateau leading to the true summit. Total distance from the park entrance to the summit parking lot is 6 miles. Buildings and radio towers just below the observation tower are relay facilities for KVOS-TV, Bellingham.

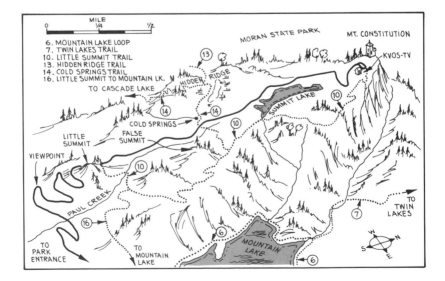

Osprey (photo by Bob and Ira Spring)

LITTLE SUMMIT

Views rivaling those from the observation tower on the higher main summit look down to Cascade Lake and Rosario Resort and out to the symmetrical humps of Entrance Mountain. Beyond are Shaw, San Juan, and Lopez islands, and in the far distance, above the Strait of Juan de Fuca, the white peaks of the Olympic Mountains.

As the Mt. Constitution road completes its last switchback and reaches the summit plateau, a pull-off on the east side of the road provides parking space for a few cars. Walk 500 feet up the trail to an open viewpoint.

A latrine and a few picnic tables are situated in the adjacent meadow. Rest on the stone and log bench and enjoy the scene, or wander across the open slopes for ever-widening perspectives—lovely even on foggy days when mists swirl around the islands, encompassing, then suddenly revealing bits of the marine view.

SUMMIT LAKE

This long, marshy lake near the mountain's main summit is only about 10 feet deep at its maximum. During winter it sometimes freezes over and islanders go ice-skating here. There is only enough space to park

View from Mt. Constitution northeast to Clark and Barnes islands

two or three cars along the road where it meets the lake; be careful not to block or obstruct the vision of drivers.

Drop a canoe or inflatable boat into the water to commune with the frogs and explore the half-mile-long lake, or drift quietly and watch for eagles, hawks, and waterfowl. There are no fish. The marshy shoreline makes hiking around the lake impossible.

SUMMIT OBSERVATION TOWER

Perched atop the hard-rock, 2,407-foot summit of Mt. Constitution, the stone lookout tower is one of the most unusual and interesting features of Moran State Park. Children especially delight in climbing the many flights of stairs inside the tower, exploring the cell-like rooms, peering out the narrow window slits barred with wrought iron, and firing imaginary crossbows at imaginary armored knights (or laser guns at alien intruders) in the forest below.

Originally designed as both a fire lookout and public observation tower, the 50-foot-high structure is a facsimile of military fortifications built by mountain tribes in the Caucasus Mountains of Russia during the twelfth century. Orcas Island quarries supplied the sandstone blocks for the CCC crews that erected the tower in 1936. A display just inside the tower tells of its history.

From the top, the highest point in the San Juan Islands, views spread in all directions; displays identify visible landmarks. Look down to Twin and Mountain lakes shimmering below, surrounded by dense green forest. Look out in all directions to the array of green and brown islands scattered in the azure fabric of the sound. Especially striking is the stratified geological pattern of the northern San Juans and Canadian Gulf Islands. Toylike boats dot the water, their silver wakes leaving long streaks on the smooth surface. To the east massive Mt. Baker looms, and to the south, through the smog of civilization, Mt. Rainier.

From the viewing area at the base of the tower peer over the stone railing for an added thrill—a dizzying view straight down the precipitous 1,000-foot face of the mountain.

LITTLE SUMMIT TRAIL

Hike from north to south along the mountain rim, looking downward into lakes and forest, outward to islands and sea—but take time to enjoy the quiet forest, too. The character of the vegetation changes rapidly as the trail traverses the gradually sloping summit plateau. It is thought the abrupt changes in the timber are caused by localized variations in the depth and permeability of the soil.

At one time a number of small ponds dotted the summit; many of these filled in with organic material and are now meadows. Hemlock and fir edge these former marshes, sustained by water seeping in the soft peat. In areas where sandy soil covers the hard summit rock, crowded stands of lodgepole pine with shallow root systems grow, but most only reach fifteen feet in height and two to three inches in diameter. Thickets of manzanita growing in the loose sandy soil attract birds who dine on their tiny apple-like fruit.

Near the brow of the plateau where dirt lodges in the spaces between rock outcroppings, mountain hemlock and Rocky Mountain juniper with tenacious roots grow. Strong winds buffeting the face of the mountain twist these trees into beautiful Japanese "bonsai" shapes. In the valley of Paul Creek near Little Summit, moistness creates another forest type   the soaring big-trunked timber of Western red cedar and Western hemlock.

The signed trail departs from the top of the mountain behind the KVOS-TV buildings. Watch the route carefully at the beginning as there are several confusing side trails. After two downhill switchbacks and a short traverse, a spur trail leads to an open rock with limited views to the south. The main trail descends steeply to a larger moss-covered rock, ¼ mile from the start, with a 180-degree outlook encompassing the nearby summit cliffs and the distant shores of the mainland.

From vantage points such as this look for eagles and osprey circling on updrafts, and swallows and flocks of swifts performing high-speed aerial acrobatics. Common nighthawks, who dart about at dusk capturing night-flying insects, nest in thickets along the top of the summit.

Views change as the route edges along the brow of the summit. The final open vista is southeast down to Mountain Lake, then the route turns west into the forest. At about ¾ mile the trail crosses a trickling stream on a crude log bridge—the dam at the outlet of Summit Lake can be seen through the trees on the right. The Cold Springs trail intersects in another ¼ mile, 1 mile from the summit trailhead.

Continuing southeast toward Little Summit, the trail passes east of False Summit, barely noticeable through the trees, and then descends for

Summit tower, Mt. Constitution

some distance to a grassy knoll with an eagle's eye view down to Mountain Lake. Here the lowest point of the trail is reached, some 400 feet below the summit.

The trail continues on, traversing a sidehill and climbing slightly. In ¼ mile watch carefully for another trail intersection that is signed, but easily could be missed. The trail to the left heads downhill above the gully of Paul Creek, following the path of an old telephone line through heavy timber to emerge at the kitchen shelter at Mountain Lake Campground. The desired route to Little Summit turns right sharply at the intersection, contouring the slope.

The path, almost a road now, crosses Paul Creek and in a short distance reaches Little Summit, 2¼ miles from the trailhead, 400-feet elevation loss.

MT. CONSTITUTION TO TWIN LAKES

One of the steepest trails in the park, losing over 1,000 feet in a mile, but what scenery! Leave the hoards of car-bound tourists at the summit for challenging trails and rugged vistas.

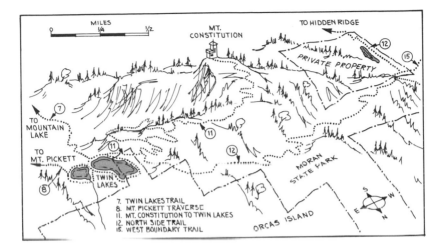

Find the signed trail on the north side of the turn-around loop at the summit. After a few switchbacks it crosses a wooded flat and zigzags down again to an opening at the end of a switchback looking north to Matia Island and Canada. The trail now turns eastward, traversing a saddle. Occasional glimpses through the trees reveal the craggy face of Mt. Constitution looming above.

At ¾ mile a short side trail on the right leads to an east-oriented rock outcropping, with the long outlines of Barnes and Clark islands seen just below, Lummi Island farther in the distance, and Mt. Baker on the horizon. Another ¼ mile down the main route a second spur trail leads right to the last viewpoint, the best one of all. These two spurs are actually the ends of a short overgrown side loop south of the present main trail. There is space here to rest and picnic, enjoying the wide views east and south—Mountain Lake, Obstruction Pass at the tip of Orcas Island, the mid-channel hump of Obstruction Island, thickly forested Blakely Island beyond, and to the far right an impressive view upward of the vertical summit cliffs.

More switchbacks—now reaching a gully with a signed trail junction with the North Side trail. Take the fork on the right, arriving at Big Twin Lake in another 500 yards. Total distance from the summit 1½ miles; elevation loss, 1,240 feet.

NORTH SIDE TRAIL

Swing wide around the north flank of Mt. Constitution through cool forest, past marshes and ponds. Views are few, but majestic eagles and hawks may frequently be seen in this oft-ignored section of the park. The trail is not heavily used and not regularly maintained; route finding in brushy areas may pose a problem.

Forest scene on Moran State Park trail

Begin the hike on the Twin Lakes trail from the top of the mountain. At the trail junction 1¼ miles below the summit turn left onto the trail signed to Cold Springs. The route heads northwest through open second growth, maintaining a gradual but steady ascent; as it swings over a ridgeline and heads west watch for an impressive grove of cedar below, along a stream bed. The trail then switchbacks uphill, occasionally obscured by growths of short fir.

Just beyond a marsh on the right the trail is clear again and a long traverse begins. Suddenly, an incongruous sight beside the trail—a deteriorating park bench of hewn logs. Perhaps Robin Hood and his men gather here to plot their next foray against the Sheriff of Nottingham!

The trail slowly climbs, traversing steep slopes covered by open stands of tall hemlock, and 2 miles from the Mt. Constitution/Twin Lakes intersection crosses a rough jeep road that can be followed downhill (for no particular reason) to the park boundary; private property lies beyond.

The trail continues its traverse and in 300 yards crosses a power line right of way that is the north end of the West Boundary trail. At this point the trail turns south along the edge of a section of private property lying within the park boundary. Beyond a lake and marsh the trail takes a short switchback up a rise. At a concrete post marking the corner of the private land the route turns southeast along the crest of Hidden Ridge.

The way is virtually flat now, through alder, fir, and sword fern, to the intersection 4 miles from the starting point. The right-hand fork switchbacks steeply down to Cascade Lake. Bear left here, continuing along the level plateau of Hidden Ridge to Cold Springs and the road.

Total distance is 4¾ miles. Elevation loss from the summit to the Twin Lakes trail intersection is 1,000 feet; elevation gain from that intersection to Cold Springs is 650 feet. For a mostly downhill trip, reverse the route, starting at Cold Springs; at the lower intersection continue downhill

to Twin Lakes and then on to Mountain Lake Landing. Total distance is
5½ miles; 1,130-foot elevation loss.

Cold Springs and Hidden Ridge

An isolated picnic area in open forest is reached by driving 3¾ miles
up the mountain from the Olga-Mt. Constitution road intersection to a gate
at an old service road. There is parking space for a couple of cars at the
gate and along the roadside. Just inside the barrier is a rustic shelter with
picnic tables and a stove, and downhill south of the shelter a log-and-cedar-
shake gazebo protects what was once Cold Springs. At one time this area
was a campground, but it has been closed to overnight use for some time.
The old-fashioned hand pump that supplied spring water was so frequently
vandalized that park rangers gave up efforts to keep it operational and
capped the spring. Picnickers must now supply their own water.

West of Cold Springs a trail wanders out to Hidden Ridge through a
cool marsh with cedar, hemlock, deciduous alder, and maple. Ferns
thickly cover the forest floor, and in season trilliums, skunk cabbage, and
marsh marigolds brighten the green carpet with their blossoms. Several
ponds along the way are nearly dry in summer, but during the wet season
they offer sanctuary for migrating waterfowl. In the forest look for varied
thrush and several species of warblers.

The trail is broad and gentle for nearly a mile as it meanders the length
of Hidden Ridge. It continues on to join the North Side trail.

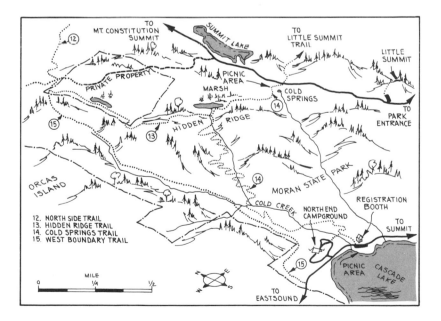

COLD CREEK TRAIL

Zigzag downhill, crossing and recrossing the branches of Cold Creek—or for a real workout begin at Cascade Lake and hike uphill, gaining 1,700 feet of elevation in 2 miles.

For the downhill route, find the trailhead by the Cold Springs shelter on the south side of the picnic area. Hike west through the swampy flat to a trail intersection in ½ mile; bear left on the trail signed to Cascade Lake.

As the steep descent begins, the vegetation immediately changes from wetland to dry, open forest. Curious squirrels edge headfirst down trees, circling out of sight around the trunk when hikers approach.

An open moss-covered bluff ½ mile from the trail intersection is a good place to rest, snack, and enjoy the view of Cascade Lake, Rosario Resort, and points beyond. Aside from occasional glimpses of scenery through the trees while on the trail, this is the only viewpoint along the route.

Pump house at Cold Springs

In about 1¼ miles the two branches of Cold Creek are crossed on log bridges. A traverse begins and the trailside growth changes from open forest to tangled vine maple, berry bushes, and nettles. At the end of the final switchback, just below the North End Campground, the creek cascades prettily over water-worn boulders overhung by ferns. Cold Creek is a natural spawning ground for native trout; fishing is not permitted.

Cascade Lake recreation center is reached 2¾ miles from the Cold Creek trailhead; elevation loss, 1,700 feet.

WEST BOUNDARY TRAIL

This is not really a trail per se, but a jeep road along the power line going up to the radio towers at the summit of Mt. Constitution. Since the West Boundary trail is extremely steep throughout its entire length, with little in the way of scenery except glimpses northwest through trees on top of the steep cliffs forming the western bastion of the mountain, its primary appeal is to hard-core hikers seeking a remote wilderness experience.

The upper end of the trail starts at its intersection with the North Side trail 1¾ miles north of Cold Springs. The power line drops briefly to the west, then heads south near the top of a 600-foot-high cliff. In ½ mile the head of the west fork of Cold Creek is reached, and the road and power line start an uninterrupted 1 mile drop down the drainage — very steep in places.

In another 1¼ mile the trail heads west, then south another ¼ mile to meet the county road at the northwest park entrance. Total distance from Cold Springs to Cascade Lake is 4½ miles. Elevation loss is 1,700 feet.

Around the Mountain

Although Moran State Park's trails were designed for day hikes, and backcountry camping restrictions preclude tenting by the trail, a determined hiker can complete a circuit of the park by planning ahead to stay in one of the established campgrounds where the trail meets the road. In summer make reservations in advance for campsites, and check in with the ranger. Remember that dogs must be kept on leash, even in the backcountry, so it might be best to leave your best friend at home.

Two possible routes are listed here, although a number of variations are available. Hikers can choose the shorter, somewhat easier scenic route, or opt for the more challenging, less-traveled outer loop which may involve some brush beating, trail-finding problems, and along with it, more solitude. Either circuit could be completed in one day by a seasoned hiker, with little time taken for sightseeing. Refer to the preceding pages of this chapter for descriptions of specific sections of the trail.

Carry water, and in case of backcountry emergency, a rucksack with the Ten Essentials: extra clothing, sunglasses, first aid kit, extra food, flashlight (and extra cells), map, compass, matches, firestarters, and pocketknife.

Both hikes described here begin and end at the top of the mountain, with overnight stops at South End Campground on Cascade Lake. Cars may not be left overnight at the summit, so it would be necessary to park them at the campground and prearrange transportation up and down the road with a friend, or resort to the expedient of an extended thumb.

Elevation loss via each route on the first day is slightly over 2,000 feet, all of which is regained the following day.

ROUTE A: THE SCENIC CIRCUIT

From the parking lot below the observation tower take the Little Summit trail south and turn right onto the trail spur signed to Cold Springs. Follow the Cold Springs trail along Hidden Ridge to the junction in ½ mile and head downhill to the Cascade Lake recreation center. Cross the road and turn right onto the trail circling the north and west sides of Cascade Lake, finally reaching the South End Campground, the first night's destination. Total day's distance is 5¼ miles.

Begin the second day with a hike along Cascade Creek from Cascade Lake to Mountain Lake, reaching the dam at the Mountain Lake outlet. At the trail intersection turn right along the east side of the lake, and at the north end head up-valley to Twin Lakes. From Twin Lakes climb the trail back to the Mt. Constitution summit. Total day's distance is 5½ miles; total distance of the circuit is 10¾ miles.

ROUTE B: FAR FROM THE MADDING CROWD

Begin the hike on the trail descending to Twin Lakes from the observation tower parking lot. Just before reaching the lakes turn left onto the North Side trail, which is signed to Cold Springs. The route swings around the northwest corner of the park, reaching the intersection with the Hidden Ridge Trail, which eventually joins the Cold Springs trail. From here hike downhill to Cascade Lake, then turn right onto the trail around the north and west shores of the lake, arriving at the night's destination. Total day's distance is 7½ miles.

On the second day take the trail on the west side of the campground signed to Mountain Lake and follow it along Cascade Creek to the point where it joins the dirt service road. Follow the road past Hidden Falls and continue on the service road over the top of Mt. Pickett. Beyond Mt. Pickett the road narrows to a trail as it approaches Twin Lakes. End the day by returning to the main road via the steep trail from Twin Lakes up to the summit. Total day's distance is 7¾ miles; total distance of circuit is 15¼ miles.

Water-carved rocks at Fox Cove, Sucia Island

9. The Northern Boundary

Dotting the sea like scattered gems of a broken necklace, a scenic string of islands—Patos, Sucia, Matia, Clark, Barnes, and their attendant smaller islets and rocks—form the northern boundary of the San Juans. Although early settlers lived on the larger of these islands from time to time, none were ever officially opened for homesteading. In early days, cobblestone for Seattle streets was quarried on Sucia, and later foxes were commercially raised there and on Matia.

During the late 1800s, after the settlement of the boundary dispute with Britain, the U.S. government set aside some of the islands as lighthouse reservations or military reserves for coastal defense. When modern warfare made the concept of fixed coastal defense fortifications obsolete, many of the islands were converted to wildlife sanctuaries and state marine parks. Sucia, made available for private development in the 1950s, was purchased in part by the state and in part by an association of boating clubs under the leadership of Ev G. Henry, and turned over to the State Parks and Recreation Commission for use as a marine park.

These two dozen islands and rocks share a common geological history. Tilted beds of shale and sandstone, believed to have been deposited as a river estuary during the Cretaceous Period, 65 million years ago, were covered by layers of gravelly till from glaciers that twice covered this region in more recent times. Sea animals such as clams, snails, and ammonites that were buried in the sediment of the estuary became the well-known fossils of Fossil Bay. Erosion of the folded beds of alternating hard and soft material accounts for the long parallel ridges enclosing slender bays.

The glacial till provides good support for vegetation, thus the larger islands are thickly covered with trees and brush. One of the most common is the Pacific madrone, with broad evergreen leaves and peeling red bark. Its gracefully twisted trunks overhang many of the islands' shores, picturesquely framing marine views.

Sandstone beds exposed on the edges of the islands have been eroded to fantastic shapes and patterns lovely enough to make a sculptor envious. Caves formed were used by early-day smugglers and today delight beach explorers. The pitted rocks provide nesting areas for a variety of marine birds, such as pelagic cormorants and pigeon guillemots, while seals and

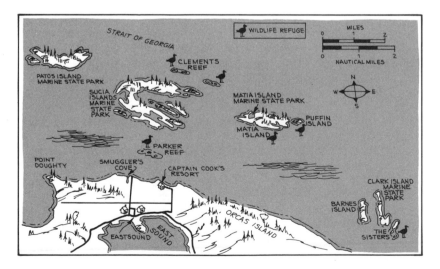

North shoreline of Patos Island; Mt. Baker beyond

sea lions haul out on the smooth, sun-warmed rocks of the more secluded beaches and nearby reefs.

All or part of Patos, Sucia, Matia, and Clark islands are now state parks, with mooring and camping facilities for visiting boaters. Camping is permitted only in designated sites — a stiff fine may result for those who pitch tents in unauthorized areas. There is no garbage collection at Patos and Clark islands; while Sucia and Matia do have receptacles, visitors are encouraged to take their trash with them to ease the problem of garbage disposal.

The marine parks are accessible only by boat. Sucia Island, which generally is the major destination for boaters, lies 2 nautical miles north of the north shore of Orcas Island. Active Cove on Patos Island is 2½ nautical miles northwest of Sucia's Shallow Bay. To the east, Matia lies 2¼ nautical miles from Fossil Bay on Sucia, while Clark is 4 nautical miles farther southeast.

The nearest put-in for small craft is at the resort on the north shore of Orcas Island, where boats also may be rented. Tidal current in the channel can be strong, and rough water may occur near the middle at Parker Reef. In a small or unpowered boat, crossing at slack tide is recommended, with a careful eye to the weather as the crossing can be quite risky when the direction of the wind opposes that of the current. Once Sucia Island is reached, small boats can island hop, timing their open-water adventures for favorable tides. Strong tidal currents and tide rips occur at many points on these passages; kayakers should not attempt these trips unless trained and experienced in open-water paddling.

Patos Island Marine State Park

Island area: 209 acres
Park area: 207½ acres; 23,234 feet of shoreline
Access: Boat
Facilities: 3 campsites, picnic tables, fireplaces, pit toilets, mooring
   buoys, *no water, no garbage collection*
Attractions: Fishing, hiking, beachcombing, tidepools

Patos Island, the northern outpost of the San Juan Islands, commands sweeping views of boundary waters heavily plied by commercial vessels, and Canadian lands. A lighthouse occupies 4 acres of the western tip at Alden Point, while the remainder of the mile-long island is a marine state park. On the eastern end parallel ridges of erosion-resistant rock extend far out into the water, like toes on a foot, hence the name Toe Point. Slightly removed from the boating mainstream and lacking the many protected anchorages of Sucia and Stuart, Patos attracts few boaters, and the beaches are uncrowded.

Patos can be reached only by boat; the nearest launching area is at a resort on the north side of Orcas Island, 5 nautical miles across President Channel. Heavy tide rips occur off Alden Point, along the north side of the island, and around Toe Point.

The east entrance to Active Cove, the only protected harbor on the island, is narrow, shallow, and filled with large rocks, so entry should be made from the west. The deep, narrow cove holds two mooring buoys and has room for a few additional boats to drop anchor. At the head of the cove on a grassy spit are three campsites and a few picnic tables. Pit toilets are nearby.

Eroded sandstone cliffs, 10 to 20 feet high, edge the south side of the island, making beach walking there difficult, except on the rock beach im-

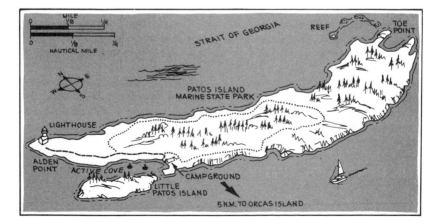

Anchorage in Active Cove

Patos Island Lighthouse

mediately east of Active Cove. In contrast, the north-side beaches are a
true delight. At the west end of the north shore eroded rock beaches offer
tidepools; eastward, gravel beaches separated by small headlands of sandstone and conglomerate stretch along the shore to Toe Point. These north-
side beaches can be walked at all but an extreme high tide, when the
headlands would have to be crossed by short inland scrambles. Watch for
seals fishing the turbulent waters of offshore tide rips.

Beaches on the north side of the island can be reached from a loop
trail that heads east from the campground, along the bluff edge above the
south shore. In ¼ mile the trail turns inland, continuing east through dense
alder, fir, and cedar. The nearly level trail skirts east of the highest point of
Patos (100 feet), then swings north and west, finally emerging to north
beach accesses near mid-island. The trail completes its loop with a short
climb over the west end of the center island rib before reaching an unmarked intersection with an overgrown service road connecting the lighthouse area to the campground at the head of Active Cove. Total trail loop
is about 1¾ miles.

Patos Lighthouse was established in 1893; the present structure was
built fifteen years later. The light is now automated, as are all such navigational warning devices throughout the San Juans. Only a few boarded-up
quarters amid unmown, waist-high grass recall the days when humans
were needed for this duty.

Patos Island is the setting for Helene Glidden's book *The Light on the
Island*. Mrs. Glidden lived here as a child at the turn of the century when
her father was lighthouse keeper; her book is based on her childhood adventures and the early history of the San Juans. The vivid accounts of

smugglers, Indians, visits by Colonel Teddy Roosevelt, rowing to Bellingham in a skiff, and the day-to-day routine on this far outpost give readers insight into early life in the islands. The book is now out of print, but is available in many public libraries.

Eagles seem to have become quite accustomed to visitors at Patos Island, and sometimes can be seen sitting on rocky points as they calmly watch passing boaters. Such apparent acceptance of humans should not be interpreted as domesticity, however. The birds are very susceptible to disturbance during nesting season, and should not be harassed, even in the spirit of curiosity.

Sucia Island Marine State Park

Islands' area: 749 acres
Park area: 564 acres; 72,429 feet of shoreline
Access: Boat
Facilities: 51 campsites, picnic tables, picnic shelters, fireplaces, water, pit toilets, docks with floats, mooring buoys
Attractions: Beachcombing, fossils, clamming, crabbing, swimming, hiking, fishing, scuba diving

Mile-long rocky fingers protecting shallow bays form the group of eleven islands known as the Sucias. Over a twenty-year period, beginning

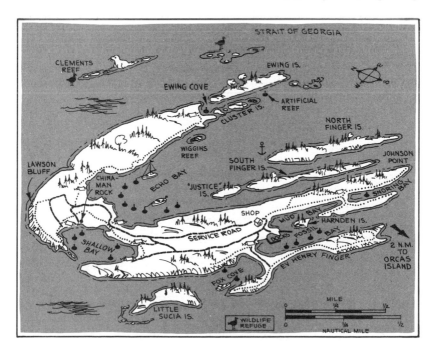

in 1952, portions of the present parkland were purchased by the state for recreational use. During the 1960s, 319 acres were bought by the Puget Sound Interclub Association of boaters and entrusted to the care of the State Parks and Recreation Commission for use as a marine park. All of Sucia Island, Little Sucia, Ewing, and the Cluster Islands are now park property.

The latest park addition consists of two acres on the westernmost of the South Finger Islands. In 1986 the property was turned over to the state after being confiscated by U.S. marshals in 1982 when the owner was convicted of trying to run a drug-smuggling operation there. The island, which some recommend calling "Justice Island," is a nesting area for eagles and pupping ground for seals, so public use is discouraged. The remainder of the Finger Islands in Echo Bay, and tiny Harnden Island, at the mouth of Mud Bay, are privately owned.

With nearly 9 miles of waterfront, 6 bays, and extensive boat and camping accommodations, Sucia Island State Park provides one of the best public marine recreational facilities in the San Juans. Located 2 nautical miles north of Orcas Island, the nearest point where boats can be rented or launched, Sucia is inviting to boaters in vessels ranging from kayak to luxury yacht. Two docks with floats in Fossil Bay and 48 mooring buoys scattered around the island are heavily used by boaters. Small boats can be beached at the head of any of the bays.

Boaters in small craft will need to exercise caution en route, carefully considering the weather and tidal currents. Heavy summer traffic or larger boats can also be a hazard. The trip is recommended only for experienced sea kayakers and canoeists.

During summer, facilities can be very crowded at Sucia, with well over 100,000 visits by boaters annually. Be prepared to anchor if necessary. Buoys and floats are first-come, first-served and the practice of "reserving" a buoy or float space by tying a dinghy to it for the later arrival of a friend or for the return of the mother craft is neither courteous nor legal—it can result in your tender being cast adrift.

Camping areas, connected by trails, are situated around Sucia Island at Fossil Bay, Echo Bay, Shallow Bay, Snoring Bay, and Ewing Cove, for a grand total of 51 sites. Camping is permitted only in designated sites. In the summer, drinking water is available at Fossil Bay, Fox Cove, and Shallow Bay; however, from November through March all water pipes except those at Fossil Bay are shut off to avoid their freezing.

The Spanish name "Sucia" is correctly pronounced *Su-see'-ah*, although few people (even residents), say it that way. The common pronunciation is *Sué-shuh*—not as melodious, but perhaps more logical to an Anglicized tongue. The name, meaning "dirty" or "foul water," was given to the island by early explorers who noted the dangerous rocks and reefs near the shores. Boaters today should take warning from the name and be wary of submerged rocks offshore and in the bays. Deep draft boats should be especially careful that they have enough depth throughout the swing of their anchorage during low tide.

Fossil Bay

Sucia has some of the finest examples of the eroded cliffs that are typical of these northern San Juan Islands. The rocks are sculpted by the chemical action of salt water on sandstone, assisted by the wearing action of wind and waves. Low-level wearing of the beaches here and on many of the other San Juan Islands is limited by tide rips offshore—only at high tide do storm waves reach shore without being broken up by tide rips; beaches at the high tide level demonstrate the cutting action of the waves.

The fierce wave action can occasionally present problems to boaters at Sucia. When a southeaster blows into any of the bays on the southeast side of the island, the anchorages are at best uncomfortable, and possibly dangerous. West-facing Shallow Bay offers the best protection during these conditions. It may be necessary to go elsewhere if it is impossible to secure a safe moorage.

The fashion once was to spray-paint the name of visiting boats on the sandstone cliffs of the island. All this graffiti has been cleaned from the rocks, and the fad hopefully is now past, so that today all visitors can enjoy the natural beauty rather than the ugly scrawls of insensitive yachtsmen.

SUCIA BAYS

Fossil and Mud Bays. Fossil Bay is the hub of park activity, with its floats and buoys filled nearly every night of the summer season. Campsites with water, picnic tables, stoves, and a small picnic shelter can be found in the sparse trees near the docks, while more are nearby on the sandspit between

Chinaman Rock at Shallow Bay

Fossil Bay and Fox Cove and on the finger on the south side of the cove.

Mud Bay, offset from Fossil Bay, nearly empties at low tide; other times the water is just deep enough for dinghying. Harnden Island at the entrance to Mud Bay is private property.

Fox Cove. Across a low sandspit from Fossil Bay, Fox Cove faces westward, sheltered by Little Sucia Island. Worn cliffs on the north side of the bay form marvelous shapes, including an 8-foot-high rock mushroom where children can pretend to be Alice in Wonderland. The sandy beach at the head of the cove is the best on the island for wading and swimming.

Row out to Little Sucia Island from Fox Cove for a private picnic and evening views of blazing sunsets. Currents in the channel between the islands can be strong; use care. Little Sucia is primitive, with no formal trails. The island is an eagle preserve, and fires or overnight camping are not permitted.

Shallow Bay. Indenting the western end of the horseshoe-shaped island, Shallow Bay has three distinct sandy beaches with a campground on each, separated by rocky headlands. Enter the bay with care as submerged rocks extend out from the points at either side of the entrance. Seven buoys and numerous good anchorages attract boaters; however the bay is extremely shallow; check water depth and the predicted tides before settling down for the night.

Shallow Bay offers driftwood, clams, and crabs to beachcombers. Large cockles may be picked up right on the surface at low tide, while other clams hide deeper in the sand. Dungeness crabs lurking in the eelgrass of the cove can be trapped with crab pots in deep water or routed out of the seaweed (carefully) during a minus tide.

Observe size and sex restrictions on Dungeness crabs. Return undersized crabs to the water or to a spot where they can burrow for protection. Crabs left unprotected in the air quickly dry out and die. In any place in the San Juan Islands it is illegal to collect or kill any live marine animal except for food use.

Chinaman Rock, on the northeast side of Shallow Bay, is a striking example of the wave- and chemical-eroded sandstone and subsequent uplifting so characteristic of these northern isles. The rock is mostly obscured by a growth of trees, but can be found by going to the east end of the northmost beach, then walking into the trees at the edge of the cliff.

Body-sized hollows have been obviously geologically uplifted at least 30 feet since they were formed. Legend is that during the late 1800s Chinese aliens smuggled into the U.S. from Canada often hid in the recesses from patrolling immigration officials. Do not scratch names and deface the rock, so others may enjoy this fascinating spot in its natural state.

Echo Bay. The largest bay on the island, Echo contains fourteen mooring buoys with ample space for additional boats to swing at anchor. The large blue-striped buoy in the center of the bay is reserved for Coast Guard boats when they are stationed in the area. Since this is the most open of Sucia's anchorages, it is exposed to waves and surges, and can be uncomfortable during some wind and tide conditions. The two long forested islands in the bay, appropriately named North Finger and South Finger, are privately owned, except as noted earlier.

Snoring Bay. Tiny Snoring Bay on the south side of Johnson Point, generally scorned by powerboaters, is a haven for paddlers seeking refuge from the noise and fumes of motors. The story goes that the bay received its name when park officials visiting the island discovered a ranger there en-

Shallow Bay

joying a siesta. Snoring Bay has two mooring buoys and two campsites on shore.

Ewing Cove. Boaters seeking privacy may find it in Ewing Cove, on the north side of Echo Bay, snuggled between Ewing Island and the Cluster Islands. Although less protected and more difficult for larger boats to navigate, the cove nonetheless boasts the same rugged cliffs and sandy beaches that make the rest of the island so popular. Four mooring buoys are available, and three campsites and a pit toilet are located above the beach at the west end of the cove. The outermost mooring buoy, when entering Ewing Cove, is over an underwater marine park area. Three sunken vessels are below the buoy and several yards to the east in 45 feet of water.

At Ewing Cove an added bonus for bird-watchers is Clements Reef and adjoining rocks, part of the San Juan Islands National Wilderness Refuge, lying less than ½ mile to the north. Hundreds of seabirds congregate here, some of them nesting on Sucia and Matia, others merely resting on their migratory flights. Be content to identify them with strong binoculars from shore, for waters around the reef can be treacherous and any approach by man disturbing to the birds. Seals and sea lions, too, can be seen on the reefs in large numbers, snoozing in the sun or warily eyeing passing boaters.

Looking inland, bird-watchers can often spot bald eagles or turkey vultures perched high atop scraggly fir trees or soaring the skies above them. Although quite rare, brown pelicans have been seen here, foraging the shores. Cormorants, known colloquially as "shags," sit on vacant buoys, overseeing harbor activities.

Cormorants are not completely waterproof, thus they must perch with wings hanging loosely or slightly outspread to dry their "sails." Their lack of oily waterproofing makes them less buoyant, enabling them to dive underwater to depths of several hundred feet to capture food. When winds are high, pelagic cormorants can be seen with their long black bodies plastered against sandstone cliffs; in good weather they frequently fly as flocks in sinuous V-formations.

HIKING TRAILS

A dirt service road loops through the wooded main section of the island, with branch trails stretching from it to all ends of the island fingers. Except for park service equipment, motorized vehicles and bicycles are prohibited on park roads and trails. The rock quarry near the service buildings at Fossil Bay is particularly dangerous and park personnel attempt to keep visitors out of the area. The loose cliffs are extremely hazardous to climb on—accidents have occurred here.

Fox Cove and Ev Henry Finger. The trail around the north side of Fox Cove stays high on the bluff above the bay, while paths on Ev Henry Finger, Johnson Point, and the northern edge of Echo Bay skirt the water. Wear sturdy shoes on any long hike; deck "tennies" or sandals do not provide adequate footing on steep, slippery trails. Search shoreline rocks, especially on Ev Henry Finger, for fossilized clams, snails, and ammonites 75 million years old. Such specimens may be collected if they are loose, but digging in the banks with pick, shovel, or any other device is illegal.

Lawson Bluff. A short but very scenic loop trail skirts along the edge of Lawson Bluff on the northwest side of the island. Find the signed trail out of the northernmost campsite at Shallow Bay, near the latrines. A network of side paths leading to open viewpoints confuse the route as it rounds the point north of the Shallow Bay entrance. All eventually lead back to the main route along the edge of the bluff. The way climbs gradually, staying just above the precipitous cliffs of Lawson Bluff. Keep a hand on the kids —the trail is easy enough, but in places it is so near the edge that a misstep could cause a bad fall.

Aerial views stretch down the sheer cliff to the ocean glimmering 100 feet below, and north to the long stretches of Patos Island and the rugged outlines of the Canadian Gulf Islands. After about ½ mile the trail turns inland, joining the northmost loop of the service road at a signed trailhead in another 200 yards. Turn right to return to Shallow Bay, left to reach the head of Echo Bay (the easiest return to Fossil Bay). Total distance of loop hike from Shallow Bay is about ¾ mile.

Ewing Cove. The most beautiful hike on Sucia, and possibly in the entire San Juans Islands, is the 2-mile trail along the north side of Echo Bay to Ewing Cove. The signed trailhead leaves the park service road about 300 yards east of its spur to Chinaman Rock.

After a few hundred yards through thick brush, the path breaks out to the edge of the bluff above Echo Bay, which it follows for the remainder of the hike. No beach access at first, as the trail winds along the 100-foot-high cliffs whose eroded sandstone cavities are used as nesting sites by hordes of darting swallows.

In ¼ mile a grassy knob, so tempting that is must be signed "No Camping," provides views down the sinuous waterways between the Finger Islands. Pocket coves have steep, somewhat hazardous scrambles down to beaches framed by wave-sculpted sandstone. Graceful madronas and gnarled white, long-dead junipers frame pictures of the myriad shapes and forms carved in the soft rock. Small rocks and islets just offshore await the visit of kayakers.

Incessantly cawing crows warn eagles, woodpeckers, and gulls of a hiker's pending arrival. As the trail nears its destination at Ewing Cove, the cliffs moderate and ready beach access is available. No moderation, however, in the fantasy of wave-carved sandstone forms continuing out along the Cluster Island chain. The cove itself is a remote and peaceful retreat — difficult to leave for the trip back to the hubbub of the main island campgrounds.

Echo Bay from the Ewing Cove trail

Matia Island Marine State Park and Wildlife Refuge

Island area: 145 acres; 20,000 feet of shoreline
Park area: 5 acres
Access: Boat
Facilities: 6 campsites, dock with float, mooring buoys, picnic tables, fireplaces, composting toilets, porta-potty dump, *no water*
Attractions: Clamming, crabbing, tidepools, fishing, beachcombing, hiking, birdwatching

Although Matia may well be the loveliest of these jewellike northern isles, it is often passed over by visiting boaters as it has limited overnight space. Only 5 acres facing on Rolfe Cove on the west end of the island are open to camping; the remainder is designated as National Wildlife Refuge. Picnic sites with tables and fireplaces are located at several coves in the refuge area.

The U.S. Fish and Wildlife Service permits use of the small area of the island as a state park, in hopes that such limited use of the land will be compatible with wildlife preservation. If the presence of the public on Matia ever becomes a threat to the birds and mammals living there or on nearby Puffin Island, all human intruders will be asked to pull up their tent stakes and anchors and go elsewhere. Treat the land with tender, loving care and strictly observe all regulations, or risk losing it.

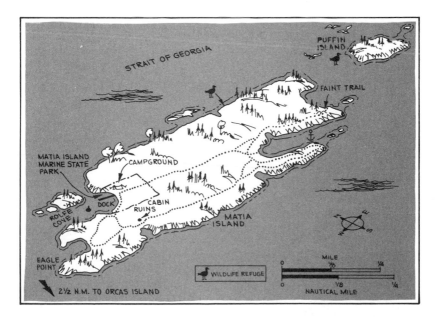

Anchorage in the southeast cove at Matia Island

Matia Island lies 2½ nautical miles northeast of the resort on the north shore of Orcas Island, where boats may be rented or launched. For day excursions small boats can be beached in any of several coves on the island; however, overnight camping is allowed only on state park land.

Rolfe Cove holds a dock with a 45-foot float and two mooring buoys, with room for only a few more boats to drop a hook. Hovering at the mouth of the cove, a rocky islet gives some protection from northerly wind, but it also causes peculiar current flows that disrupt confident anchoring. The bottom of Rolfe Cove is deep and quite rocky; in a strong blow it may be difficult to secure a safe anchorage. The float is removed during the winter months to prevent damage from storms.

On the bank at the head of the cove are picnic tables, garbage cans, six campsites, and ingenious composting toilets; a porta-potty dump is also provided to preserve the composting toilets from chemicals that would destroy their effectiveness. A sign tells you all you ever wanted to know about composting toilets—and then some. Drinking water once was available from a nearby pump; problems with adequate purification caused it to be capped, so bring your own.

The exposed walls of the coves at Matia Island are naturally sculpted masterpieces. Hollowed and smoothed by wind and waves, the stony banks are accentuated by banded patterns of layered conglomerate.

Boats also may anchor in a long narrow bay on the southeast end of the island; however, the end of the bay is extremely shoal at low water. Several rocks lying in the entrance are an additional hazard.

"Matia" has undoubtedly the most varied and disputed pronunciation of any San Juan Island. The Spanish pronunciation of the word, meaning "no protection," is *Mah-tee´-ah*. However the name is often corrupted as *May-shuh*, *May-tee*, or *Mat-ty*.

THE HERMIT OF MATIA

In early years this island was the longtime home of the San Juan's most interesting character, known as the "hermit of Matia." His name was Elvin Smith, and even though local newspapers of the day referred to him as a hermit, he was in truth not antisocial, for every week, in all but the foulest of weather, he rowed his skiff to North Beach on Orcas Island. From here he hiked a 2-mile trail to East Sound to collect his mail, buy supplies, and gossip with his cronies.

The pioneer recluse had gained a reputation as a mystic and mail-order faith healer. His weekly mail included dozens of letters, and sometimes money, from supplicants all over the country seeking his assistance. At home, on the retreat of his island, Smith claimed to spend hours each day in prayer on the behalf of his correspondents.

Elvin Smith lived for nearly thirty years on this briny paradise. From time to time other pioneers showed interest in the land, but one occupant on a 150-acre island was considered quite crowded enough for the time, so they settled elsewhere. One stormy February in 1921, Smith (who was then 86) and a visiting friend, their boat heavily laden with supplies, cast off from Orcas Island for the return trip to Matia. They were never seen again. Stones marking two vacant graves in an Orcas Island cemetery commemorate their lives.

Several trails on the island pass by the remnants of Smith's early settlement. A wide path leaves the dock at Rolfe Cove and heads south near the edge of the cove, reaching another cove near Eagle Cliff in about ½ mile; a picnic site is located above the beach. About 200 yards after leaving Rolfe Cove, a branch trail to the left leads to still another diminutive cove. Debris of old buildings can be found near the marsh at its head.

The tree-shaded path continues eastward, edged by skeletons of ancient fences. Although Smith was a vegetarian, he kept sheep for wool, chickens for eggs, and rabbits, perhaps for companionship. At the head of the southeast bay, and in a small cove south of it, are two more picnic sites. Here trails branch in many directions. One path leads to the head of the finger of land on the south side of the bay; others flank its northern edge, climbing through wind-tormented madronas and hemlock to high bluffs.

This large, shallow bay may also be reached more directly by a ½-mile trail from Rolfe Cove east from the campground to the head of the southeast bay. Clams may be dug in the tidal flat at a low tide.

PUFFIN ISLAND

One of the prettiest beaches on the island is a sandy crescent facing Puffin Island. To reach it, watch carefully for a branch trail, largely overgrown, just north of the southeast bay. Pick your way through the brush for

Beach at the east end of Matia Island

about 500 yards to emerge at a more discernible trail along the edge of the bluff. Even this trail requires a watchful eye occasionally as it proceeds easterly above the cliffs defining the bay. At the south rim of the cove opposite Puffin Island, the faint trail switchbacks down to a grassy flat above the beach; here is another picnic site.

Sandy sections of the shore harbor clams. At low tide, rocks jutting out on the south side of the bay display spectacular tidepools, with multitudes of starfish, sea anemones, limpets, barnacles, tiny crabs, and other creatures. Bring along a picnic lunch for all-day enjoyment of the island.

The cove looks out to Puffin Island, just a stone's throw offshore. This steep, rocky island, topped with a scraggly pompadour of trees and grass, is one of the islands of the San Juan Islands National Wildlife Refuge; going onshore is prohibited. Seals and sea lions can often be seen lolling about in the warmth of the sun, and with binoculars, squawking gossipy seabirds can be identified—ungainly murres and auklets, bizarre puffins (known as sea parrots), and shy pigeon guillemots.

From mid-March to mid-September these birds gather in colonies and lay their eggs in rock clefts, tending them until the downy chicks feather out and are able to fly. During this nesting time any close approach by boats or people is disturbing to the families; if the birds become alarmed by your presence, you are too close.

Early-day Lummi Indians from the Bellingham region paddled dugout canoes to Matia and Puffin islands to collect eggs, which they packed in the cool, moist leaves of sea lettuce to safeguard against spoiling and breakage. The sea lettuce, too, was later eaten or dried for winter use. Today visitors may sample the green, tissuey seaweed (if they do not go close to the birds to collect it), but Uncle Sam protects the eggs.

Clark Island Marine State Park

Park area: 56 acres; 6,000 feet of shoreline
Access: Boat
Facilities: 8 campsites, picnic tables, fireplaces, pit toilets, mooring
  buoys, *no water, no garbage collection*
Attractions: Clamming, mussels, beachcombing, scuba diving, fishing,
  tidepools, birdwatching

Swept by the waters of the Strait of Georgia, shadowed by the mountains of Orcas Island, a group of rocks and islands cluster together like the big brothers and small sisters of a family. On the southwest, the smaller, barren rocks are known as the Sisters, with the southernmost wedge-shaped rock named Little Sister.

The largest of the rocks once sported a single pine tree, prompting the name Lone Tree Island, but the tree has long since surrendered to the sea, leaving the islet to some tenacious grass and hundreds of nesting birds. The rock is now marked by a navigational light.

The Sisters are included in the San Juan Islands National Wildlife Refuge. In spring and summer, cormorants, pigeon guillemots, glaucous-winged gulls, and other pelagic birds nest here. At other seasons gulls gather on the rocks, occasionally in enormous numbers, for reasons known only to gulls —perhaps an approaching storm, perhaps feeding is poor, or perhaps for an afternoon coffee (or herring) klatch. Whatever the reason,

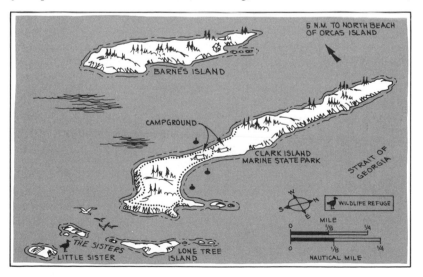

Gulls feeding on herring

the cacophony of their conversation at such times is overwhelming, even on the shores of Clark Island.

Barnes Island, second in size of the island group, lies on the west. While the uplands at Barnes are private, all the surrounding tidelands below the mean high water level are public. Do not stray above the driftwood level onto private property.

Less than ½ mile east of Barnes is the largest of the island family, 56-acre Clark Island, a marine state park. Although it is located less than 2 miles from the shores of Orcas Island, the nearest boat launching area is 5 nautical miles to the west at the resort at North Beach. The distance from populated areas, the lack of fresh water for campers, and the lack of protected anchorages make this one of the less frequented of the San Juan marine state parks.

The slender island is a mile in length, but scarcely 300 yards across at its widest point. Its southern end hooks sharply eastward to form a small broad bay; here six mooring buoys offer easy, although exposed, anchorages. Skippers approaching this bay should use care, as several rocks lie just beneath the surface along its east side; boats have been known to have run aground. Refer to a good navigational chart for location of hazards. A slight indentation on the opposite side of the island holds three additional mooring buoys, sheltered from the west by Barnes Island and from the southeast by the end of Clark.

Madronas at Clark Island Marine State Park

Clark Island Marine State Park; Barnes Island beyond

Campers may pitch tents in one of seven campsites above the beach on the east side of the island. Two more campsites can be found in the trees along the cross-island trail connecting the two anchorages. The west beach, one of the few true sand beaches in the San Juans, is a day-use picnic area. Camping or building fires on the beach is prohibited in order to keep it as natural as possible.

Timber on the southern end of the island is sparse, with graceful red-barked madronas leaning over the banks. A bluff-top trail can be followed around this end of the island, with views down to the beaches and tiny steep-walled coves; numerous side trails drop down to the water.

Clark Island is reputed to have the nicest beaches of any of these northern island state parks. Sand and mud flats to the south, exposed at low tide, are good for clamming and summertime wading; mussels cling to protruding rocks. The steeper rocky northern beaches hold an array of marine life—purple starfish, pastel sea anemones, barnacles, sea squirts, purple and green urchins, and more—to be admired by skin divers and tidepool explorers.

Afoot & Afloat

Appendices

A. Emergency Phone Numbers
and List of Contacts

All numbers listed are area code 206

Fire (Alarms Only)

Blakely Island—375-6121
Lopez Island—911
Orcas Island—911
San Juan Island-911
Shaw Island—911
For fires on remote islands, call the Department of Natural Resources—
    1-800-562-6010. (If calling by radio, notify the U.S. Coast Guard.)

Medical Emergencies

Blakely Island—375 6121
Lopez Island—911
Orcas Island—911
San Juan Island—911
Shaw Island—911
Poison Information Center—1-800-732-6985

Sheriff

Lopez-Shaw Island—911 (Emergencies)
                468-2333 (Other business)
Orcas Island—911 (Emergencies)
            376-2207 (Other business)
San Juan Island—911 (Emergencies)
            378-4141 (Other business)

U.S. Coast Guard

Marine and Air Emergency—1-800-592-9911

Hotlines (Toll Free)

Red Tide Hotline—1-800-562-5632
Whale Hotline—1-800-562-8832

Radio Contacts

Marine V.H.F.: Coast Guard distress and hailing—Channel 16
Coast Guard liaison—Channel 22A
Marine Operator; Bellingham—Channel 28, 85
Victoria, B.C.—Channel 27
Citizens Band: Distress—Channel 9

U.S. Customs

Friday Harbor—378-2080 (After hours—1-800-562-5943)

Washington State Ferries

Information— 1-800-542-0810 or 1-800-542-7052 (toll free)
Seattle—   464-6400
Anacortes terminal—293-2188
Lopez terminal—468-2252
Orcas terminal—376-2134
Friday Harbor terminal—378-4777
Shaw terminal—468-2288

Parks

San Juan Island National Historical Park; P.O. Box 549, Friday Harbor, WA
98250. Phone—378-2240.
Washington State Parks and Recreation Information Service; 7150 Cleanwater
Lane, Olympia, WA 98504. Phone—1-800-562-0990 (toll free, May 1
through Labor Day only) or 753-5755.
Eastern San Juan State Parks (Spencer Spit, James I., Saddlebag I., Turn I., Doe
I.); Spencer Spit State Park, Lopez Island, WA 98261. Phone—468-2251.
Northern and Western San Juan State Parks (Sucia I., Matia I., Patos I., Freeman
I., Reid Harbor, Prevost Harbor, Turn Point, Jones I., Posey I., Lime Kiln
Lighthouse); Sucia Island State Park, 6158 Lighthouse Road; Friday Harbor,
WA 98250. Phone—378-2044.
Moran State Park; Moran State Park Office, Eastsound, WA 98245. Phone—
376-2326.
San Juan County Park; 380 West Side Road, Friday Harbor, WA 98250.
Phone—378-2992.
Odlin County Park; Lopez, WA 98261. Phone—468-2496.

Museums

Lopez Island Historical Museum—468-2049
Orcas Island Historical Museum—376-4849
San Juan Island Historical Museum—378-4587
Shaw Island Historical Museum—468-2637
Whale Museum; 62 First St. N., Friday Harbor, WA 98250. Phone—378-4710

Other

University of Washington Marine Field Laboratories; 620 University Road, San
Juan Island, WA 98250. Phone—378-2165

B. Nautical Charts and Maps

Sketch maps for this book are intended for general orientation only. When traveling by boat on any of the San Juan waters it is imperative that the appropriate nautical charts be used. The following list of charts covers the area included in this book. They may be purchased at map stores or many marine supply centers.

NOAA Chart 18423, Bellingham to Everett, including the San Juan Islands
(Scale 1:80,000—folio of charts including some detailed insets).
NOAA Chart 18421, Strait of Juan de Fuca to Strait of Georgia
(Scale 1:80,000—covers all areas included in this book).
NOAA Chart 18425, Friday and Roche Harbors (Scale 1:20,000)

Although it would be difficult to get seriously lost on any of the islands, the USGS topographic maps listed below are useful and interesting.

7½' series maps—Mt. Constitution, Blakely Island, Lopez Pass, Lummi Island, Eastsound, Shaw Island, Richardson, Waldron Island, Friday Harbor, False Bay, Sucia Island, Stuart Island, Roche Harbor.

C. Quick Reference to Facilities and Recreation

Some kinds of marine facilities such as boating, fishing, and beachcombing are found throughout the San Juan Islands. Others, however, are more specific to particular areas. The following table provides a quick reference to needed facilities and specific activities in the major areas covered by this book.

Marine Services include marine supplies and repair; in some places they may be of a very limited nature.
Floats/Buoys refers to marinas that have transient moorage, as well as public facilities at marine parks.
Launch Facilities may be only a shore access for hand-carried boats. Hoists and slings are always at commercial marinas. Ramps may be at either commercial or public facilities.
Point of Interest includes historical or educational displays, museums, and self-guided nature tours.

Some facilities listed may be entirely at commercial resorts or marinas; some may close off-season. For detailed information read the description of specific areas in the text.

( ) = Nearby; [ ] = Freshwater
Fuel: D = On Dock; S = Service Station
Launch Facilities: H = Hoist; R = Ramp; C = Hand Carry
Camping: B = Bicycle Only
Walking/Hiking: BW = Beach Walk

	U.S. Customs	Fuel	Marine Services	Groceries/Shopping	Restaurants	Floats/Buoys	Launch Facilities	Fishing	Shellfish	Paddling	Scuba Diving	Swimming	Camping	Picnicking	Walking/Hiking	Point of Interest
1. THATCHER PASS																
Blakely Island		D	•	•		•		•						•		
Decatur Island							R									
James Island Marine State Park						•		•		•	•		•	•	•	
2. LOPEZ ISLAND																
Odlin County Park						•	R	•	•	•	•	•	•	•	•	
Bella Tierra Park						•			•					•	BW	
Lopez Village	S			•	•											•
Fisherman Bay		D	•	(•)	•	•	R/H	•	•	•		•		•		
Otis Perkins Park							C							•	BW	
Hummel Lake							[R]	[•]		[•]						
Spencer Spit State Park						•	C	•	•	•	•		•	•	•	
Hunter and Mud Bays						•	R	•	•	•					BW	
Shark Reef Recreation Site										•				•	•	
Richardson		D/S			(•)						(•)					
Mackaye Harbor							R									
Agate Beach Picnic Area							C			•	•			•		
3. THE CENTRAL CHANNEL																
Shaw Landing		D/S		•		•	C			•						(•)
Blind Island Marine State Park						•			•	•			•	•		
Shaw Island County Park							R	•	•	•		•	•	•	•	
Yellow Island										•					•	•
Jones Island Marine State Park						•			•	•	•		•	•	•	
4. SAN JUAN ISLAND																
Friday Harbor	•	D/S	•	•	•	•	H			•			(•)	•		•
Turn Island						•			•	•	•	•	•	•	•	
Turn Point Road Access							C									
Jackson Beach							R							•		
Sportsman and Egg Lakes							[R]	[•]		[•]						
Lakedale Campground			•				[C]	[•]		[•]		[•]	•			
Reuben Tarte Picnic Area											•			•		
Roche Harbor	•	D/S	•	•	•	•	R			•		•		•	•	•

	U.S. Customs	Fuel	Marine Services	Groceries/Shopping	Restaurants	Floats/Buoys	Launch Facilities	Fishing	Shellfish	Paddling	Scuba Diving	Swimming	Camping	Picnicking	Walking/Hiking	Point of Interest
Posey Island Marine State Park										•			•	•		
Westcott Bay								•	•	•				•		
Mitchell Bay (Snug Harbor)		D	•	•		•	R					•				
San Juan County Park				•			R	•		•	•		•	•		
Lime Kiln Point State Park												•		•	•	•
Pedal Inn Bicycle Camp													B			
Eagle Cove Public Access							C				•	•		•	BW	
Griffin Bay Campground													•			
Cattle Beach Picnic Area														•	•	
Cattle Point															•	•

5. SAN JUAN ISLAND NATIONAL HISTORICAL PARK

	U.S. Customs	Fuel	Marine Services	Groceries/Shopping	Restaurants	Floats/Buoys	Launch Facilities	Fishing	Shellfish	Paddling	Scuba Diving	Swimming	Camping	Picnicking	Walking/Hiking	Point of Interest
British Camp							C	•	•					•	•	•
American Camp							C			•				•	•	•

6. NORTH FROM SPIEDEN AND PRESIDENT CHANNEL

	U.S. Customs	Fuel	Marine Services	Groceries/Shopping	Restaurants	Floats/Buoys	Launch Facilities	Fishing	Shellfish	Paddling	Scuba Diving	Swimming	Camping	Picnicking	Walking/Hiking	Point of Interest
Harbor Marine State Parks						•		•	•	•			•	•	•	•
Stuart Island Marine State Parks								•	•	•	•		•	•	•	•
Turn Point State Park															•	•

7. ORCAS ISLAND

	U.S. Customs	Fuel	Marine Services	Groceries/Shopping	Restaurants	Floats/Buoys	Launch Facilities	Fishing	Shellfish	Paddling	Scuba Diving	Swimming	Camping	Picnicking	Walking/Hiking	Point of Interest
Orcas Landing		D/S	•	•	•	•								•		•
Killebrew Lake							[C]	[•]		[•]						
Deer Harbor		D/S	•	•	•	•	C			•		•				(•)
West Sound		D	•	•	•	•	H	•		•						
Obstruction Pass				•		•	R	•		•						
Obstruction Pass Campground						•			•	•			•	•	•	
Doe Island Marine State Park						•				•			•	•	•	
Doe Bay			•	•						•	•		•			
Olga			(•)	(•)	•					•						
Rosario		D	•	•	•	•	R			•		•			•	•
Eastsound		S	•	•	•	•	C			•				•	BW	•
North Shore		D	•	•	•	•	R/C	•		•	•					
Point Doughty										•	•		•	•		
Freeman Island Marine State Park											•			•		

	U.S. Customs	Fuel	Marine Services	Groceries/Shopping	Restaurants	Floats/Buoys	Launch Facilities	Fishing	Shellfish	Paddling	Scuba Diving	Swimming	Camping	Picnicking	Walking/Hiking	Point of Interest

8. MORAN STATE PARK

	U.S. Customs	Fuel	Marine Services	Groceries/Shopping	Restaurants	Floats/Buoys	Launch Facilities	Fishing	Shellfish	Paddling	Scuba Diving	Swimming	Camping	Picnicking	Walking/Hiking	Point of Interest
Moran State Park							[R/C] [•]			[•]		[•]	•	•	•	•

9. THE NORTHERN BOUNDARY

	U.S. Customs	Fuel	Marine Services	Groceries/Shopping	Restaurants	Floats/Buoys	Launch Facilities	Fishing	Shellfish	Paddling	Scuba Diving	Swimming	Camping	Picnicking	Walking/Hiking	Point of Interest
Patos Island Marine State Park						•		•	•	•			•	•	•	•
Sucia Islands Marine State Park						•		•	•	•	•		•	•	•	•
Matia Island Marine State Park						•		•	•	•			•	•		•
Clark Island Marine State Park						•		•	•	•			•	•		•

D. Selected References

History

Haskett, Patrick. *The Wilkes Expedition in Puget Sound—1841*. Olympia, Washington: Western Interstate Commission for Higher Education and The State Capitol Museum, 1974.

Majors, Harry. *Exploring Washington*. Holland, Michigan: Van Winkle Publishing Co., 1975.

Meany, Edmond S. *Vancouver's Discovery of Puget Sound*. New York: The Macmillan Company, 1907.

Murray, Keith. *The Pig War*. Tacoma, Washington: Washington State Historical Society, 1968.

Richardson, David. *Pig War Islands*. Eastsound, Washington: Orcas Publishing Company, 1971.

Beaches and Marine Life

Kozloff, Eugene N. *Seashore Life of Puget Sound, the Strait of Georgia, and the San Juan Archipelago*. Seattle and London: University of Washington Press, 1973.

McLachlan, Dan H., and Ayres, Jak. *Fieldbook of Pacific Northwest Sea Creatures*. Happy Camp, California: Naturegraph Publications, 1979.

Puget Sound Public Shellfish Sites. Olympia, Washington: State Department of Fisheries, 1978.

Scott, James W. and Reuling, Melly A. *Washington Public Shore Guide*. Seattle and London: University of Washington Press, 1986.

Sheely, Terry W. *The Complete Handbook on Washington's Clams/Crabs/Shellfish*. Snohomish, Washington: Osprey Press.

Smith, Lynwood S. *Living Shores of the Pacific Northwest*. Seattle, Washington: Pacific Search Books, 1976.

Your Public Beaches—San Juan Region. Olympia, Washington: State Department of Natural Resources, 1985.

Nature

Angell, Tony, and Balcom, Kenneth C. III. *Marine Birds and Mammals of Puget Sound*. Seattle, Washington: Washington Sea Grant Program, 1982.

Atkinson, Scott, and Sharpe, Fred. *Wild Plants of the San Juan Islands*. Seattle, Washington: The Mountaineers, 1985.

Lewis, Mark G., and Sharpe, Fred A. *Birding in the San Juan Islands*. Seattle, Washington. The Mountaineers, 1987.

Wahl, Terence R. and Paulson, Dennis R. *A Guide to Bird Finding in Washington*. Bellingham, Washington: T.R. Wahl, 1981.

Boating, Paddling

Bultman, Phyllis and Bill. *Border Boating*. Seattle, Washington: Pacific Search Press, 1979.

Cummings, Al, and Bailey-Cummings, Jo. *Gunkholing in the San Juans*. Edmonds, Washington: Nor'westing, Inc.

Furrer, Werner. *Water Trails of Washington*. Lynnwood, Washington: Signpost Publications, 1973.

Hilson, Stephen E. *Exploring Puget Sound and British Columbia*. Holland, Michigan: Van Winkle Publishing Co., 1975.

Pacific Boating Almanac: Pacific Northwest and Alaska. Ventura, California: Western Marine Enterprises, Inc., published annually.

United States Coast Pilot: 7 (Pacific Coast: California, Oregon, Washington and Hawaii). Washington, D.C.: U.S. Department of Commerce, published annually.

Van der Ree, Frieda. *Exploring the Coast by Boat, Vol. I*. Mercer Island, Washington: The Writing Works, 1979.

Washburn, Randel. *Kayak Trips in Puget Sound and the San Juan Islands*. Seattle, Washington: Pacific Search Press, 1986.

Bicycling

Kirkendall, Tom and Spring, Vicky. *Bicycling the Pacific Coast*. Seattle, Washington: The Mountaineers, 1984.

Woods, Erin and Bill. *Bicycling the Backroads around Puget Sound*, Second Edition. Seattle, Washington: The Mountaineers, 1981.

Hiking

Darvill, Fred T., Jr. and Marshall, Louise B. *Winter Walks and Summer Strolls, I*. Lynnwood, Washington: Signpost Publications, 1977.

Sterling, E. M. *Trips and Trails, 1: Family Camps, Short Hikes and View Roads around the North Cascades, Third Edition*. Seattle, Washington: The Mountaineers, 1986.

Scuba Diving

Fischnaller, Steve. *Northwest Shore Dives*. Edmonds, Washington: Bio-Marine Images, 1986.

Pratt-Johnson, Betty. *141 Dives in the Protected Waters of Washington and British Columbia*. Mercer Island, Washington: The Writing Works, 1976.

Ward, Peter. *Beneath Puget Sound*. Seattle, Washington: Peanut Butter Publishing, 1974.

Fishing

Haw, Frank, and Buckley, Raymond M. *Saltwater Fishing in Washington, 2nd Ed.* Seattle, Washington: Stan Jones Publishing, Inc., 1981.

Olander, Doug. *Northwest Coastal Fishing Guide*. Seattle, Washington: The Writing Works, 1984.

General

San Juan Islands Almanac. Friday Harbor, Washington: Long House Printcrafters and Publishers, published annually.

Index

About the authors:

Seattle residents, the Muellers have been active in the outdoors around Puget Sound for well over twenty years. Both Marge and Ted are long-time mountain climbers and worked with Mountain Rescue Council; they have also instructed in mountain climbing through the University of Washington. More than a decade ago they added sailing to their round of interests and, with their two children, began wandering the inlets and outlets of the Sound year round.

Researching and writing the *Afoot & Afloat* series took the Muellers more than eight years, and included visits to every beach, bay, island and "point of interest" covered in the text, plus many hours spent in libraries and museums and contacting land management agencies for historical and useful information.

The Muellers' first book, *Northwest Ski Trails,* was also published by The Mountaineers.